A MILITARY HISTORY OF MODERN SPAIN

A MILITARY HISTORY OF MODERN SPAIN

From the Napoleonic Era to the International War on Terror

Edited by Wayne H. Bowen and José E. Alvarez

Foreword by Stanley G. Payne

PRAEGER SECURITY INTERNATIONAL
Westport, Connecticut • London

Library of Congress Cataloging-in-Publication Data

Bowen, Wayne H., 1968–
    A military history of modern Spain : from the Napoleonic era to the international war on
    terror / Wayne H. Bowen and José E. Alvarez ; foreword by Stanley G. Payne.
        p. cm.
    Includes bibliographical references and index.
    ISBN 978–0–275–99357–3 (alk. paper)
1. Spain—History, Military—20th century. 2. Spain—History, Military—19th century. I.
Alvarez, José E., 1955– II. Title.
DP78.5.B69 2007
355.00946—dc22   2007028019

British Library Cataloguing in Publication Data is available.

Library of Congress Catalog Card Number: 2007028019
ISBN-13: 978–0–275–99357–3

First published in 2007

Praeger Security International, 88 Post Road West, Westport, CT 06881
An imprint of Greenwood Publishing Group, Inc.
www.praeger.com

Printed in the United States of America

The paper used in this book complies with the
Permanent Paper Standard issued by the National
Information Standards Organization (Z39.48–1984).

10 9 8 7 6 5 4 3 2 1

Contents

Foreword

In no other country is the historical importance of the military greater than in the case of Spain, for it is the only Western country founded by eight centuries of intermittent but continuing warfare against another civilization. Geography is destiny, as the saying goes, and this is absolutely the case with Spain, whose position as the southwestern frontier of Europe has determined much of her history and her military affairs. Thus, one American historian termed medieval Spain "a society organized for war" to a greater extent than other Western lands. Once the united monarchy of Spain metamorphosed into the government of the first world empire, military action remained of prime importance, both to maintain the integrity of the European crownlands and to sustain the struggle against a powerful and aggressive Ottoman Empire in the Mediterranean and in north Africa. It is scant exaggeration to say that the expense of the military burden bankrupted the state and helped to precipitate a disastrous economic decline. During the last imperial century—the eighteenth —this burden was reduced yet remained significant.

In the nineteenth and twentieth centuries, Spain for the first time ceased to be a military power—something that a lagging economy could not possibly afford—yet the military remained important, and during this period played a significant role in political affairs as well. Though the country had fallen from the ranks of the major powers, the combination of foreign invasion, complications of imperial decline, remarkably severe internal conflict, and continuing hostilities on the Moroccan frontier created a situation in which what had become a second-rank army and navy spent more years engaged in warfare during the nineteenth century than was the case with any other country. Protracted involvement in international, colonial, and civil wars proved a heavy burden once more for both the state and the economy, and was undoubtedly a major factor in the country's lagging economic growth during that era.

Spain entered the era of liberal and parliamentary politics in 1810, earlier than most countries, yet the weakness and division of the new political forces quickly summoned the military as political arbiter, especially during the chaotic "era of pronunciamientos" between 1820 and 1875. A "praetorian" role for the military returned again during the dictatorship of 1923–30 and then during the civil war of 1936–39 and the long Franco regime that followed. A praetorian military was nonetheless rarely "militarist"—that is, given to the hypertrophy of the military for purposes of war—at any time during this era, as Spain remained apart from the European alliance systems and neutral during both world wars.

The result was to produce a singular Spanish military history in modern times, the subject of this book. Between 1810 and 1944 Spanish forces were frequently active on a variety of fronts, yet rarely engaged in full and direct international warfare. In no other European land did the army play such an important role in political affairs, and yet there was never a completely clear-cut military dictatorship until 1936. Throughout this period the military remained weak as a fighting force, significantly under-budgeted, disproportionate resources being devoted to paying the normally meager salaries of a very bloated officer corps. The final paradox was that it was the Franco regime that largely disciplined the military and removed them from political life, finally reducing the military budget to less than the amount devoted to education for the first time in Spanish history.

Both the size and the influence of the military have been reduced even more under the democratic governments that have ruled since 1978, so that it is possible to define the main modern era of the Spanish military as lasting from the beginning of the French invasion in 1808 to the abortive pronunciamiento of 1981. The contemporary period is characterized by the incredibly shrinking Spanish military, which receive even less attention than in most other European countries, so that at the time this is written the government would be hard-pressed to place more than 70,000 troops in combat. For the first time since the eighth century it would be unable to defend its own southern frontier.

The present volume presents a succinct but comprehensive account of this singular modern military history. It makes available to a broad audience a clear, objective treatment that will be useful not merely to students of Spanish history but also to those interested in the broader study of modern Europe and of comparative military affairs.

Stanley G. Payne

Introduction

Wayne H. Bowen and José E. Alvarez

Spain's modern military history is one of the lessons learned and then quickly forgotten. The nation's army remained mostly stagnant and unresponsive to new tactics and doctrines even though it was called upon to fight wars both at home and abroad. It is also the history of an organization that in the early nineteenth century served as an instrument for liberal reform and progress, then by the end of the century, and into the twentieth century, became a vehicle for political conservatism and reactionary politics. In its nine chapters, this book takes a critical and analytical look at the Spanish military from the Napoleonic invasion in 1808 to the ongoing war on terror.

In "The Spanish Army at War in the Nineteenth Century," Geoffrey Jensen astutely details how the Spanish military responded to Napoleon's invasion of Spain in 1808, known in Spain as the War of Independence (1808–14), as well as to the postbellum period. During the Napoleonic War, the Spanish Army performed poorly. Even though in some cases units adopted modern military tactics, such as changing from linear formations to a combination of lines and attack columns, the army as a whole failed to realize the importance of combined arms, effectively employing artillery and cavalry, to support the infantry. With the exception of their victory over the French at Bailén in 1808, the Army was unable to repeat this triumph for the remainder of the war. It would be the combination of Spanish guerrilla fighters and the Duke of Wellington's British regulars that would drive the French invaders from Spain. In Spanish history, the guerrilla fighter attained near mythical status in harassing and tying down thousands of Napoleon's soldiers in a vicious war, particularly in the northern half of the country.

Jensen continues his essay describing the role of the Spanish Army during the period of civil wars. The three Carlist Wars (1833–40, 1846–49, and 1872–76), fought between the followers of Don Carlos and the government forces of Queen Isabel II (*Cristinos*), again showed the poor fighting capability of the Spanish Army. This time, as Jensen notes, the

Carlist guerrillas were the opponents of the central government. While the military had tried to institute reforms after the Napoleonic War, by establishing military academies and training manuals for recruits, one area of military science that was overlooked was mountain warfare. It would be in the mountainous regions of Navarre and the Basque Country that the Carlists would have their strongest base of support. The use of irregular warfare by the Carlists would prove difficult and costly for the liberal army to overcome. It is interesting to note that despite having fought and defeated the Carlists, the Army ignored the lessons learned in fighting an insurgency campaign in favor of emphasizing conventional war in its doctrine. In addition, the cumulative effect of the Carlist Wars and military coups (*pronunciamentos*) was the politicization of the officer corps, resulting in a tremendously deleterious practice within the ranks of the officer corps: rewarding loyalty to the government by awarding promotions. This had the effect of creating a bloated and top-heavy officer corps that would plague Spain well into the twentieth century.

In the international arena, the Spanish Army, under the leadership of the then Prime Minister, General Leopoldo O'Donnell, became involved in a short war against the Berbers in Morocco in 1859–60. When local tribesmen attacked the Spanish *presidio* of Ceuta, Spain responded by declaring war. Although the war brought Spain control of the Moroccan cities of Tetuán and Tangiers, it had been at the cost of thousands of lives, the great majority to cholera. The military had also clearly demonstrated that it was still disorganized and had gained little from the Carlist Wars. Nevertheless, the Army did learn a few lessons from the Moroccan campaign such as using skirmishers to counteract indigenous guerrillas and employing flanking attacks to surround the enemy.

Lastly, Jensen recounts the actions of the Spanish Army in its two wars against Cuban insurgents seeking independence. In the Ten Years' War (1868–78), the military was able to defeat the *independentistas* and impose a peace treaty, the Pact of Zanjón. This first campaign in Cuba was greatly overshadowed by the much more important Cuban War of Independence (1895–98) which gave Cuba (as well as Puerto Rico, the Philippines, and Guam) its independence from Spain. The commanding Spanish general, Arsenio Martínez Campos, who had been successful in winning the Ten Years' War, did not meet the same success in 1895–96. A combination of poor training, tropical diseases, and highly motivated Cuban insurgents had led to Spanish setbacks in the campaign. Unable to adapt to and counter the guerrilla tactics of the Cuban rebels, Martínez Campos was recalled and replaced by General Valeriano Weyler y Nicolau in 1896.

Weyler's arrival in Cuba and his counterinsurgency tactics in Cuba began to turn the tide of the war in favor of the government. His introduction of "reconcentration" was a way of separating the guerrillas from the local peasantry by forcing the civilian population into camps, thus severing the lifeline between the two groups. Reconcentration led to the deaths of thousands of Cubans due to disease and starvation, but it was an effective military strategy. Negative international newspaper publicity, especially in the United States, and serious political pressure in Spain led to the removal of Weyler in 1897. Less known about Weyler, and Jensen notes this in his chapter, is the creation of a very effective counterinsurgency unit known as the *Cazadores de Valmaseda*. An elite, multinational, light infantry unit, the *Cazadores de Valmaseda* was able to move rapidly and fight the style of war their enemies would choose. In the end, the involvement of the United States in 1898 ended Spain's overseas empire in the Caribbean and in the Pacific. The "Disaster" of 1898 would shake Spain and its military to the very core and produce tremendous consequences for the twentieth century.

The deplorable state of the Spanish military is covered comprehensively in José E. Alvarez's "From Empire to Republic: The Spanish Army, 1898–1931." It is the story of an army trying to cope with the loss of its overseas empire (*ultra mar*) to the newly emerging United States of America, while at the same time trying to preserve what little remained of its pride and dignity. With its Navy having been destroyed in Manila Bay and Santiago de Cuba, Spain's possibility for overseas operations was terminated and future naval careers were dashed, a good example being that of Francisco Franco. The best the Army could do now was to focus on Morocco and Equatorial Guinea for any semblance of an overseas empire. Moreover, the Army had to reinvent itself as the defender of the fatherland from internal enemies such as Catalan separatism and working-class political movements such as anarchism, socialism, and communism. It had to emerge from the ignominious defeat of 1898 and make itself relevant to the nation. However, the Army was in a calamitous state burdened by too many senior officers, promotions based on seniority, poor pay for junior officers, inadequate training, and obsolete equipment. To make matters worse, the Army was also internally divided by branches of service: those that required technical training, such as artillery, engineers, and medical personnel, who perceived themselves as being superior to the combat branches of infantry and cavalry, who saw the greatest amount of combat. This sentiment would later lead to the creation of *Juntas de Defensa,* basically military unions for each branch of service. Another internal stress was the division between those who served in Spain (*peninsulares*) and those who served in Morocco (*Africanistas*). For those who sought a military career of adventure and rapid promotions, Morocco became the place to pursue those dreams and aspirations. Starting in 1893 and then again in 1909–10, the situation in the Spanish *presidios* of Ceuta and Melilla in northern Morocco became the site of constant small-scale engagements with the local tribesmen. The Army increased its call for reserves and for draftees to fight in Morocco which triggered outbreaks of antigovernment violence in Barcelona and other cities.

One constructive thing that came out of the 1909–10 Melillan campaign was the creation of the *Regulares* by Lieutenant Colonel Dámaso Berenguer Fusté in 1911. The *Regulares* was a unit of Moroccan troops led by Spanish officers, and it would be the officers who began their careers with the *Regulares* such as José Millán Astray, Francisco Franco, Emilio Mola, and Juan Yagüe that would later go on to serve in the Spanish Foreign Legion or continue their careers with the *Regulares.* In addition, many of these officers would later serve as senior commanders of the Nationalist army during the Spanish Civil War. Because of their service and rapid promotions received as a result of combat duty with the *Regulares* and the Legion, these officers became known as *Africanistas* (Africanists), an identification which differentiated them from those officers who had served entirely on the Spanish peninsula (*peninsulares*).

Following the signing of the Treaty of Fez in 1912, Spain became even more involved in expanding its Protectorate in Spanish Morocco. While its conscripts fared poorly in fighting the Berbers and defending blockhouses trying to keep supply and communication networks open, the *Regulares* fared much better. Spanish policy in Morocco by 1920 was to pacify the rebellious tribesmen either through military power, bribes, or a combination of both, and to penetrate into the interior as much as possible. While Spanish advances in the Western Zone under the command of General Berenguer progressed smoothly, the situation in the Eastern Zone, under the command of General Manuel Fernández Silvestre, did not. General Silvestre had recklessly moved his army westward from Melilla with the goal of reaching the coastal town of Alhucemas Bay, deep in Riffian territory, without taking the necessary precaution of disarming the local tribesman and securing his flanks. Just after Silvestre reached the main camp at Annual in the summer of 1921, the Riffian chieftain, Sidi Mohammed ben Abd-el-Krim el Khattabi, and his fighters attacked and destroyed the Spanish force. What started as an orderly retreat became a flood of panic-stricken soldiers who dropped their weapons and ran for their very lives. Having lost his command and honor, General Silvestre took his own life. The Annual disaster was the worst colonial defeat since the defeat of the Italians at Adowa, Ethiopia, in 1896. Estimates of casualties range from a conservative 8,000 to a high of 15,000 not to mention enough small arms, heavy weapons, and ammunition to equip an army. Only the arrival of two *banderas* (battalions) of the recently created Spanish Foreign Legion kept the Spanish city of Melilla from being overrun by the Riffians and its inhabitants put to the knife as had happened to soldiers and civilians alike in other Spanish outposts.

The Annual disaster caused the fall of the ruling government, and a move by the Army to avenge their fallen comrades, recapture the territory which had been lost to the Riffians, and regain their lost honor. With the Legion and *Regulares* serving as the "spearhead" for Spanish operations, the military was able to very slowly regain what had been lost. Abd-el-Krim's army grew larger with every victory and the war in Morocco continued to drag on for years. There was no end in sight and great disagreement between politicians, *peninsulares*, and *Africanistas* on how the war should be fought. In 1923, General Miguel Primo de Rivera carried out a successful *pronunciamiento* (pronouncement). This type of military rising had occurred with some frequency during the nineteenth century, but during that period it had been most often a form of military pressure exerted to force the government to change its policies, rather than as a method to seize power in an armed coup d'etat. In this regard, General Primo de Rivera's dictatorship was with few precedents. As Spain's new ruler, Miguel Primo de Rivera's first order of business was to bring the war in Morocco to a close. At first his plan was to abandon the Protectorate, later his policy changed to withdrawing from isolated outposts to more secure positions behind the so-called "Primo de Rivera Line" (his detractors called it the "Abd-el-Krim Line"). Thousands of lives were lost trying to evacuate these vulnerable outposts, but it was accomplished by 1924. What began to bring the war in Morocco to an end was when Abd-el-Krim made the fatal error of attacking the French zone as well, which gained the insurgent leader a powerful new enemy and a broader front. This overly ambitious move pushed the French and the Spanish to join forces against the common foe, and a Spanish amphibious landing at Alhucemas Bay in 1925, supported by French naval gunfire, doomed the Riffians. During the next two years, the combination of Spanish and French forces defeated the Riffians and Abd-el-Krim was forced to surrender to the French who sent him into exile on Reunion Island off the coast of Madagascar.

Primo de Rivera would serve as dictator of Spain from 1923 to 1930. He is best remembered for ending the Moroccan War (1921–27), but he is also responsible for reforming the Army by, among other measures, reducing the size of the officer corps, acquiring better weapons and equipment, raising salaries, placing greater emphasis on merit promotions over seniority, and establishing the GMA (General Military Academy) in Zaragoza with General Francisco Franco as its first director in 1927.

However, opposition to Primo de Rivera's reforms, particularly from the artillery branch, caused him to lose the Army's support as republicanism began to increase in Spain. In 1931, having lost the support of his people and King Alfonso XIII, Primo de Rivera was forced to abdicate and go into self-imposed exile in Italy. The incoming government, the Second Republic (1931–39), would greatly affect the leadership of the Army, eventually leading to the start of the Civil War in 1936.

Spain was still a weak state as the Great War was beginning in 1914, recounted in Javier Ponce's chapter, "World War I: Unarmed Neutrality." The Spanish Army and navy were in no condition to be significant participants in the conflict, and the nation's infrastructure was so dilapidated that the French declined initial offers to use its roads and railways to transit to Africa. Within Spain, many of the higher ranking aristocrats and military officers supported Germany, inspired as they were by Wilhelmine Germany's martial traditions and rise to industrial prowess. Prime Minister Eduardo Dato also sympathized with the Central Powers. The Spanish king, Alfonso XIII, related by blood and marriage to the German and British royal families, initially favored the Allies, but once the war began seriously considered German entreaties, which hinted at the expansion of Spain's colonies, the annexation of Portugal, and other forms of assistance. Although hopeful that Spain might break from its benevolent neutrality toward the Triple Entente, Germany realistically expected Alfonso XIII to do little more than remain a mediator between the two warring coalitions, and retain his freedom of maneuver for any eventuality. In public, the king and his government proclaimed Spain's strict neutrality. The British and French received more support from Spain's business leaders, middle classes, and republicans, identified as these three groups were through commercial and political ties to the Entente. As the war continued, most of even those few Spaniards who had supported Germany and Austria-Hungary realized that the Allies would emerge victorious from the war. Spain's increasing trade with Britain and France, and the profits that ensued, also won support for the Allied cause.

Whatever the inclinations of Spain's political class, the government had almost no means to intervene successfully in the European war, or even defend its own territory. On paper, the Spanish Army boasted 140,000 soldiers, but this force of mostly poor conscripts lacked modern weapons, strong leadership, adequate budgets, or even a clear mandate. Half of the army remained in Morocco and also received most of the limited modern equipment purchased by the Spanish government, undermining the ability of the military to conduct peninsular defense. The navy, despite several naval building programs, had still not recovered from the disaster of 1898 and remained unable to defend Spanish waters, much less conduct offensive operations in the Atlantic or Mediterranean. Spain did attempt to leverage its weakness into strength, by serving as a locus for mediating efforts between the two sides, and profiting from trade to both warring sides. The Spanish government did not manage the increased trade effectively, however, leading to significant military and working class unrest in 1917. The Spanish military emerged from World War I in essentially the same weak position as when it had begun, as the central government had proved unable to capitalize on the war to strengthen

Spain's economy, allocate resources to provide for a real defense, or identify sufficiently with the Allies to share in the spoils of war. While Spain's military did not collapse during World War I, the conflict exposed yet again the deep fissures within the armed forces, divisions that would explode less than two decades later.

On July 17, 1936, elements of the Spanish Army rose up in revolt against the Popular Front government (a coalition of left-wing political parties), which had gained control in the February elections. The conspirators, led by General Emilio Mola, stationed in Pamplona at the time, were opposed to the military reforms which had been instituted by the leadership of the Second Republic since 1931. What the rebel generals expected would be a very quick coup d'etat turned into a three-year bloody, brutal, fratricidal conflict that involved not only Spaniards (liberal vs. conservative) but the major powers of Europe as well. In the "Spanish Civil War: Franco's Nationalist Army" by George Esenwein and "The Popular Army of the Spanish Republic, 1936–39" by Michael Alpert, we are able to see the war from both sides. Esenwein begins his chapter on the Spanish Civil War by detailing how the Second Republic's Minister of War, Manuel Azaña, moved quickly to dismantle what had previously been done by Primo de Rivera. As Esenwein notes, Azaña's goal was twofold: to democratize the Army and to keep it out of politics. His reforms included reducing the number of senior rank officers by offering them early retirement and creating a new category for NCOs, as well as closing the anti-Republican GMA in Zaragoza and military journals. As ministers of war changed depending on elections, reforms were done and later undone. The military grew restless as they felt that their positions in the military and within society in general were threatened, while generals considered to be "dangerous" to the Republic were posted to Spanish Morocco (Mola), the Canary Islands (Franco), and the Balearic Islands (Manuel Goded) far from the peninsula.

By early July 1936, the plan to overthrow the government was coming together under Mola's leadership. The revolt (*Alzamiento*) began prematurely, launched on July 17 by officers of the Foreign Legion in Melilla in Spanish Morocco, and quickly spread to the rest of the Protectorate and to the peninsula. In the conservative and strongly Catholic north, the revolt found support and the Carlist *Requetés* provided a highly motivated and loyal militia to support the rebellion. However, the rebellion failed in the three major cities of Spain: Madrid, Barcelona, and Valencia. There, trade unions and their politicized militias refused to let the government be overthrown by disaffected generals. Leftist and anarchist trade unions rallied their workers, men and women, to defend the Popular Front government. While the revolt failed in the principal cities, Spanish Morocco became crucial to the nascent uprising. The battle-hardened and tested "Army of Africa" composed of the Moorish troops of the

Regulares and the Foreign Legion (roughly 34,000 officers and men) went over to the rebel Nationalists. With its experienced officer corps that had led units not only in Morocco but also against working-class Spaniards in the Leftist Asturias revolt of 1934, the Nationalists were in a much better position to exercise command and control over their forces. Transporting the Army of Africa across the Strait of Gibraltar would be the key to keeping the revolt from fizzling out. As the Navy had remained loyal to the Republic, after pro-coup officers had been murdered by their working-class crews, the only way to get the Army of Africa to the peninsula was by air. With only the gunboat *Dato* providing a naval escort, Franco was able to airlift his troops from Morocco to Seville where General Gonzalo Queipo de Llano had secured the city for the Nationalists. With the use of Italian and German bomber-transports, as well as a few Spanish *Breguet* transports, the Army of Africa was rapidly transferred from Tetuán to Seville. The 17th Company of the Vth *Bandera* of the Legion became the first military unit in history to be airlifted into combat on July 20. It has been said that Hitler told Franco that he should build a monument to the Junkers Ju-52 as it was this bomber-transport that allowed him to ferry the Army of Africa to Spain and thus kept the uprising from failing during the first days.

In both chapters, Alpert and Esenwein discuss the course of the war. During the first days and weeks of the conflict, the government was caught by surprise. Some trade union militias mounted an effective resistance to the rebels, and many local units of the *Guardia Civil* and other constabulary forces remained local to the Popular Front government in key cities such as Madrid and Barcelona. On the Nationalist side, Carlist and Falange militias also served a similar purpose as a force in existence. By the late summer of 1936, the battle lines had stabilized and Spain was divided. With Mola commanding the "Army of the North" and Franco the Army of Africa in the south, the aim of both was to take Madrid and end the war quickly. This was not to be as Franco's forces were diverted away from Madrid to relieve a Loyalist siege at the Alcázar in Toledo where rebel colonel, José Moscardó, and about 1,000 others were trapped. Instead of proceeding to attack Madrid as Colonel Juan Yagüe of the Army of Africa advised, Franco replaced Yagüe with the highly decorated *Africanista* José Varela and moved to rescue those besieged in the Alcázar. The relief and rescue of those in Alcázar provided Franco with a great propaganda victory, but cost him the opportunity to capture Madrid since during this time, the Republic, and the people of Madrid, had been equipped with Mexican and Soviet weapons, and the people of Madrid had dug trenches and prepared other defenses that withstood repeated assaults by Franco's troops.

As both authors write, the Spanish Civil War did not remain exclusively Spanish for long as Italy and Germany sided with the insurgent

Nationalists, while Mexico and the USSR supported the Republic. At first, weapons and equipment were shipped by both sides to Spain, while later Italian and German "volunteers" and technicians, as well as Soviet military officers, political commissars, and NKVD officials were sent by their respective governments. The Soviets went further via the Comintern when the call went out around the world for volunteers to come to Spain to fight fascism. Thousands of socialists, communists, and idealists heeded the call to arms as the International Brigades played a crucial role in defending the capital from the rebels.

In his chapter on the Army of the Republic, Alpert describes the difficulties faced by the government in trying to find qualified and experienced officers since the majority of these had opted for the Nationalist side. In the beginning, the militias served as the backbone of the government's army and of those, the Spanish Communist Party's (*Quinto Regimiento*) were the most disciplined and politically motivated. Also noted by Alpert is that during the Civil War, the Republicans were not only fighting the Nationalists but each other as the pro-Stalinist Spanish Communist Party tried to, and succeeded in eliminating its leftist rivals such as the *Partido Obrero de Unificación Marxista* or *POUM*. The Soviet Union would provide military support and other aid only to the Communists in Spain, not solely to defeat the rebels but to eliminate its enemies as well. So it can be said that the Republic was fighting a two-front war, one against Franco and another against itself.

Aside from describing the principal highlights of the war, such as the major battles and fronts, the bombing of the Basque town of Guernica by Germany's Condor Legion in 1937, and the foreign military equipment that was tried and tested out in Spain, the authors also detail the impact the war had on the nation and its peoples. One excellent observation made by Esenwein is what can be referred to as "Franco's way of war." Franco believed in a military strategy that focused on the slow, methodical advance making certain that those areas to your rear had been totally "pacified." Enemy combatants had been killed in combat, summarily shot, or in fewer cases, taken prisoner. All enemies and/or potential enemies of the *Cruzada* in a certain town or province had to be eliminated before further operations could proceed. While this strategy infuriated Franco's fascist allies (particularly the Germans who insisted that he drive for the enemy's *schwerpunkt*), it perfectly suited the nature of this civil war where great hatred and animosity, based on social class, politics, and religion, had been festering at least since the start of the twentieth century. This was a war that could only be won through the physical eradication of the enemy. Moreover, Franco had lived through the disaster which had befallen General Silvestre at Annual in 1921, where Silvestre had failed to disarm those in his rear and had advanced too rapidly thus not protecting his flanks. Silvestre's mistake was not one Franco was going to repeat.

The Spanish Civil War (or as the Nationalists called it—the War of Liberation) ended in 1939 with total victory for the Nationalists. Four months later, the outbreak of World War II in Europe would eventually engulf much of the world. Wayne H. Bowen's chapter, "The Spanish Military During World War II," examines the structure, operations, and politics of Spain's armed forces during this global conflict. As it had been during World War I, Spain was officially neutral during World War II. However, the regime that governed Spain—that of General Francisco Franco—was clearly sympathetic to the Axis, providing moral and material support to Nazi Germany for the first few years of the struggle. Not only did Spanish soldiers and airmen serve in the German military, at the initiative of Spain's government, but Madrid also aligned its diplomatic and commercial efforts alongside those of the Axis. While this identification with Nazi Germany and Fascist Italy faded with the declining fortunes of Hitler and Mussolini, military and economic collaboration continued, albeit in reduced forms, until the end of the war.

The primary combat role of the military during World War II was on Spanish soil, however, fighting attempts by communist-led guerrillas to overthrow the Franco regime in the immediate postwar period. Spanish members of the French Resistance, who had fought against the Nazis in France, began to cross the border as early as late 1944, hoping to rally peasants and workers, as well as to force intervention by the Allies, to bring down the Spanish government. Along with the *Guardia Civil*— Spain's national constabulary—the Spanish Army conducted operations in northern Spain to crush these incursions. By early 1946, the guerrilla movement failed, and the Franco regime reasserted its authority over the mountain valleys of northern Spain.

For most of the Spanish military, however, the war was one spent on the sidelines. Underfunded, underpaid, equipped with mediocre weapons, and filled with unwilling conscripts, the armed forces nonetheless played a vital role in the regime. As the force that had won the Civil War for Franco, the military held a special place of honor within the regime. Although its enlisted soldiers did not benefit from this association, its officer corps received special privileges and treatment, including food and housing allowances and opportunities to hold other salaried government and political positions without surrendering their commissions. Officers also understood that they were the foundation of the state and, with the Catholic Church, one of two key pillars ensuring the survival of Franco's government.

The Spanish dictator was keen to maintain high morale among the officers of his military, recognizing that his own survival as Head of State depended on their forbearance. As the only institution with the means to overthrow Franco, the army was at once all-powerful and vulnerable to manipulation. Although he had significant flaws as a leader, Franco was a master at ensuring his own endurance, primarily through keeping his enemies divided. Several times during World War II, groups of senior officers urged Franco to resign or surrender some of his power to accommodate a monarchical restoration. At other times, Naziphile military factions attempted to pressure Spain to enter the war on the side of the Axis. In each case, Franco sidestepped the central question, instead dividing the conspirators through selective promotions, demotions, and the use of internal and external exile. Despite his military background, Franco considered the military in ways similar to other institutions of government, awarding key positions based on loyalty rather than competence and giving primacy to political considerations at the expense of military necessity and efficiency.

During World War II, Franco had entertained dreams of expanding the Spanish empire through collaboration with the Axis. With the failure of that venture in 1945, Spain found itself diplomatically, commercially, and militarily isolated from the Great Powers and at odds with both Superpowers. Rather than a vast colonial empire, encompassing most of Northwest Africa, Spain entered the postwar era with modest imperial possessions. The development and eventual decline of this empire is the focus of Shannon E. Fleming's chapter, "Decolonization and the Spanish Army, 1940–76." The Spanish Empire, truncated after the debacle of 1898, remained central in the mentality, career, and operations of the Spanish military during these years. With Franco himself being an *Africanista,* loath to abandon Morocco and other overseas territories, the Spanish military struggled mightily against the wave of decolonization that began after World War II.

Spanish Morocco held a special place in the minds of many officers, including Franco, who had earned his early promotions and medals in the territory. Believing that they had a special link to the Berbers and Arabs of the colony, Spanish soldiers and colonial officials tolerated the presence of pro-independence leaders, with the unrealistic expectation that these Moroccans would only target the neighboring French colony. Franco's pro-Arab policies also included funding development projects, refusing to recognize Israel, and encouraging "a paternalist rapport" with indigenous leaders. As the campaign for independence gained support in French Morocco, however, these ideas spread to the Spanish territory. By the mid-1950s, it became obvious that Spain's hold on its Moroccan enclave was untenable, and in 1956 Spain followed France in recognizing independent Morocco.

Despite the loss of its Moroccan territory, Spain still held its colonies of Equatorial Guinea, Spanish Sahara, Ifni, and the cities of Ceuta and Melilla, the latter three entirely surrounded by Morocco. Unlike Spanish Morocco, these three colonies had mostly Spanish populations, thus increasing resistance by Madrid to the idea of giving up sovereignty.

Moroccan forces supported unsuccessful guerrilla operations against Ifni in the late 1950s, but Spain retained control of the enclave until 1969. Unlike Spain's North African territories, Equatorial Guinea never developed indigenous rebel groups, allowing Spain to move the colony toward independence without any crises or humiliations. In 1968, Spain granted independence.

Even after the Spanish surrender of its part of Morocco and Ifni, the kingdom of Morocco still hoped to gain control over Spanish Sahara, especially given the rich deposits of phosphates in the territory. By the early 1970s, Spain also confronted the *Polisario* movement, a rebellion of native *Saharawis* who wanted independence, rather than union with Morocco. Unable to crush this insurgency, and fearing open war with Morocco, in late 1975, as Francisco Franco lay in a persistent coma, the Spanish government began to negotiate the surrender of the colony. In early 1976, Spain withdrew the last of its military and civilian personnel, leaving Spanish Sahara to be divided between Morocco and Mauritania. The North African cities of Ceuta and Melilla, populated almost entirely by Spaniards, did not fall to the colonization process, remaining in Spanish hands.

From the 1950s to the 1970s, as Spain was dismantling its colonial empire, it was also successfully attempting to reenter the political and economic sphere of Western Europe. This movement is the subject of Chapter 8, "Rejoining Europe: From Isolation to Integration, 1945–2006," by José M. Serrano and Kenneth W. Estes. The authors present the modernization of the Spanish military over the sixty years after World War II as a series of modest steps, each of which brought Spain closer to Western Europe and NATO in terms of equipment, structure, and doctrine. By the early twenty-first century, the Spanish armed forces were nearly comparable to those of Britain and France, in terms of their quality and capabilities, and were fully integrated into the NATO system.

After more than a decade of military isolation, inadequate funding, poor training, and weak leadership, in 1953 the Spanish government signed several cooperation agreements with the United States. Not only did these accords allow the United States to base strategic aircraft in Spain, but they also committed the United States to provide military equipment and training to the Spanish military. While this assistance was modest and did not live up to the expectations of Franco and his commanders, U.S. military sales and transfers to Spain began the process of modernization. U.S. restrictions on the types of equipment—only defensive—and its employment—only within the Spanish peninsula—rankled, but the aid was nonetheless a significant improvement.

The growing economy of the 1960s allowed Spain to increase its acquisitions of modern equipment, and its increasing ties with Western Europe demonstrated in its purchases from the United Kingdom, France, and other NATO states. At the same time, the Spanish military became an increasingly professional and depoliticized force. Despite being the bulwark of the Franco regime, and having triumphed during the Spanish Civil War, after the mid-1950s officers increasingly viewed their role as defenders of Spain against the external threat of the Soviet Union, rather than as guardians of internal security.

The death of dictator Francisco Franco in 1975 and the nearly simultaneous loss of the last of the Spanish colonial empire accelerated Spain's integration into Europe and the modernization of its military forces. After holding democratic elections and surviving an attempted military coup in 1981, Spain joined the alliance in 1982. Now under an elected Socialist government, Spain began to distance itself from the more visible terms of its 1953 agreements with the United States, voting by referendum in 1986 to close U.S. air bases, while maintaining membership in NATO. In 1988, Spain joined the Western European Union and accelerated its full military integration into NATO.

Throughout the 1980s and 1990s, Spain reduced the size of its forces, while increasing the capabilities of its forces through better equipment and training. The Spanish military provided important support to Coalition Forces in the Gulf War, and Spain became a major participant in the NATO-led peacekeeping operations in Bosnia (1995) and Kosovo (1999). Conscription ended in late 2002 under a conservative government, and the increasingly professional armed forces continued to be a significant tool of Spain's foreign policy, participating in operations in Afghanistan and Iraq after 9/11, although the latter involvement ended with the election of a Socialist government in 2004.

The final chapter focuses on the roles of the Spanish military in struggles against terrorism, especially the Basque movement ETA (*Euskadi Ta Askatasuna*). From its beginnings in the 1950s, ETA emerged as a serious threat to internal security in northern Spain, with national and international capabilities. Using bombings, assassination, political coercion, and extortion, ETA became one of the most important terrorist groups in Western Europe. The response by the Spanish government, and the Spanish military, involved a combination of military operations, law enforcement, and political pressure against ETA and its collaborators, culminating in successful campaigns to arrest most of the group's key leaders, bans on political activity by movements tied to ETA, and increasing autonomy for the Basque region as a way to co-opt more moderate Basque leaders, such as those in the largest legal movement, the PNV (*Partido Nacionalista Vasco*—Basque Nationalist Party).

ETA's most spectacular early success was the assassination of Admiral Luis Carrero, Franco's chief adviser and rumored successor, in 1973. The regime immediately began a fierce, although somewhat incoherent, military, and law enforcement campaign against ETA, an effort which continued through the years of transition to democracy. Under the new democratic system of the late 1970s, however, the granting of autonomy to the Basque region greatly undermined ETA's maximalist demands for an independent state in northern Spain and southern France. The height of ETA violence, and counterreaction by the state, was from the late 1970s to the mid-1980s. After that point, ETA's terrorism, however bloody, was of decreasing effectiveness in rallying Basque popular opinion or convincing the Spanish public to grant independence. ETA's freedom of movement continued to decline throughout the 1990s and early twenty-first century, with increasingly effective law enforcement, collaboration from other European states, and divisions within the underground movement.

Other terrorist movements also were active in Spain during the 1970s and 1980s, including the revolutionary communist faction GRAPO (*Grupo de Resistencia Antifascista Primero de Octubre*), smaller regional separatist movements, and antidemocratic movements on the extreme right. None of these rose to the importance of ETA, either in the national consciousness or in the impact on politics, although for a brief period the extreme violence of GRAPO brought it national attention and clandestine (and sometimes illegal) action against it by the Spanish government. Most recently, Spain experienced terrorist attacks linked to supporters of Al-Qaeda, most infamously in the March 2004 commuter train bombings in Madrid.

The role of the Spanish military in the war on terrorism has been of decreasing internal importance, despite Spain's deployment of forces to Afghanistan and Iraq after 9/11. While during the Franco regime and early years of the democratic transition, the military played a significant role in counterterrorism operations, by mid-1980s the army's involvement was reduced to a minimum. Instead, the national police and *Guardia Civil* took the lead against ETA, GRAPO, and other terrorist movements, even though ETA continued to target military officers for assassination in its campaign to gain recognition as an active belligerent.

In the two centuries since 1808, the history of the Spanish military has been the history of Spain, from its mythical role during the Napoleonic occupation, to the clefts of the Carlist Wars, to its mixed record as a colonial power, to the military regimes established by its generals through coups and rebellions, to its final integration into Western Europe as a professionalized force. For most of this history, the Spanish Army was a failed institution, divided by political factions, poorly equipped, and vulnerable to external invasion and internal dissent. Prone to military coups in the nineteenth century, it was an irony that the most enduring government established through an attempted military coup, General Francisco Franco's (1936–75), set the stage for the professionalization, depoliticization, and integration into Europe of the Spanish military.

CHAPTER 1

The Spanish Army at War in the Nineteenth Century:

Counterinsurgency at Home and Abroad

Geoffrey Jensen

The role of the Spanish Army in shaping its country's history was probably as great as that of any European armed force in the nineteenth century. In addition to fighting an invasion by Napoleon's armies, two major civil wars, and colonial conflicts in the Americas, the Pacific, and Africa, the Spanish Army also exercised decisive, long-term influence on Spain's political scene. Indeed, it is the military's political influence in Spain that has received the most attention from historians, especially those studying the country after the final expulsion of the Napoleonic invaders in 1814.[1]

This chapter, however, focuses on the wars themselves and the fighting methods of the Spanish Army, discussing the politics, social composition, and cultural characteristics of the armed forces only insofar as they influenced military operations. It is of course impossible to tell the whole story of nineteenth-century Spanish military history in a single chapter, and most of the Latin American wars of independence are not covered here. Yet even a relatively short overview of the evolution of the army and the wars it waged can shed light on certain patterns in tactics, operations, and strategy, many of which reflected or even influenced other aspects of Spanish history.

As we will see, some kinds of failures on the battlefield repeated themselves tragically and unnecessarily, in large part because Spanish Army leaders proved unable or unwilling to accept the primacy of irregular warfare to their work. It did not help, moreover, that Spain's military institutions suffered from a constantly changing political scene; between 1814 and 1899, Spain had 129 ministers of war, including interim ministers who sometimes held their positions for only days or even hours.[2] In part for this reason, the leadership of the same officer corps that produced some of the country's most prominent political figures failed to adapt to the form of warfare in which politics plays an especially prominent role: counterinsurgency.

The French Revolution and the wars that followed affected the Spanish military as much as they affected most European armies, although in different ways. Whereas many other countries—most famously Prussia—reformed their armed forces in the wake of defeats by France's new mass armies, in Spain the changes in military organization that came after 1789 often had less to do with adapting to new ways of warfare than with domestic political and economic developments. The French revolutionary and Napoleonic victories may have influenced internal politics in other countries as well, especially as nationalism became an increasingly powerful force, but such pressures often helped stimulate the kind of military reforms that had no counterpart in Spain. While other European leaders accepted, for instance, the need to raise large armies to counter France's new mass force of citizen-soldiers, in Spain even the most vigorous military reformer in the wake of the French Revolution, royal advisor Manuel de Godoy, rejected the idea of a universal draft.[3]

The difficulties the Spanish Army would face in the struggle against Napoleonic occupation—known in Spain as the War of Independence (1808–14)—stemmed in no small part from the legacy of the late eighteenth century. As in much of Europe, the quality of the rank-and-file soldiers in Spain was low, but to make matters worse the number of cadres had fallen dramatically as well, which meant that if a major war came the army would be forced to rely heavily on new and untrained soldiers. The officer corps, moreover, was professionally divided, often lacking in technical expertise, and resented by civilians because of the privileged status officers had attained under the Bourbons.[4]

Correspondingly, Spanish tactics at the beginning of the nineteenth century were outdated, even though Godoy and others had made some attempts to modernize the tactical system. The French revolutionary armies had replaced some of their traditional linear formations with attack columns, typically units made up of one or two companies, with a front of some fifty to eighty men arranged nine to twelve men deep. This innovation eventually prompted a Spanish response, with some officers advocating the replacement of traditional lines with offensive columns of its own. However, resistance to change persisted in some segments of the army, which meant that the older tactical system would still see use in the War of Independence. Furthermore, those attempts to institute tactical changes that did take place were often flawed. The 1807 Spanish infantry manual (*Reglamento*), for example, recognized the need for attack columns, but it failed to appreciate the crucial role combined arms had to play in the actual employment of these columns in battle. Not only did it say little about how artillery and cavalry support would facilitate the columnar operations, but it also paid scant attention to the place of skirmishers in the new combat system.[5]

The employment of skirmishers by French revolutionary armies would, of course, attain near mythical status in the eyes of the many military historians who have stressed how France's transformation into a nation in arms facilitated the implementation of new skirmish tactics conceived but not used before the revolution. Although more recent studies have questioned whether the employment of skirmishers and other individual methods of the French revolutionary armies were really so novel after all, France's mass armies after 1789 combined lines, columns, and skirmishers on the battlefield in new and often devastating ways.[6] Godoy, however, failed to take account of such tactical developments in his reforms of the Spanish infantry. Furthermore, at a more fundamental level, he failed to grasp that the Spanish Army desperately needed major transformations in structure, organization, and size.[7]

The consequences of Godoy's failure in this respect would become painfully clear after May 2, 1808, less than two months after King Charles IV—along with Godoy himself—had lost power to Charles's son Fernando VII. On this day, the popular uprising against Napoleon's occupying troops began, famously portrayed in Goya's paintings and soon serving as a source of inspiration to anti-Napoleonic nationalists elsewhere in Europe. The ensuing War of Independence would subsequently form the basis of much nationalist and military mythology in Spain, but the Spanish Army itself garnered relatively little glory in the struggle. Although the soldiers of the regular armed forces and militias were certainly not incapable of fighting hard and bravely, the far more loosely organized Spanish guerrilla fighters and the British army of Arthur Wellesley—later the Duke of Wellington—earned most of the credit for Napoleon's eventual defeat in Spain.

Spanish civilians had little faith in the regular army's leadership when the war began, and as conditions rapidly turned revolutionary many made it clear that they opposed the existing military hierarchy altogether. Not surprisingly, many generals first offered their services to the French, in no small part because they feared the radical developments unleashed by the insurgency. Most senior officers, however, found that the explosion of anti-French sentiments was too powerful—and personally dangerous—to resist. They thus had little choice but to join the war effort against Napoleon, hoping that they might thereby at least control and channel some of the violent popular sentiments that had been let loose around them. They feared not only revolution but also that a nonprofessional army of untrained masses would lack the skills necessary to wage war successfully—the successes of the earlier French revolutionary armies not-withstanding.[8]

In the end, however, it was the guerrilla fighter who came to symbolize Spanish military resistance to the French, and the most famous Spanish figures of the war were mainly independent guerrilla leaders such as Juan Martín Díez, or "El Empecinado." Their endeavors combined with those of Wellington's regular army ultimately to doom Napoleon's forces in Spain. By constantly threatening their enemies' lines of communication, the guerrillas seriously hindered the French prosecution of the war against Wellington. At the same time, the presence of Wellington's forces on the peninsula meant that the French could not devote all their resources to the large-scale counterinsurgency campaign that the situation demanded.

Yet Napoleon could not ignore the Spanish Army either, even if its role in this war has been largely overshadowed by Wellington and the guerrillas. In spite of the behavior of many of their generals, most of the Spanish Army's rank-and-file and its officer corps, especially at the lower grades, supported the popular resistance to French occupation, albeit for varying reasons. Not least of their motives was the widespread fear that French rule in Spain would bring with it their own incorporation into Napoleon's *Grande Armée*, which might mean being forced to fight far from home. Many soldiers exhibited the same dislike of the French occupation seen in Spanish civilians, and they also expressed loyalty to the new and still-popular king, Fernando VII. Furthermore, junior officers hoped that a war would bring with it new possibilities of promotion.[9]

Thus, of the 28,000 Spanish troops under French command abroad or in garrisons within Spain that the French had occupied by spring 1808, remarkably few came to serve in Napoleon's imperial force. Instead, regiments experienced widespread desertions, went over as a whole to the insurgency, or sometimes simply disbanded rather than join the French. Officers who resisted such actions by their soldiers did so at considerable risk, being cast aside or suffering bodily harm for their actions. The resistance to service in the Grande Armeé even spread as far as Denmark, where Godoy had sent some 13,000 Spanish troops under the command of the Marqués de la Romana, Pedro Caro, as part of his policy of collaboration with France. There, news of the French invasion of Spain had fueled enough discontent among Spanish soldiers that Napoleon had ordered the garrisoning of extra French forces in Hamburg and Schleswig-Holstein in case the Spanish detachments in Denmark rose up. His concerns were not unwarranted. Although La Romana tried at first to appease the French, he soon found himself—probably under considerable pressure from his own officers and troops—organizing a mass escape of his forces with the help of the Royal Navy. Shortly after receiving the news of the Spanish victory over the French at Bailén, which we will turn to shortly, a convoy set sail from Denmark, and the first ships finally made it to Santander on October 10. Several thousand of the Spanish soldiers in Denmark did not make it to the departure point in time, however, and their unhappy fate was to join Napoleon's ill-fated invasion of Russia.[10]

After May 2, provincial committees, or *juntas*, sprang up all over Spain to direct the revolutionary war against the French. Their members understandably distrusted the generals, but this attitude led to the replacement of experienced military leaders by men who lacked the skills necessary to organize and run an army, regardless of how strong their devotion to the cause may have been. The generals who remained, moreover, found themselves in command of forces that, while often very large thanks to new levies, lacked military experience. To make matters worse for the regular army leaders, the *juntas* broke up existing units or deprived them of recruits, to the benefit of the more than two hundred new infantry regiments that formed in 1808. Such actions ensured the political loyalty of the new regiments' officers, who had a personal stake in the revolution, but it obviously hindered military effectiveness.[11]

As had been the case with the early French revolutionary armies, the inexperienced but enthusiastic character of the new Spanish regiments had its positive aspects. Although the French found it easy to outmaneuver or overrun these units when they faced them in battle, in stationary positions where the cavalry was insignificant, the Spanish soldiers could withstand even strong French attacks. The initial failure of the French to take such cities as Zaragoza and Gerona, which subsequently resisted long and horrible sieges before finally falling, attests to the high fighting spirit of the Spanish soldiers. Early in the war, the Spaniards prevailed in the battle—really more of a campaign—of Bailén in July 1808. Bailén was a crucial victory over the French imperial army, which up to this point had not surrendered, and it attracted more volunteers for the struggle against the French. It was not, however, a sign of things to come. Instead, the Spanish commander, General Francisco Javier Castaños, benefited from a unique combination of fortuitous encounters and French failings, even if he deserves credit for seizing opportunities when they appeared and exacting some very grueling marches from his men.[12]

Yet Bailén would be an exception, and things went so badly in general, that provincial *Junta* leaders eventually agreed to the creation of a new national congress, the *Junta Central*, in September 1808. This change did not, however, bring with it noteworthy improvements in military operations. At the tactical level, the army continued to perform badly. An important weakness lay in its cavalry, which suffered from a lack of experience. As one historian writes, even when the infantry performed well on offensives, on the flanks the Spanish cavalry would be put to flight with monotonous regularity, thereby opening the way for a torrent of French horsemen to burst in upon the flanks and rear of the unfortunate infantry. Caught entirely by surprise, the infantry would not have the time to form square, and could only flee for their lives, to be ridden down or captured in their thousands.

The Spaniards also lacked sufficient skirmishers, especially during the early part of the war, and as a result, their French counterparts tended to drive them back with relative ease, then firing upon the stationary Spanish lines behind them. When those lines began to falter, the French columns would charge forward to finish the story.[13]

At the strategic level, the political predicament of the *Junta Central* severely hindered the army's effectiveness. It had gained a respite in late 1808 thanks to the British army under Sir John Moore, who led much of the French force in a strategically fruitless chase from central Spain to the northwestern coastal city of La Coruña. However, the *Junta*'s need for the political capital that military victories would bring with them prevented the adoption of an appropriate defensive strategy. It thus called for taking the offensive, but this meant taking on the French in the open geography of central and northern Spain, thereby playing to the enemy's strengths in maneuverability and set piece battles. Even Wellington's plea to the contrary had no effect.[14]

It would have made more sense to adopt a defensive posture, in which regular armies would remain mostly in the mountains preparing for later encounters while guerrillas continued to harass the French. Indeed, the Marqués de la Romana practiced a form of this strategy with considerable success. In a microcosm of the successful coalition of the British army and the Spanish guerrillas throughout Spain, his regular army camped out in the mountains near the northern Portuguese border while guerrillas wore away at the French. Because of potential threat of his relatively large force, the French could not devote all their forces to counterinsurgency against the guerrillas, who in turn prevented the French from concentrating against Romana. However, the methods of the Marqués earned him the ire of many critics, who went as far as to accuse him of cowardice and a lack of patriotism for his unorthodox strategy.[15]

Inevitably, the Spanish Army did poorly on the battlefield, reaching its lowest point in November 1809 in the defeats at Ocaña and Alba de Tormes, when it lost 40,000 men and 59 artillery pieces. These losses and the subsequent French victories in Andalusia led to the fall of the Central *Junta* in January 1810. Henceforth, the British army's role in the war increased significantly, with Wellington relying upon the Spanish Army as little as possible. At the same time, the rise to power of Spanish liberals did not bring with it an improvement in the patriot army's effectiveness.

The famous Constitution of Cádiz (1812) that grew out of the Spanish liberal revolution may have represented a monumental development in the history of liberalism, but the attitude of its authors toward the professional military did not help the army. They opposed in principle regular, professional armies, favoring citizen militias in their place. Unfortunately for the anti-Napoleonic Spaniards, however, in the War of Independence this argument had not proved operationally viable, regardless of its ideological appeal to liberals. Indeed, regular, professional forces of the sort that liberals opposed had fought at Bailén, "the only field battle won by the Spaniards."[16] Thereafter, as the army increasingly assumed the character of a "people's force," it encountered scant success on the battlefield. From 1810 until the final French defeat in 1814, the British army's importance in the struggle against the French only grew, easily eclipsing that of its Spanish counterpart.

The guerrillas, on the other hand, continued to play a key role in sapping Napoleon's forces of their military strength, even if some historians argue that their overall role in defeating the French was minor compared to that of Wellington's army. In fact, the British would not have fared nearly so well if the French had not had to deal with the horrendous insurgency problem. Thanks to the guerrillas, during the summer of 1811, the French needed 70,000 troops to keep the communications line between Madrid and the French border open.[17] The guerrilla war may not have been the selfless, patriotic, and popular struggle that Spanish nationalists would later claim, but it did severely limit French operations.[18]

In the Spanish Army's next major conflict, the First Carlist War (1833–40), guerrillas would be opponents rather than allies, marking the beginning of a recurring pattern of counterinsurgencies that the army would wage throughout the century. In this case, the conflict was a civil war, with the insurgents, or Carlists, fighting in the name of the rival Bourbon line of Don Carlos against Queen Isabel II and, more generally, in favor of ultraconservative religious and political values over the relative liberalism associated with the queen's rule. Although they never succeeded in placing their rival dynastic line in power, the movement in support of Carlos and his descendants would cause several major civil wars and exercise significant political influence well into the dictatorship of Francisco Franco.

Over 65,000 government soldiers lost their lives in the First Carlist War, and total casualties on the government side (including wounded and missing in action) numbered some 175,000. The Carlists probably lost at least an equal number of soldiers, and the total military casualties for both sides—not including civilians—may have been as high as 2.5% of the total population. Given these figures, it is not surprising that the army underwent significant changes during the course of the conflict. Above all, the government army grew dramatically after the war's outbreak. By the war's end, the government casualty count alone was more than twice as high as the number of men who had been in the Spanish Army in 1828.[19]

Why did the insurgency prove so difficult to suppress? A multitude of social, economic, political, and cultural forces all played a role in the course and outcome of the war, and it is not possible here to cover them all. Yet the condition and performance of the government army itself should not be overlooked either. As we will see, the army entered the conflict unprepared for a civil war of this magnitude or character, even if its effectiveness did improve with time.

During the decade before the Carlists took up arms in 1833, leading Spanish officers devoted substantial efforts to raising the professional and educational standards of the army. Their main instruments were the various military academies and other instructional centers that they revived during this period, and the literature they produced often stressed the instruction of recruits, as well as military science in its more technical aspects. They did not, however, pay particular attention to mountain warfare, which is what the army would face in abundance in its struggle to subdue the Carlists. In late 1834, slightly over one year after the war began, a book on the subject finally appeared, most likely because of the sudden relevance of the topic. Although the work's author, former general staff officer Santiago Pascual y Rubio, focused on mountain warfare, aspects of his analysis apply equally well in broader terms to many of the counterinsurgencies that the army would wage throughout the century.[20]

The mountain warfare he described had little in common with the regular warfare for which the army had been preparing. According to Pascual, in the mountains extensive experience and knowledge of military science often means little, for such conditions entail "extraordinary qualities" in commanders far different from those needed in more traditional battles. Even the most skilled commanders, he wrote, can commit grave errors when they try to apply the principles of fighting on flat land to mountain warfare. At the more practical level, he advocated equipping the individual soldiers as well as the cavalry lightly, reasoning that the latter needed the ability to dismount easily and fight on foot if surprised. Pascual's march tactics involved using columns to move through valleys and ravines, while light infantry provided cover by occupying high positions. In the case of enemy fire, only the skirmishers were to answer in kind, while the columns would stay in close formation and attack with bayonets. The main aim, however, was to outflank the enemy through the use of multiple columns, thereby obscuring the main thrust of the attack. The weakness of this method would become deadly clear in practice, as the Carlists learned that ascertaining the army's intentions allowed them to take advantage of their interior lines and defeat the Spanish forces in detail.[21]

When the war began, the government forces numbered only 45,000 veteran soldiers, not counting the militias and the 20,000 draftees who were soon raised. The army was widely dispersed, with some troops covering the Portuguese border to prevent Don Carlos himself from entering the country, some guarding penal colonies spread around Spain, others manning the *cordon sanitaire* that the government had created in response to cholera outbreaks, some guarding supply and ammunition dumps, and others disarming the Royalist Volunteers, whom the government quickly acted against when the war broke out, justifiably suspicious of their loyalty to the new queen.[22]

The Carlists, on the other hand, had to create their own army from scratch; not one unit of the regular army went over to their side. Because they were scattered all over the peninsula, the Carlists ended up creating three major forces: the army of the north, the army of Cataluña, and the army of the Maestrazgo. Through a combination of volunteers and draftees, by the end of 1834 the Carlist armies had only about 18,000 troops all together, but by 1839 the three armies probably numbered over 70,000 men, in addition to perhaps some 15,000 guerrillas. For most of the war, there was scant communication between the three armies and most of the guerrilla bands, or *partidas,* that sprung up elsewhere across the country.[23] Although the liberal army would always outnumber the Carlists, the insurgency would prove very difficult to break.

The war began in earnest in the Basque city of Bilbao, where word of Ferdinand VII's death arrived around 0300 hours on October 2, 1833. By the evening of the next day, the Carlists had gained firm control of the city.[24] They would receive some of their strongest support in the rural, more mountainous areas around Bilbao and elsewhere in the Basque Country and Navarre, areas that—not coincidentally—had supplied the guerrilla *partidas* with much manpower during the War of Independence over two decades earlier. The insurgents found it very difficult to hold on to cities, however, and they relinquished Bilbao without a fight in November with the arrival of the government forces, also known as the queen's army or *Cristinos,* for their loyalty to the new queen Cristina. The Carlists also gave up Logroño and Vitoria, which they had initially controlled.

Yet the war was far from over. As Napoleon's forces had discovered after 1808 and numerous regular armies have found out since, even loosely organized guerrillas with no formal training and inferior weapons can be very tenacious opponents. The Carlists in the Basque Country may have worn makeshift uniforms, including their signature red berets and hemp sandals, and lacked sufficient weaponry and ammunition, but they were mountaineers well suited for irregular warfare, and such tasks as casting bullets and making cartridges came easily to them. Even more importantly, the Carlists in northern Spain soon gained a very effective commander, Tomás de Zumalacárregui, who ended their early series of defeats. Zumalacárregui's task was made easier by geography and the popular support he enjoyed, as he benefited from the help of local priests, community leaders, and the tradition of resistance to central authority that characterized the region in which he operated. He was certainly not adverse to employing force when necessary; it was, after all, a horribly brutal civil war in which civilians suffered greatly and both sides employed terror and shot prisoners. Nevertheless, Zumalacárregui endeavored to foster good relations with local leaders whenever possible, and his hearts-and-minds work in general was more profound and effective than that of the *Cristinos*.

He proved his leadership skills on December 21, 1833, at Guernica, the emblematic Basque town that would suffer a horrible air attack during another civil war a century later, its destruction famously portrayed by Picasso. Under Zumalacárregui, the Carlist forces at Guernica held their ground, inflicting some 300 casualties to their own 100. Although he decided to withdraw when government reinforcements approached, his withdrawal did not bring with it a strategic victory for the *Cristinos*. Instead, Zumalacárregui put into practice a more general, classical guerrilla approach that would prove effective: shunning battle except when conditions favored his own side. To the consternation of the Spanish Army commanders, he avoided battle and led his troops into the mountainous area around Navarre instead, where he organized them into battalions.

On December 29, he decided to take on the government's army again, this time near the village of Asarta. His force of some 2,500 men, divided into seven battalions, was not well armed, but its location between Asarta and the neighboring village of Nazar fits well into his conception of what he thought might unfold. Not only did the terrain make his position difficult to outflank, but all the roads on which his troops might flee in a worst-case scenario led to the same place, thus making it easy for him to form them up again if necessary. Not unexpectedly, the *Cristinos* eventually forced a general withdrawal of the Carlists.

Yet Zumalacárregui did not deem the battle of Asarta a defeat. His army had for a while stood up and fought against an enemy of roughly equal size but with much better arms, equipment, and training, and he believed that his men had suffered fewer casualties than the *Cristinos*. It was now clear that they could stand firmly against an initial attack, withdraw in a relatively orderly fashion if necessary, and then reassemble without much loss. Up until this point, Carlist soldiers had typically deserted after battles. This time, the battle's end brought with it new volunteers, and some officers in the queen's army actually went over to the Carlists. Zumalacárregui would continue to prove an insurmountable obstacle to the government army's success until his demise in the summer of 1835, when he died from wounds suffered during his ill-advised siege of Bilbao—an action he had reluctantly undertaken under pressure from the ruling Carlist *Junta* and Don Carlos himself.

More important for our purposes, however, is how the regular Spanish Army responded to Zumalacárregui and the Carlist insurrection in general. Its counterinsurgency methods evolved over time, including certain methods that would repeat themselves in other wars during the rest of the century. Early in the war, after the battle of Asarta, Cristino army leaders wisely elected not to pursue Zumalacárregui, who took his battalions to the Navarrese valley of Amescóa, about thirty-five miles southwest of Pamplona. Surrounded by mountain ranges but relatively well connected with the Basque Country, it was good guerrilla terrain.

The strategy of the queen's army was to build a line of forts at key points along the Ebro River between Pamplona and Logroño, thereby boxing the Carlists into the southwest corner of Navarre while also securing their own communications line with Madrid. But the forts were hardly sufficient to root out the insurgents, who may have lacked resources but benefited from superior local intelligence, knowledge of terrain, and a lack of burdensome supply trains. As a result of the failure of this counterinsurgency strategy, a new supreme commander, General Vicente Gonzalo de Quesada, took over the government's army in February 1834. He came up with a new plan for subduing the Carlists in the north that, while theoretically sensible, in practice proved more difficult to realize than he had expected.

He too aimed to take away some of the Carlists' mobility and force them to concentrate into smaller areas, where he could then wield his superior force against the insurgents on his own terms. To achieve this goal, he sought to place large and well-armed columns at key points, create smaller, mobile—or "flying"—columns that could be brought together or separated as necessary, and build more forts to better secure his own communications. The problem lay in the human and logistical resources that such a strategy entailed. The mobile columns he envisioned would require 10,000 troops and 400 horses, and garrisoning the forts as necessary required another some 3,000 men. Maintaining security in the cities of San Sebastian and Pamplona, moreover, required about 2,500 troops. Such numbers were simply too high, even as the Spanish government called up another 25,000 men in addition to the regular draft in February.

In late June, José Rodil replaced Quesada as the *Cristino* commander in chief in the north, and he modified the government's counterinsurgency strategy in the north once again. Believing that key individuals lay behind much of the rebels' fighting spirit and success on the battlefield, he divided his forces into three parts, two of which he devoted to pursing Zumalacárregui and Don Carlos, respectively. The third's task was to garrison the existing forts. Unfortunately for Rodil, the gamble did not pay off. Although at one point he came close to capturing Carlos, in general his strategy was counterproductive, as it exacted grueling marches from his men for little gain.

To make matters worse for the *Cristinos,* Zumalacárregui organized some of his best and most audacious officers and sergeants into very small, highly mobile units—or flying bands—that severely hindered government communications, and these units would grow in size with time. Taking advantage of their local knowledge, they made communications very dangerous for the *Cristinos,* harassing them, monitoring their movements, and intercepting messages. Much like the Spanish guerrillas fighting the French decades earlier, the Carlists thereby tied down an increasing number of the queen's troops. In this way, the Carlists compensated at least in part for their relative lack of numbers, which were too small to blockade the government garrisons in a traditional fashion.

After Zumalacárregui's death in June 1835 and the defeat at Mendigorría one month later, the Carlists in the north suffered a notable loss of momentum. They gained almost complete control of the interior of the Basque provinces, but the concurrent shift from Zumalacárregui's strategy of roving operations to one of occupation also led to a decline in Carlist morale, and a stalemate ensued. After another failed attempt by the Carlists to besiege Bilbao and a major *Cristino* victory at Luchana at the end of 1836, the queen's army attempted to break the stalemate with a decisive offensive in the north. However, their plan, which called for a simultaneous advance on Carlist territory in Guipúzcoa from Pamplona, San Sebastian, and Bilbao, presupposed an operational-level competence that the army simply did not have, and all three columns suffered high losses and had to return to their bases. From this point on, it was clear that the war's center of gravity no longer lay in the north.

The army also failed in its attempts to crush the famous "expeditions" later launched by the Carlists, which consisted of several large columns—one led by Don Carlos himself—that made their way through various parts of Spain. Although they made their presence known all over the peninsula, motivating the existing guerrilla *partidas* and garnering much popular support, they did not change the military balance directly. They did, however, draw attention to the seeming impotence of the government forces that pursued them, thereby publicizing their cause in Spain and abroad and helping weaken the position of the Queen's government in Madrid. To make matters worse for the *Cristinos,* in lower Aragon, Valencia, and Catalonia the government forces struggled with increasing difficulty against not only independent guerrilla bands but also troops under the command of Ramón Cabrera, a former seminarian who proved to be one of the Carlists' most effective military leaders. The *Cristinos* created a new force—the so-called army of the center—in response to the growing difficulties they faced in the east.

In the end, though, internal rivalries within the Carlist camp facilitated the end of this long and bloody civil war. In early 1839, the commander in chief of the Carlist forces, General Rafael Maroto, asserted his authority over the theologically extremist and intransigent faction of the movement by having four rival Carlist generals shot. Negotiations between him and the leader of the Cristino forces, General Baldomero Espartero, ensued. The two men signed an armistice on August 29, and the war-weary north could finally return to peacetime. In the east, Carlists continued to fight, but the queen's army could easily concentrate on this area now, effectively crushing all remaining resistance by the summer of 1840.

Thus, when all was said and done, victory had come not through brilliant counterinsurgency planning or operations, but rather from improvised strategy and attrition. Yet during the course of the conflict, the Spanish Army had experimented with various counterinsurgency tactics, and its operations had improved over time. The question remained, then, what the army would learn from the experience. Did this victory herald institutional change in the Spanish Army? Unfortunately for subsequent Spanish governments, it did not. Instead, army culture remained very much oriented toward regular war. Moreover, political interests and conflicts continued to plague the officer corps, which only grew in size as promotions were handed out to reward loyalty.

The less-than-ideal condition of the Spanish Army revealed itself again in the Moroccan campaign of 1859–60. The grandiose name that it soon assumed in Spain—the "War of Africa"—reveals more about its relationship to Spanish nationalism than the actual scale of the military operations.[25] In fact, the war was a limited response to attacks by Moroccan tribesmen around Spain's North African cities of Ceuta and Melilla. Although such small attacks had taken place off-and-on over the last few decades, most recently in August 1859, this time public opinion clamored for a vigorous response. Spanish Prime Minister Leopoldo O'Donnell, in need of a political boost at home, declared war on October 22, later taking command of the operation personally. The Spanish forces would succeed in their objective of taking Tetuán and the port of Tangier, both near Ceuta, forcing the Moroccans to sue for peace in late March 1860. Under British pressure, the Spaniards had to relinquish Tangier and Tetuán in the final peace settlement of late April, but they were allowed to expand their territory around Ceuta and Melilla and—in theory, at least—establish an Atlantic fishing settlement at Santa Cruz de Mar Pequeña, or Ifni, although they would not effectively occupy the area until 1934. Yet Spain's spoils and O'Donnell's political benefits from the war came at a high price: more than 4,000 of its sons perished in the conflict.[26] To understand why, it is necessary to analyze aspects of the war in more depth.

In spite of its ultimate success in Morocco, the Spanish Army demonstrated that the experience of the Carlist Wars had not made it a more effective force. Many commentators, including Friedrich Engels, then a war correspondent for the *New York Daily Tribune,* commented on the slow pace of Spanish military operations during the war. First, it took over a month just to transport the Spanish soldiers across the eight-mile Strait of Gibraltar, during which weather conditions combined with a shortage of adequate ships held back the operation. Thereafter the troops remained at the El Serrallo base next to Ceuta until January 1, when the move toward Tetuán finally began. This delay prompted Engels to comment that "[n]o matter what O'Donnell may say by way of apology, there can be no excuse for this continued inactivity." It then took a month for the troops to make the twenty-one-mile trip between the two cities.[27]

At the tactical level, the army made some improvements during the four-month campaign, even if its conditions were far from ideal when operations commenced. Part of the problem stemmed from the nature of Spanish military culture then, which emphasized personal bravery to an absurd degree while discounting the guerrilla tactics used by Carlists as cowardly. Such arguments help drown out those officers who advocated serious, rational study of Spanish campaigns from the recent past, thereby hindering doctrinal development. Thus, each new campaign meant relearning lessons that should have been absorbed earlier.[28]

At first, the infantry showed itself completely unprepared for the enemy's guerrilla tactics, and in some cases it took only forty or fifty Moroccans to tie down an entire Spanish battalion. Engels, in fact, would view the Spaniards's performance so negatively that in March 1860 he wrote: "This much is certain: the Spaniards have much to learn yet in warfare before they can compel Morocco to peace, if Morocco holds out for a year."[29] Of course, Engels was somewhat off the mark with this appraisal. The Moroccans actually sued for peace at the end of that month, and over the course of the conflict, the Spaniards in fact adapted to the Moroccan fighting methods. They learned, for instance, to deploy extensive chains of skirmishers to prevent the long, spread-out lines of enemy soldiers from enveloping them. Along the same lines, on the offensive the Spanish forces increasingly emphasized flank attacks aimed at enveloping the enemy.[30] As we will see, the future commander in chief of the Spanish Army in Cuba, Valeriano Weyler, would similarly stress outflanking as a way of defeating guerrillas.

Also like in Cuba decades later, disease could be as deadly of a threat to the Spaniards as the Moroccan soldiers. Cholera became a problem early in the campaign, and it would reach epidemic proportions in Tetuán. During the forty days in which the army remained at El Serrallo, cholera killed more Spanish soldiers than enemy fire would during the entire campaign. Of the some 2,000 Spanish deaths by late December 1859, a majority were the result of cholera. Overall, well over 38,000 soldiers out of a force of around 55,000 were hospitalized because of illness or combat wounds, the vast majority because of the former. Another some 3,000–4,000 Spanish soldiers died in the campaign, a number that might have been even higher had the Moroccans possessed better weaponry.[31]

Yet even with its many faults, the Spanish Army could at least view the Moroccan War of 1859–60 as a relatively straightforward operation in which it fought at the behest of a single government and with largely undivided popular support. The same could not be said of its next war, this time another civil war against the Carlists once again. The Carlists had already staged another uprising since the First Carlist War, the so-called "War of the 'Early Risers'" ("*Matiners*" in Catalan or "*Madruga-dores*" in Spanish), or Second Carlist War of 1846–49, which took its name from the insurgents' early-morning guerrilla attacks. This insurgency was nowhere near the scale of the First Carlist War, taking place only in Catalonia and then Galicia before the government put it down, granting the Carlists amnesty.

The Third Carlist War of 1872–76 (called the Second Carlist War by those who deem the "Early Risers" uprising too minor to have been a war) was a much bloodier affair. Thanks to the Spanish Revolution of 1868 and the various regime changes that followed, it took place in a political climate even more tumultuous than that of the previous Carlist insurgencies. By the time the army finally defeated the Carlists, it had fought in the name of the governments of King Amadeo I, who reigned from 1871 through early 1873; the First Republic of 1873; General Francisco Serrano, who ruled for most of the next year; and finally King Alfonso XII, who in 1875 brought the Bourbon dynasty back to Spain. To further complicate matters, with the declaration of the First Republic many monarchists went over to the side of the Carlists, where they would remain until the Bourbon restoration. In the summer of 1873, moreover, the Spanish Army also had to confront a left-republican "cantonalist" revolt, inspired in part by the Paris Commune of several years earlier.

The war against the Carlists began when Don Carlos de Borbón y Austria-Este, known as Carlos VII to his followers, crossed the French border into Navarre on May 2 to lead an uprising in his name. Two days later, however, the governor general of the region surprised him and his followers at their base, and he had to flee back across the border. The Carlists then rose up again but with more success in December, and soon the war spread throughout two main theaters of operation, the so-called northern and eastern fronts. As before, the rebel movement was strongest in the former, located in the Basque Country and Navarre, but the eastern, or Catalan, front was a crucial theater of operations as well. But unlike in the north, in Catalonia the insurgents would fail to establish even the beginnings of a state based on local rights, or "*fueros*," as called for by Carlist doctrine. This failure would eventually contribute to a growing sense of disenchantment there, which in turn contributed to the Carlist defeat. Another difference in the two theaters lay in the character of the Carlist leadership: in the northern front the Carlist leadership included many professional military men with considerable experience, including two who had served as colonels in the 1859–60 African campaign and one who had held the rank of major general during the conflict (field marshal according to the Spanish nomenclature then).[32]

The government army was organized according to traditional Spanish military practice, although it also included two relatively new battalions of special light infantry, or *cazadores,* assigned to the forward positions of armies on the move and to the first line of attack or defense in combat. Their equipment and training was equal to that of the normal line infantry, but each battalion included eight companies of fusiliers, as opposed to the standard six. Their *cazadores* officers were all career military men, and they owed their positions at least somewhat more to merit than to political favoritism, which was not the case in the rest of the army. Indeed, gross favoritism, which had stymied the promotion of many officers suspected of disloyalty to the central government, contributed greatly to the low morale within the officer corps as a whole. As the war raged on and political turmoil reigned in Madrid, discipline among the rank-and-fire became a growing problem within the army, which experienced continually more desertions and acts of insubordination, especially after the establishment of the First Republic and then the outbreak of the Cantonalist revolt. When such problems among the troops occurred, the many officers who had little faith in the government they served, often because they had been denied promotions for political reasons, felt no strong compulsion to help reestablish order.[33]

On the other hand, the army benefited from a strong pool of experienced NCOs that the Carlists could not match. Here one of the traditional regional rights, or "*fueros,*" that the Carlists were fighting to preserve actually came back to haunt them: they were exempt from the obligatory military service demanded in the rest of Spain. Thus, in spite of the undeniable guerrilla skills of many Carlists, when organized into regular units they lacked the kind of experience that made it possible for government troops to withstand continual harassments, food and supply shortages, and poor leadership at times.[34]

The cavalry of the government army also exceeded that of its opponents in both quality and quantity, thanks in large part to the privileged position it held during the years prior to the Revolution of 1868. Although terrain and deadly defensive firepower prevented it from effectively carrying out all the tasks for which it had been trained, the cavalry did continue to see use for reconnaissance, harassing enemy flanks, and the exploitation of gaps in enemy lines. Although it would not play a decisive role in the government victory, it was definitely superior to the enemy cavalry.[35]

The government's artillery, on the other hand, performed very badly during much of the war, but not for lack of guns. Instead, its problem stemmed from conflicts between its elitist officer corps and relatively radical political leaders, including Prime Minister Manuel Ruiz Zorrilla. In 1873, Ruiz Zorrilla pushed a proposal to reorganize the artillery—which essentially called for its dissolution—through parliament, resulting in the substitution of all artillery colonels, majors, and captains by officers from other arms and the navy. Ruiz Zorrilla's desire to tame the artillery made political sense, especially in light of its officers highly questionable loyalty and ties to his opponents, including anti-abolitionists—slavery was a major issue in Cuba—who exercised much influence within the officer corps. Yet by acting against the artillery, he left this technically demanding arm with few experienced officers.[36]

In any case, it was the infantry that played the most important role in deciding battles. Once again, infantry officers began a new war with doctrine and an institutional culture in general more apt for regular European warfare than fighting guerrillas in mountainous terrain. As they soon discovered, the traditional European tactics that their leaders had emphasized were simply not possible given the conditions, a state of affairs from which they ironically benefited in at least one way. During the second half of the nineteenth century, defensive firepower increased tremendously, as the American Civil War had already made clear. Yet European armies still preserved many tactical methods that presupposed a more like relationship between the offensive and the defensive, in some cases breaking through fortified enemy positions only by using powerful new artillery not available to the Spanish Army, such as the rifled steel Krupp guns the Prussians directed against the French in 1870. Thus, if the terrain had facilitated the employment of "classical" infantry tactics in the Third Carlist War, even more blood may well have been shed in futile offensives. In addition to geography, the smaller size of the Spanish forces also discouraged the use of costly frontal attacks. Whereas Prussian generals fighting against the French in 1870 were not averse to suffering huge casualties if victory came in the end, in Spain neither side could afford these kinds of losses. Thus, Spanish military leaders had scant choice but to avoid this aspect of the German way of war.[37]

Until the last part of the conflict, the Spanish government forces experienced many of the same difficulties they had encountered in earlier wars, such as an inability to engage the enemy except on his own terms, a lack of security and control in rural and mountainous areas, and a political context that severely hindered the ability of commanders to prepare and use their forces effectively. To add to the problems with morale and insubordination already mentioned, in February 1873—while the Carlist War and a long separatist war in Cuba continued—the leaders of the First Republic decided to eliminate the draft and establish an all-volunteer force. Shortly thereafter, it created a new militia, the "Volunteers of the Republic." This militia attracted far fewer recruits than government leaders had expected, and those who joined often did so in hopes of fomenting indiscipline within the regular army. Some were even Carlists. As Daniel R. Headrick writes, whereas the French Revolution had found success on the battlefield thanks to the *levée en masse,* the Spanish Revolution of 1873 would fail in no small part because it abolished the draft.[38]

The situation was even worse in Catalonia, where the Provincial Delegation of Barcelona (*Diputación Provincial de Barcelona*) forced the Madrid government to cede control over the army of the eastern front in return for withdrawing the Delegation's demand for the independence of Catalonia. After immediately purging 400 officers it suspected of monarchist sympathies, the Delegation then dissolved the regular army in anticipation of replacing it with a new volunteer militia. Whereas the Madrid government's elimination of the draft had at least kept currently serving soldiers within the army, in Catalonia the authorities had gone much further.[39]

Predictably, enough, more desertions and uprisings followed, while commanders found the new militia soldiers to be largely unreliable. The Carlists took advantage of the situation by coming down from their fortified positions in the mountains to attack urban areas. In Gerona and Igualada, soldiers refused to go into battle against the Carlists, and in Murviedro a colonel died at the hands of his own troops. At Alpens, government troops abandoned their general in the middle of a battle, and he then lost his life to the Carlists. In June, General Arsenio Martínez Campos would go as far as to resign his command due to exasperation over the unreliability of the militias. In many other cases, however, commanding officers did little to bring the situation under control, as most felt scant loyalty to the central government they found themselves serving. The army's situation in Catalonia began to improve only with the arrival in mid-August of a new captain general, General José Turon y Prats, but even with his vigorous measures to reinstill discipline, months passed before the government's forces began to regain their operational usefulness.[40]

Of course, the government army finally defeated the Carlists in 1876, and it deserves credit for prevailing under political and social conditions particularly trying even for a civil war. Nevertheless, for most of the conflict the army's operational-level planning had been poor, such as in the so-called central front around lower Aragon and the Maestrazgo, where a lack of unified command prevented any effective coordination of tactical movements and battles into broader strategic planning.[41] Furthermore, the Carlists had committed some major errors, and in any case they lacked the numbers—especially outside their core areas—to achieve a decisive victory. The most they probably could have hoped for was to wear out the enemy over time, but it was unlikely that this would have occurred given the absolute nature of the end goal they sought to impose on all of Spain.

As is often the case in successful counterinsurgency, the key to victory had been political as much as military. With the restoration of the Bourbon monarchy under Alfonso XII in 1875 and the new regime's good relationship with the Church, the Carlists lost many supporters who had perceived the movement as the most viable way of combating liberalism and republicanism. Even Ramón Cabrera, the famous veteran of the First Carlist War, recognized Alfonso's legitimacy in 1875, receiving a promotion to captain general in return. General Martínez Campos, now head of the government army, extended mass pardons to Carlist soldiers who gave up, thereby helping bring about mass desertions. The government army could thus concentrate its forces against the remaining insurgents still fighting, and in late February 1876, Carlos himself crossed back to France as the army mopped up the last resisters.[42]

Of course, the Spanish Army's next—and last—major conflict of the nineteenth century, this time in the form of wars against Cuban *independistas,* ended with a dramatic defeat by the United States in 1898, thereby bringing Spain's once great empire in the Americas and the Pacific to an end. Yet the enormity of the final defeat and its consequences should not overshadow the many operations against Cuban separatists that the Spanish forces had been waging for years before the United States stepped in. Although they cannot all be covered here, some aspects of the last war of Cuban independence against Spain (1895–98) merit mention, as they highlight the continuity in the nineteenth-century Spanish Army's failure to assimilate the lessons of counterinsurgency.

Thanks in no small part to inadequate training, grossly unfair and wildly unpopular recruitment methods, administrative incompetence, widespread disease, and poor leadership, the Spanish Army in Cuba suffered some major setbacks at times. Using classical guerrilla tactics, including ambushes, dispersal, and the refusal of battle with large Spanish forces, the Cuban rebels could be formidable opponents. At the most basic level, moreover, the Cubans often employed their rifles better than the Spanish soldiers, who lacked proper training in the use and maintenance of their weapons, sometimes arriving on the island with no live-fire rifle experience whatsoever.[43] Spanish soldiers also suffered far more from disease on the island than their Cuban enemies.

With time, however, operations against Cuban insurgents became notably more effective, especially after the Spanish leadership finally recognized that the insurgency demanded a new approach. Initially, General Arsenio Martínez Campos, charged with putting down the Cuban rebellion that broke out in 1895, could not, or did not want to, adapt Spanish strategy or tactics to the enemies' irregular methods. Under political pressure to spread his forces thin to protect property owners, he made no serious effort to separate the enemy from the areas and people from which it derived its resources, apparently because he could not bring himself to implement a policy that would devastate the civilian population. He also failed to promote adequate tactical responses to the situation he faced. These failures were symptomatic of his attitude toward the conflict as a whole, the very nature of which he despised because it bore so little resemblance to his conception of what war should be. He hated the jungle conditions, the guerrilla tactics of the enemy, and irregular warfare in general. As he had complained during the previous, failed struggle for Cuban independence in the Ten Years' War of 1868–78, he was stuck in a war that, in his view, "cannot be called a war."[44] His successor, however, had far less difficulty adapting to the conditions in Cuba.

When General Valeriano Weyler replaced Martínez Campos in 1896, the situation changed dramatically. Above all, he implemented a counter-insurgency strategy that proved very effective against the Cuban rebels, and the Spanish forces were on the verge of military victory when Weyler was recalled because of developments back in Spain.[45] His infamous strategy of "reconcentration," which entailed forcibly moving 300,000 people into specific locations in order to isolate the guerrillas, brought with it mass disease, starvation, and death. The response of the rebel Cuban military leadership to reconcentration, moreover, only increased the numbers and suffering of its victims, and Weyler continued to reconcentrate very large groups of civilians even after the terrible consequences of such measures were clear. All together, reconcentration probably killed from 155,000 to 170,000 civilians, or about 10% of Cuba's population.[46]

Yet from a purely military perspective, Weyler's actions were a logical reaction to the insurgent strategy, which had called for its own form of reconcentration, thereby helping to provoke Weyler's brutal response. Reconcentration as a military strategy was not, moreover, unique. Indeed, the Spaniards themselves had drawn up a reconcentration plan in Cuba during the Ten Years' War, although they failed to implement it completely. Weyler knew, as did the rebels who themselves had already cleared territories and forcibly relocated their inhabitants in their prosecution of total war, that economic warfare could be decisive in achieving victory, and in his view, the ends justified the means.[47]

Even before Weyler became known for his reconcentration strategy, at the tactical level he had pushed for innovations in the Spanish way of colonial war. Shortly after the outbreak of the Ten Years' War in 1868, General Blas Villate, Count of Valmaseda, embraced a new march formation that Weyler promoted for use against guerrillas, derived from his earlier experiences in Santo Domingo. Although it met with some resistance, it proved reasonably effective in defending columns against enemy attacks. At the request of Valmaseda, Weyler prepared a report on his tactics for use by the rest of the Spanish forces in Cuba. In this report and the others that followed, he elaborated on the use of what the Spaniards then called "guerrilla formations" (really counterguerrilla formations), the smaller units or skirmishers that moved forward in advance of the main columns.[48]

Weyler seems to have studied counterinsurgency tactics more systematically than his colleagues did, and after the outbreak of the Ten Years' War he prepared plans, reports, and instructions for the general staff on a regular basis about how to operate against the insurgents. As a commander in the field, he endeavored to train his soldiers in these ideas. Among other things, they called for going beyond the standard use of the so-called guerrilla formations by, after making contact with the enemy, charging ahead in the jungle in pursuit, thus taking the initiative from the insurgents. He also emphasized the importance of rapid maneuver as a general principle of war, an often-unattainable goal for large, regular armies in colonial campaigns, which tend to plod through enemy territories in ways that make them and their supply lines perfect targets for the hit-and-run tactics of small, highly mobile guerrilla forces. In Weyler's view, dispersed guerrilla forces were unlikely to offer much resistance in the face of skillful maneuver.[49]

Although Weyler has been portrayed as a visionary in the development of Spanish—and even European—counterinsurgency, such praise is exaggerated.[50] In the eighteenth century, European armies had already developed methods and even several manuals devoted to counterguerrilla warfare.[51] As we have seen, moreover, more recently some Spanish officers had already learned to emphasize maneuver and outflanking tactics as part of counterinsurgency during the Carlist and Moroccan wars. Yet Weyler's emphasis on them in his reports suggests that these earlier experiences had not found their way into the institutional culture of the army.

Weyler knew that such tactics required highly adept and motivated soldiers, and he created special units with these needs in mind. His *Cazadores de Valmaseda*, named after his former commander who had been so receptive to his ideas, anticipated José Millán Astray's Spanish Foreign Legion of the 1920s in several ways. A multiracial force manned by Cubans as well as Europeans from various countries, its ranks included more than a few fugitives from justice. Like Spain's legionnaires in North Africa years later, the *Cazadores* quickly earned a reputation for effective counterinsurgency that set them apart from the bulk of Spanish forces. He later recounted that his men's performance in combat consistently met or exceeded his expectations, giving him ample reason to praise their toughness, loyalty, and overall performance in battle.[52]

Yet in the end neither Weyler's tactical reforms nor his strategy of reconcentration prevailed and the latter's genocidal consequences brought with them no decisive advantage, especially after Weyler's recall to Spain in 1897. Thereafter the government made political concessions to the *independistas* that, while too late to win them over, were accompanied by a lull in Spanish military operations that allowed the insurgent forces to begin to recover and rebuild.[53] With the subsequent intervention of the United States in 1898, the fate of the Spanish Army in Cuba was sealed.

Of course, the Spanish Army was not the only European force to fail to carry out necessary reforms in the wake of defeat. Army officers, normally conservative by nature, tend to distrust radical innovation, and efforts to reform any large bureaucratic institution often meet with failure anyway. In nineteenth-century Spain, the constant political turmoil, frequent civil wars, and deep involvement of leading officers in politics made it especially difficult to affect significant changes.

Furthermore, to affirm that counterinsurgency merits as much attention as traditional strategy and tactics is to acknowledge something about the basic identity and purpose of an army that many military leaders are not willing to concede. Although the British army may have assumed the task of "colonial policing" with relative ease, many others have not forsaken the primacy of traditional battle tactics and strategy so easily. During the nineteenth century, the institutional culture of the U.S. army, for instance, remained oriented toward regular warfare waged by professional forces, even though in practice it spent far more time on irregular campaigns against American Indians than with the Napoleonic- or Prussian-style tactics taught at West Point and elsewhere. Of the two major exceptions—the Mexican War and the Civil War—only the former really fit the pattern of the kind of wars army leaders expected.[54]

In Spain, the institutional culture of the army also resisted absorbing the lessons of its counterinsurgency campaigns, but the consequences for the country were graver. After the lost Santo Domingo war of 1863–65, Weyler himself lamented that by promptly forgetting the lessons of the campaign, Spain had failed to gain "the one good thing that comes from the bad: learning to avoid past mistakes."[55] His words could apply to much of nineteenth-century Spanish military history.

CHAPTER **2**

From Empire to Republic:
The Spanish Army, 1898–1931

José E. Alvarez

The defeat of 1898 brought to light the deplorable state of the Spanish military, both before the international community and to the Spanish people. Conscript soldiers died abroad in the thousands due to disease and neglect. The fault lay with the government, which failed to equip and supply the troops properly, and with the officer corps, which refused to reduce its bloated ranks.[1]

Geopolitically, the loss of her overseas empire to the United States left Spain with only her Moroccan *presidios* and claims to territories in the Western Sahara and Equatorial Africa. At a time when overseas possessions were a mark of a great, powerful, and modern nation, Spain had lost most of hers. This international humiliation had a powerful impact on Spain's psyche as a nation but was most strongly felt within the ranks of the armed forces. The loss of these overseas colonies took away the opportunity for active service and therefore deprived the army and navy (which had lost both its Atlantic and its Pacific fleets in the war) of any chance of restoring the loss of prestige and honor which the Army had suffered. It appeared as if all military adventure outside Spain was gone, as well as the opportunities for promotion and battle pay which campaigning could provide. For officers of the regular army, it seemed as if their futures would be spent performing wearisome garrison duty throughout the peninsula.[2]

As a result of the 1898 war, the Army blamed the defeat on the negligence of the politicians in power and began to portray itself as the defender of the authentic nation against the dual threats of separatism and political radicalism.[3] However, what the Army most needed at the time was to reform its supernumerary ranks. It was top heavy, with too many officers for so few troops. It was composed of 499 generals, 578 colonels, and more than 23,000 other officers for an army that numbered around 80,000 men. Put another way, the Army had 25,000 officers for only

80,000 men, or one officer for every five soldiers. What this meant for the Army was that 60% of its annual budget went to pay officers' salaries, while inadequate resources were devoted to training or for the purchase of modern weapons and equipment.[4]

Reforming the Army would be challenging as the officer corps resisted any attempts by the government to change their established system. In turn, the Army also represented the greatest threat to the stability and authority of any restoration government. The officer class was disgruntled owing to the fact that now, without wars to fight and/or territories to protect overseas, promotions, based on seniority, would be slow in coming. This bitterness was compounded by a rise in the cost of living which led some mid-grade officers to seek outside employment, when not on duty, in order to afford their uniforms as well as to maintain their economic status. To make matters worse, the Army was continuously criticized and ridiculed in the Catalan press, both in print and in cartoons. On November 25, 1905, a gang of about 200 officers from the Barcelona garrison attacked the offices of the weekly satirical magazine, ¡Cu-cut!, destroying printing presses and office furniture, while also wounding a few workers with their swords. The "¡Cu-cut! Affair" caused a major crisis for the government. The officers were applauded and heralded by their peers and received no punishment for their actions. Emboldened, the officers demanded that the government censor criticism of the Army, as well as Catalan and Leftist newspapers, and also apply military jurisdiction to all offenses against the Army.[5]

The Army itself was internally divided between officers who had served in the Spanish-Cuban-American War and those who had remained in the peninsula; between branches of service/arms known as the cuerpos facultátivos (which required technical training like the artillery, engineers, medical corps, and the general staff) and the armas generales (the infantry and cavalry which required less education but performed the bulk of the fighting); and later between the peninsulares (those who served in Spain) and the Africanistas (those who served in Morocco).[6]

Spain's modern military and diplomatic involvement with Morocco began in 1859 when troops sent by General Leopoldo O'Donnell crushed a revolt by Moroccan tribesmen against Ceuta, a Spanish presidio since 1578. Following this brief six-month war which resulted in a series of Moroccan defeats, Spain was forced by Great Britain and its own tenuous international position to accept a series of treaties which, while extracting concessions from the Moroccan sultan, limited its territorial ambitions and restored to some degree the antebellum stability. This stability remained intact until the early 1890s.

Since 1893, the military situation around the Spanish North African enclave of Melilla had been relatively quiet. However, that quickly changed on July 9, 1909, when a force of Riffian tribesmen attacked a military outpost protecting Spanish workers building a railway to link Spanish iron ore mines to the port.[7] Four workers and one sentry were killed. This was the chance that Spanish colonialists had been anticipating. On July 13, 6,000 Riffians attacked a force of 2,000 Spaniards; ten days later, the tribesmen engaged Spanish forces for a third time. The campaign began disastrously for the Spaniards, when the 1st Madrid Chasseurs under the command of the reckless General Guillermo Pintos Ledesma were ambushed in the *"Barranco del Lobo"* (Wolf's Ravine). In the *presidios* at the time, only 15,000 soldiers could be called upon for combat so the government decided to reinforce its meager colonial forces by activating 40,000 reserves. This mobilization to protect private mining interests outside of Spain led to antiwar protests, particularly in Barcelona. The authorities suppressed these protests harshly, and the period in late July and early August 1909 came to be called the "Tragic Week."[8]

This episode visibly demonstrated the government's commitment to not only expand its influence in Morocco for political and economic purposes by reinforcing the number of troops posted there but move out from its ancient *presidios* of Ceuta and Melilla toward the Moroccan interior.[9] Moreover, it brought to light the deep divisions that existed in Spain between those who advocated overseas colonization and those who opposed it. What brought about such outpouring of resentment toward the government, especially in Barcelona, was the call-up of the poor to protect what the Spanish republicans and the socialists defined as plutocratic interests. The bulk of those who served in the ranks of the Army were conscripts and reservists, and the overwhelming majority of these came from the peasantry and the working class. It was these two segments of the Spanish population who supplied the "cannon fodder" for Spain's ambitions in Morocco. They were poorly trained, equipped, and led. It should be noted that there was little sympathy for the officers who served in Morocco, as they were volunteers who were rewarded with merit promotions (based on battlefield heroics, not seniority) and decorations for risking their lives against the Moroccans; conscripts and reservists did not have that option.[10]

With the arrival of thousands of fresh troops in Melilla during 1909–10, Spanish forces were able to move from Melilla and occupied an enclave that stretched from Cape Tres Forcas to the southern shore of Mar Chica, or about 10 kilometers into the Moroccan interior. This campaign had gained new territory for Spain, which had been losing it around the world for the last 200 years, as well as had provided the Spanish Army an opportunity to gain glory, respect, and promotions.[11] However, these African adventures were extremely costly in lives and resources. Militarily speaking, the 1909 and subsequent campaigns in northeast Morocco taught the Spanish two lessons. First, that the establishment of indigenous units such as the Moroccan-staffed *Regulares* in 1911 spared Spanish lives and provided them with tough soldiers who were better acclimated to the terrain of the Protectorate than were Peninsular troops. And second, that these campaigns created a tightly knit group of mid-level combat officers known as *Africanistas* who developed a special esprit with these indigenous soldiers and a determined commitment to Spain's new colonialism. This group, in fact, would play a significant role in Spanish politics through the 1970s. These men had not been tainted by the defeats of 1898 and from their beginnings in 1909, would earn their stars in combat with the *Regulares* and later, the Spanish Foreign Legion. They would go on to command armies on both sides of the Spanish Civil War, though mostly on the Nationalists' side. Such *Africanistas* as Francisco Franco, Emilio Mola, Miguel Cabanellas, Agustín Muñoz Grandes, José Varela, Juan Yagüe, Francisco García Escámez, Carlos Asensio, and Vicente Rojo are but a few of the leaders who emerged out of the Moroccan combat of 1911 through 1927.[12]

In November 1912, the Moroccan Sultan, Moulay Abd-al-Hafid, was forced to sign the Treaty of Fez which established the French and Spanish Protectorates. Spain received the northern one-fifth of Morocco to administer with Tangier being declared an international city. The Protectorate consisted of roughly 20,000 square miles inhabited by sixty-six tribes which were subdivided into various clans and subclans that constantly fought among themselves. The most warlike of these tribes resided in the Yebala, the northwest corner of the Protectorate under the rule of Sherif Muley Ahmed el Raisuli/Raisuni, and in the Rif, the eastern half of the Protectorate. Hypothetically subordinate to the khalif, the Sultan's deputy in Tetuán, capital of the Spanish Protectorate, the protectorate's rural tribes basically ignored the Sultan and were even more opposed to domination by foreigners. After 1912, the Spanish Army began a campaign to advance deeper into the Yebala region hoping to occupy the city of Xauen. This proved unsuccessful and it was forced to return to Tetuán.[13]

When World War I began, Spain quickly declared its neutrality, even though it had closer ties to Britain and France than to Germany. These political/diplomatic ties stemmed from the Cartagena Declarations of May 1907, whereby the three nations agreed to collaborate on the security of their respective Mediterranean and Atlantic territories. And while Spain remained neutral, the people, as well as the military, were divided over which side they favored in the conflict, the French or the Germans. This division also carried over to personal political preference/affiliation.[14]

A serious consequence of the establishment of the Protectorate and renewed military activity in Morocco was the polarization of the Army. In 1910, the Army reintroduced *méritos de guerra* (war/combat merits) which greatly benefited those officers who served in Morocco. Promotions based on *méritos de guerra* had been employed during the Spanish-Cuban-American War but were done away with due to rampant abuse by some officers. Again, the central issue which divided the officer corps was promotion based on seniority vs. battlefield promotions. This pitted the *peninsulares* against the *Africanistas.* During World War I, the situation grew more acute as junior officers who remained in Spain saw their chances for higher salary and promotion stagnate, while those who served in Morocco quickly rose in rank and pay. Inflation, provoked by the war, exacerbated the situation which in turn led to a strike by junior officers in Barcelona on June 1, 1917. These disgruntled junior officers formed a *Junta de Defensa* (committees of defense) for the Infantry branch, similar to the one that already existed in the Artillery branch. The Artillery and the Engineers, both technical services, had similar political interests, whereas the Infantry and Cavalry, who had been less organized, now created their own *Juntas*. While the *Juntas* had formed in Barcelona, they quickly spread to other garrison cities throughout Spain. Generally speaking, the *Juntas de Defensa* were anti-*méritos de guerra,* anti-*Africanistas,* and suspicious of King Alfonso XIII and his military household. In addition, they wanted the government's recognition of the *Juntas de Defensa.* For the next five years, the *Juntas de Defensa* would play a major role in the relationship between the Army and the government.[15]

While Spain was dealing with the aftermath of World War I (e.g., inflation, unemployment, political instability, and division within the military), the government resumed its push to occupy the interior of the Moroccan Protectorate which it had curtailed during the War. In the western part of the Protectorate, the new High Commissioner, General Dámaso Berenguer Fusté, employed a combined policy of arms, bribery, and "divide and rule" to deal with the tribesmen of the Yebala, principally under the leadership of the Raisuli. Under the leadership of the aggressive and dynamic military governor of Ceuta, General Manuel Fernández Silvestre, the Army was able to connect the major cities of Ceuta, Tetuán, and Larache, as well as to control the area proximate to Tangier. The aforementioned cities were linked via the construction and manning of a string of blockhouses that connected one major outpost with another. In Morocco, these blockhouses had to be frequently resupplied and were constantly under attack by hostile tribesmen. The soldiers who manned these remote and vulnerable outposts were poorly trained and equipped conscripts. The officer class and military administration fared no better as corruption was rampant, and many officers preferred drinking, gambling, and whoring in the major towns of the Protectorate to commanding their troops in the field. In reality, it was the noncommissioned officers, corporals and sergeants, who ran the day-to-day operations of the army. And while there were those in Spain who favored the government's policy in Morocco, there were those, especially the lower classes and those on the political left, who opposed the cost in lives and national treasure.[16]

Slowly and methodically, the Army had been able to advance deeper into the Yebala region. The "spearhead" troops for this operation were the *Regulares* who were better led and motivated by their *Africanista* officers than the Spanish conscripts who were mainly relegated to the mundane task of manning blockhouses and performing supply convoy duty. Whereas the *Regulares* performed admirably in the Protectorate, a new organization was in its formative state in 1919. The brainchild of an ex-*Regulares* officer, Major José Millán Astray, the soon-to-be-created Spanish Foreign Legion was to serve with the *Regulares* as the "shock troops" of the Spanish Army in Morocco. Millán Astray's proposal for a Foreign Legion, based on the more famous French Foreign Legion, would have a dual purpose: first, it would be made up of hardened professional soldiers, and second, it lessened the number of Spanish conscripts required for what seemed in the early 1920s an endless colonial conflict.[17]

The genesis of the Spanish Foreign Legion can be traced back to 1919 when Millán Astray proposed the formation of an elite volunteer force made up of Spaniards and foreigners to become the vanguard of army operations in Africa. Millán Astray was promoted to the rank of lieutenant colonel, which permitted him to command a regiment-sized unit, and was put in charge of organizing the newly founded *Tercio de Extranjeros*.[18]

The support of the king and the new Minister of War, Luis Marichalar y Monreal (Vizconde de Eza), allowed the Legion to overcome resistance from those in the army like General Silvestre and the *Juntas de Defensa*. The *Juntas de Defensa* supported the dissatisfaction of peninsular officers with "elite units" like the *Regulares* and the proposed foreign Legion. As noted previously, officers in these units (*Africanistas*) would bypass promotion through seniority by taking advantage of "*méritos de guerra.*" Officers serving in Africa believed that they deserved this privilege as they suffered the hardships of campaigning and possible death, while their counterparts in the peninsula remained in barracks throughout the major cities of Spain.[19]

With a very effective propaganda campaign in both Spain and abroad, and lured by enticing signing bonuses and a thirst for adventure, volunteers began to arrive in Ceuta in September 1920. The first group consisted of 200 men. Within a few weeks, others would follow and soon three *banderas* (battalion-size units) were created, with Francisco Franco, Millán Astray's hand-chosen deputy, commanding the 1st *Bandera*.[20] And while the Legion was in its formative stages in the fall of 1920, it would very quickly become an invaluable part of military operations in Morocco, eventually surpassing the *Regulares* as the elite "shock troops" in the Army.[21] And while the Legion was being organized, Berenguer proceeded with his operations in the West against the Raisuli. With the *Regulares* serving as the "spearhead" for this operation, the Legion was relegated to performing convoy and protection duty in the vicinity of Tetuán. The crowning achievement of Berenguer's offensive was the capture of the city of Xauen on October 14, 1920.[22]

In February 1920, General Manuel Fernández Silvestre, recently promoted to the rank of lieutenant general and transferred from the West (*Comandancia de Ceuta*) to the East (*Comandancia de Melilla*), began to carry out his advancement into the Rif with the goal of reaching Alhucemas Bay and thus pacifying the eastern half of the Protectorate. At the same time, Berenguer continued the occupation of the western half of the Protectorate. Berenguer's strategy consisted of careful and methodical advancements, using a strong hand when necessary, but never discounting diplomacy and payoffs. On the other hand, Silvestre's strategy, encouraged by his friend and supporter King Alfonso XIII, was more headlong, aggressive, and ultimately reckless. His ultimate goal was to pacify the region that extended from Melilla to the strategic Alhucemas Bay. This region, dominated by the Rif mountains and populated by the bellicose Rif tribes, offered a difficult challenge for Silvestre and his forces. Under his command, Silvestre had an army of 25,700 men, of which some 20,600 were Spaniards and 5,100 were Moroccan *Regulares.* By early 1921, Silvestre had crossed the Kert River and established a base at Annual on January 15 and the riparian post at Sidi Dris on March 15.[23] In March, Berenguer visited the Melillan front and, after meeting with some of the tribal chiefs on the beach at Alhucemas, came away feeling that the situation was favorable and that Silvestre was accomplishing his goal admirably. However, not all the tribes of the Rif were willing to submit to Spanish control. Mohammed ben Abd-el-Krim el Khattabi and his younger brother, Mahammed, of the Beni Urriaguel tribe opposed the advance of Spanish forces into the Rif. The Abd-el-Krim brothers took it upon themselves to liberate their country from foreign domination. The first step toward this objective was to destroy the army of General Silvestre.

In late May, Silvestre decided to move deeper into the Rif against the expressed advice of Berenguer crossing the Amekran River and setting up a position on Monte Abarran in early June. Abarran was located eighty miles from Annual. Militarily, the Abd-el-Krims welcomed the Spaniards advance deeply into the Rif since this would bring them farther from Melilla and thus lengthen their supply lines and making them more vulnerable to attack. As Ricardo Fernández De La Ruguera and Susana March observed in *El Desastre De Annual*: "the general had dug his own grave. All they [the Riffians] had to do was throw dirt on top of him."[24] What followed next was a series of minor defeats which inevitably led to the Annual debacle. First, the Spanish outpost at Abarran was attacked by a thousand Riffian tribesmen acting in concert with a number of native

Regulares who betrayed their Spanish officers. The Spaniards, and the *Regulares* who remained loyal, were no match for the Riffians. The position was wiped out with nearly 200 killed, and most importantly, an artillery battery was captured along with small arms and ammunition. Emboldened by their success at Abarran, the Abd-el-Krim brothers attracted other Riffian tribesmen to their side with the promise of rifles and loot.

The next Spanish position attacked was Igueriben on July 16. Situated three miles from Annual, it was quickly surrounded and cut off from the larger base. At his headquarters in Melilla, Silvestre quickly gathered what forces he could and rushed by car to Annual to take personal charge of the relief operations. Several attempts were made to break the siege and deliver desperately needed supplies, including two cavalry charges personally led by Silvestre, but withering machine gun and artillery fire from the Riffians repelled all attempts. Igueriben fell to the Abd-el-Krim's forces of roughly 4,000 men, thus sealing the fate of Annual. Silvestre, with a force of 4,000 men, was also cut off at Annual. Silvestre fired off three radiograms in a row to Berenguer asking for major reinforcements. With ammunition for small arms and cannons, as well as food and water running dangerously low, Silvestre, along with his officers, saw the possibility of having to abandon this key position. After convening a council of officers to decide the fate of Annual, a vote was taken to withdraw. On the morning of July 22, Silvestre gave the order to abandon Annual and to pull back to the next main outpost of Ben Tieb and then to Monte Arruit. What should have been an orderly, fighting withdrawal quickly turned into a rout as panic-stricken conscripts dropped their weapons and ran for their lives. The Riffians slaughtered those they caught, with soldiers and civilians alike being put to the knife. In the end, Spanish casualties numbered from a conservative 8,000 to a high of 15,000, with 570 taken prisoner and held for ransom. Silvestre perished at Annual, although it was never conclusively established whether he was killed by the enemy or died by his own hand. What had taken twelve years of blood and treasure to conquer had now been lost in a few days. Spain's ignominious rout at the hands of Riffian tribesmen was the greatest defeat suffered by a European power in an African colonial conflict in the twentieth century.[25]

On July 22, Millán Astray received orders stating that two *banderas* were to quickly proceed to Tetuán. In Tetuán, they learned that there had been a terrible disaster in Melilla and that Silvestre had committed suicide at the head of his troops. The 1st and 2nd *banderas* boarded a train for Ceuta. In the port city they boarded the steamer *Ciudad de Cádiz* the following day. On board and steaming at full speed for Melilla were General José Sanjurjo Sacanell (future *Marqués del Rif*), who led the expedition, and Lieutenant Colonel José Millán Astray, commander of the Legion's 920 men. Also aboard were two *tabores* (battalions) of the *Regulares de Ceuta,* commanded by Lieutenant Colonel Santiago González Tablas y García Herreros, and three mountain batteries.[26]

When the ship docked in the harbor of Melilla on Sunday July 24, the populace of the threatened city gathered at the pier frantically waving their handkerchiefs. Panic-stricken and hoping to get aboard the ferry in order to sail away to Spain and safety, the citizens had their fears pacified by the arrival of the highly respected General Sanjurjo and the Foreign Legion. Berenguer had arrived the previous day and had taken stock of the situation. "All has been lost, including honor!" he noted.[27] Prior to the ship's docking, Berenguer had sent a message by way of his aide-de-camp, Juan Sánchez Delgado, saying that there was nothing left of the Melillan Command; the Army had been defeated; the city was defenseless; nothing had been heard of Silvestre's second-in-command, General Felipe Navarro; and the people of Melilla were in a state of sheer terror and needed to have their spirits and morale lifted.[28]

Now began the Herculean effort of rebuilding what the Annual debacle had undone. The government fell as the people of Spain looked for someone to blame for such a humiliating defeat. The Conservative politician who had been Prime Minister during the 1909 campaign, Antonio Maura, returned as prime minister, replacing Manuel Allende-Salazar, and his associate from that same era, Juan de La Cierva, replaced the Vizconde de Eza as Minister of War. Who was responsible: the Army, Berenguer, Silvestre, the king, the politicians, or the industrialists? A commission was set up under General Juan Picasso González to investigate why the Army had collapsed and who had been responsible for it. Berenguer offered to resign, but Alfonso XIII and the new Minister of War refused to accept his resignation.[29]

During the time Berenguer was in Madrid, the plan for the future of the Protectorate began to develop. It had three phases:

> the first, to recover all the territory that was lost after Annual in the East; and in the Western Zone, to expel or contain the Raisuli, conquering Beni Aros and el Ajmas; the second, the landing at Alhucemas; and the third, the establishing, through political action or by force of arms, coastal positions in the tribal lands of the Beni Said, Tensaman, Bocoya, Peñón de Vélez y Metiua. The occupation of Alhucemas was considered, justifiably so, as paramount.[30]

Unlike the negative public reaction during the 1909 Melillan campaign, the Annual disaster initially generated a wave of patriotism and support for the war in Morocco. Spain's honor and prestige in Morocco needed to be restored. The government moved quickly to reinforce the troops in Melilla, and under the command of the battle-tested General José Sanjurjo Sacanell, the recovery of the *Comandancia de Melilla* began in late August–early September 1921. Following Annual, volunteers for the Legion grew quickly with men enlisting not only from Spain but from foreign nations as well, especially from Latin America. The king authorized the creation of two new *banderas* (the 4th and 5th) to accommodate the new volunteers.[31]

The recovery of territory lost following the Annual disaster was a long and difficult one with the Legion and the *Regulares de Ceuta* serving in the vanguard of all major operations. Outpost after outpost was recaptured; the most horrifying sights were discovered in Nador (the first Spanish town recovered), Zeluán, and Monte Arruit (site of General Navarro's surrender) where civilians and soldiers alike had been murdered and savagely mutilated by the Riffians. These abominable and sickening sights only emboldened the Spanish Army, to avenge their butchered comrades.[32]

By 1922, the Army in the Protectorate had grown to 150,000 men, the majority of them conscripts.[33] Prime Minister Maura attempted not to interpose in the conduct of the war in Morocco; however, he had little confidence that the military could carry out a full-scale offensive against the enemy. Cognizant of the difficulties in undertaking such a campaign, as well as the political troubles it would give rise to, Maura would have liked for the Army to simply defend the principal coastal cities and abandon most of the interior to the tribesmen, as had previously been the case. Berenguer, however, supported by Juan de La Cierva (Minister of War), planned to keep up the counteroffensive in the Melillan zone during 1922, prosecute the Yebala campaign against el Raisuni to a conclusive end (this was accomplished with the capture of Raisuni's mountain stronghold in Tazarut and his subsequent pact with Spanish authorities), and then occupy the Rif itself, thus shattering Abd-el-Krim's revolt and occupying the entire Protectorate. The last phase of these operations would be the most arduous, as they would almost certainly require an amphibious landing near Alhucemas Bay, close to Abd-el-Krim's capital of Ajdir, and land attacks from the east in order to capture the rebels from behind.[34]

While the military situation in the Protectorate was uneventful, the political and diplomatic one was quite active. In Spain, there were serious strains within the government concerning future military actions in the Protectorate. The Minister of War and the Foreign Minister, González Hontoria, were at odds over what plan of action to follow in Spanish Morocco. This conflict led to the *Conferencia de Pizarra*, which was held from February 4 to 6, 1922. The conference took place in the province of Málaga, in order to get away from the political climate of Madrid, as well as to keep the High Commissioner close to the Protectorate. With this reunion of governmental and military leaders, the main topic of discussion was, as Morales Lezcano succinctly put it, "the final solution to the Moroccan problem." The military was in total agreement that Abd-el-Krim and el Raisuni must be defeated decisively and that the best way to accomplish the former was by disembarking at Alhucemas Bay.[35]

The political and military situation heated up during the summer with Berenguer as the major target. He was criticized in the press by Spain's most senior general, Valeriano Weyler y Nicolau, for doing nothing to get back the prisoners from the Annual disaster. Furthermore, the Picasso Commission, which had been established after the Annual disaster to find out the reasons for it, finished its investigation on the military aspects (but not the political) of it on April 18, 1922. The investigation proclaimed that Army officers had been incapable of meeting the challenges presented by the Moroccan campaign and recommended that Berenguer, Silvestre (if he were to be found), and General Navarro (if he were rescued or ransomed) be prosecuted for Annual. The findings of the Commission were not made public but disclosed solely to the government. No one found culpable by the Commission was ever brought up on charges before military judicial authorities.[36]

On July 9, 1922, Berenguer submitted his resignation for the fourth and final time. It was accepted. The former Captain General of Madrid, General Ricardo Burguete y Lana, replaced him on July 16. Burguete had been an able field commander in previous Moroccan campaigns and, like Berenguer, was a politician, as well as a soldier. His appointment as the new High Commissioner came as quite a shock to many in the military. In the past, he had written in favor of militarism, but now, for political reasons, he changed his stance. Both the new Prime Minister, Sánchez Guerra, and Burguete responded to popular opinion to terminate offensive operations in Morocco. Burguete sought a peaceful or nonmilitary solution to the situation. This new policy was totally impractical and went against the wishes of the *Africanistas*. However, by mid-August, Burguete's policy had once again changed in favor of aggressive action in the Protectorate, and even included a major offensive aimed at Ajdir, Abd-el-Krim's Riffian capital.[37]

The political situation in Spain vis-à-vis the Protectorate in Morocco, which had steadily gone from bad to worse, finally came to a head in 1923. On September 13, 1923, Lieutenant General Miguel Primo de Rivera y Orbaneja (*Marqués de Estella*), the Captain General of Barcelona, successfully brought about a bloodless *pronunciamiento*. Taking control of the government with the consent of the king, he installed a Military Directorate composed of eight brigadiers and one admiral.[38] Although considered to be an *abandonista* by many in the Army,[39] Primo de Rivera received the support of the military to bring an end to the Rif Rebellion with honor and dignity.[40]

Primo de Rivera's *pronunciamiento* had minimal impact on the situation in the Protectorate. His statements on Morocco were vague, and it was difficult at this point to determine what specific course of action he would follow in the Protectorate. However, he did promise to bring a "quick, honorable, and sensible" solution to the conflict. On the same day that the constitutional government in Madrid changed, there was also a change in Tetuán—General Luis Aizpuru y Mondéjar (ex-Commanding General of Melilla and ex-Minister of War), a well-respected Moroccan wars veteran, becoming the seventh High Commissioner since 1912.[41]

When he became dictator, Primo de Rivera had no clear-cut plan about what to do in Morocco. Basically, it was to continue the plan that had already been in place which was to withdraw from the interior to the coastal *presidios*, while simultaneously attempting to negotiate with Abd-el-Krim. The possibilities were abandonment, semi-abandonment, or a continuation of hostilities. The abandonment/semi-abandonment option was seriously questioned when the *Africanistas* vociferously opposed it at what came to be known as the "Ben Tieb incident" of July 19, 1924. At this forward base in the Eastern Zone of the Protectorate, officers of the Legion and *Regulares* let Primo de Rivera know during a luncheon in his honor that they opposed any solution but total victory over the Riffians, and adamantly called for the restoration of honor for Spanish arms in Morocco. As they saw it, the lives of their comrades who had fallen in combat would not go unavenged. Regardless of what the *Africanistas* thought, Primo de Rivera pursued his aforementioned policy. However, his plan was altered when Abd-el-Krim decided to move into French Morocco, which in turn encouraged French–Spanish cooperation, which had not existed before, for a joint military solution to the problem in Morocco.[42]

Having been supported by *Africanista* officers in his successful bid for power, he now devoted great energy to securing the military's position there, although not as fervently as some of these officers in Morocco would have liked. On November 1, 1923, to counterbalance the large numbers of troops who were being brought back from Morocco, he gave the necessary authorization for the formation of two reserve brigades which were to be permanently stationed in the ports of Alicante and Almeria. The brigades' purpose was to be a reserve force for the Army of Africa, ready to embark men and materiel, in case of any military difficulties in the Protectorate.[43]

Primo de Rivera's plan vis-à-vis the Army was twofold. First, he supported the colonial forces (*Africanistas*) in their campaign to continue the war in Morocco by strategically withdrawing from vulnerable positions/outposts in the Yebala region (specifically from Xauen) to more defensible positions near Tetuán. And second, he moved to reform the Army (this topic will be covered later in this chapter).

The first order of business for Primo de Rivera in 1924 was the withdrawal of more than 40,000 men from the area around Xauen to more defensible positions behind what came to be known as the "Primo de Rivera Line"/"Estella Line," a journey of forty plus miles. In this most risky and dangerous operation, the Legion was used to evacuate these forward positions. With Abd-el-Krim's army of Riffians and Yebalis (roughly 7,000 strong) persistently harassing the evacuation columns (along with inclement weather), casualties were high, with estimates ranging from 2,000 to an incredible 18,000 deaths. This operation, which began in September and ended in early December, has sometimes been referred to as a "second Annual" for Spain. With Spanish forces behind the "Estella Line," Primo de Rivera and the High Command now could focus on the amphibious landing at Alhucemas Bay, which they believed would be the beginning of the end of Abd-el-Krim's rebellion.[44]

Emboldened by Primo de Rivera's strategic withdrawal from the Yebala region, Abd-el-Krim committed what would turn out to be a fatal mistake for the survival of his regime. With his army numbering around 80,000 men (according to Spanish estimates) and with more than 200 field pieces, Abd-el-Krim, no longer seeing Spain as a serious threat, launched a preemptive attack against French outposts along the Wergha River on April 9, 1925. The situation in Morocco took a new direction as Spain's problems with Abd-el-Krim and his rebellion now spilled over into the French sector as well. Nevertheless, Spanish officials were still trying to bring an end to the rebellion. According to Fleming, during the spring of 1925, Spanish agents had been discussing a settlement to the rebellion with Abd-el-Krim, but once again it had proved fruitless. He also noted that Primo de Rivera was planning to abandon the entire Protectorate except for the *presidios* (Ceuta and Melilla), but that now with Abd-el-Krim's attack on the French, the situation had changed.[45]

Along the French Protectorate border, the situation was grave for the French, as Abd-el-Krim chalked up one victory after another, threatening Taza and even coming within 30 kilometers of the royal Moroccan city of Fez. The government in Paris blamed Marshal Louis-Hubert Lyautey (France's Resident General in Morocco) for not stopping the Riffian onslaught on French positions. Lyautey who had been in poor health for many years, resigned, temporarily replaced by General Stanislas Naulin. However, Lyautey did remain as Resident General. Eventually, Marshal Henri Philippe Pétain, the hero of Verdun, would assume overall command of French forces in Morocco.[46]

Primo de Rivera declared after the retreat from Xauen that once Abd-el-Krim had finished with the Spanish, he would next turn his attention to the French. To date, France had remained indifferent to Spain's difficulties and defeats in Morocco, and as long as Spain was the victim of Abd-el-Krim's attacks, France would sit tight. Now the two European powers, facing a common foe, agreed to cooperate in putting an end to the rebellion. Representatives of the two nations met throughout June and July 1925 to hammer out an agreement on fighting the war. The Franco-Hispano Conference met first in Madrid, then again on July 25 when they reached an agreement. On July 28, Pétain and Primo de Rivera met in Tetuán to finalize their plans for a combined land and sea operations.[47]

At 0600 hours on the foggy morning of September 8, 1925, the invasion began with naval bombardment and aerial bombing and strafing of the beaches of La Cebadilla and Ixdain near Alhucemas Bay. At 0900 hours, the order was given to board the landing crafts, which would then be towed closer to the beach. The tugs would cut their lines to the landing crafts at about 1,000 meters from shore, and these crafts would proceed the rest of the way under their own propulsion. Twenty minutes later, the landing barges ran aground on rocks and shoals. The men poured onto the beach and began to quickly fight their way off of the beaches. Overwhelmed by the aggressiveness of the attack, the defenders barely resisted and fled, leaving behind a cannon, several machine guns, and their dead. By sundown on that first day, with over 8,000 men and three batteries having been put ashore, it was obvious that the surprise landing west of Alhucemas Bay had been a success. Abd-el-Krim had been expecting the landing to take place within the bay itself, but the Spaniards fooled him by landing at Ixdain/La Cebadilla, which was less well-defended and belonged to the Bucoya tribe, not Abd-el-Krim's Beni Urriaguel.[48]

The landing at Alhucemas Bay proved an overwhelming success for the new allies as the Riffians, attacked by superior Spanish and French forces (by this time, the Spanish Army had grown to 200,000 men, while the French had 300,000), quickly gave ground. On October 2, Spanish forces captured and torched Ajdir, Abd-el-Krim's capital. He fled deeper into the Rif hoping to make the conquest of the territory as costly as possible for Spain. By 1926, after a few important battles around Tetuán (Yebala), Abd-el-Krim surrendered to French forces on May 27, who promptly exiled him to Reunion Island off the coast of Madagascar. Following Abd-el-Krim's surrender, a few of his supporters continued to fight on. However, the war was pretty much over. On July 10, 1927, General Sanjurjo, the High Commissioner of the Spanish Protectorate, proclaimed the complete and total pacification of Spanish Morocco.[49] Successfully terminating the Moroccan War (1909–27) would be Primo de Rivera's greatest accomplishment as dictator.

From 1923 to 1929, Primo de Rivera worked tirelessly to reform the Army by reducing the size of the officer corps (by promoting early retirement), greatly restricting the number of cadets permitted to enter the officer corps, eliminating the council of senior generals, reducing military service to two years, acquiring new/modern small arms, supporting a pay increase for those below the rank of brigadier, abolishing the general staff as a separate corps, eliminating some inessential regiments within the artillery and cavalry corps, and placing greater emphasis on merit promotions. The medical corps, the engineers, and the artillery (*cuerpos facultátivos*) lost their right to promotion based solely on seniority

(June 9, 1926). The greatest resistance and opposition to Primo de Rivera's new promotion policy came from the Artillery. His promotions based on "battlefield merits" (which benefited the combat arms—Infantry and Cavalry) angered the Artillery Corps so much that they actively and bitterly opposed him from June to September 1926. After they tried to rise up against him and failed, he responded by dissolving six of its regiments, forcing many of its officers to retire, and compelling them to accept his new system for promotion. Later, in February 1927, he created the GMA (General Military Academy) in Zaragoza, and in 1928, Franco was chosen its first director. The GMA would provide cadets with the first two years of military instruction, followed by two more years in their own individual branch of service academies.[50]

Primo de Rivera succeeded where others had failed in trying to reform the bloated Army. By thinning out the senior ranks of the Army, he was able to appropriate a greater percentage of the military's annual budget away from salaries toward the purchase of modern weapons and equipment.[51] At the same time, he alienated the one group that had been his base of support—the Army. In 1925, he sacked the venerable Valeriano Weyler, the Chief of the General Staff, and went after other important generals like Eduardo López de Ochoa and Gonzalo Queipo de Llano (both Masons and Republicans), as well as the *Africanistas,* José Cavalcanti, and Miguel Cabanellas.[52] In addition to the Army, Primo de Rivera also badgered and alienated the Navy and Air Force. Without the support of the military, Primo de Rivera's days as dictator were numbered. On January 29, 1930, he was dismissed by Alfonso XIII and replaced by another general, the former High Commissioner, Dámaso Berenguer Fusté (*Conde de Xauen*). The Army's influence in the new government remained strong as General Enrique Marzo became the new Minister of Interior, while General Emilio Mola served as Director General of Security and General Manuel Goded as Undersecretary for War.[53]

Under Berenguer, opposition to the king and the monarchy continued. Discontent within the Army, due to the reforms carried out by Primo de Rivera, led to the formation of pro-republic groups, the best known being the AMR (Republican Military Association). In order to placate the disgruntled artillerists, the quartermasters, and the Air Force (Ramón Franco was one of the most radical AMR members), who made up the bulk of the AMR's membership and at the same time weaken the AMR, Alfonso XIII reversed many of the reforms carried out by Primo de Rivera, in particular, promotion based on seniority. Nevertheless, discontent within the Army by pro-republic elements led to an attempted coup in December 1930. The conspirators were divided into two centers: General Gonzalo Queipo de Llano (an AMR leader) and Ramón Franco in Madrid, and Captain Fermín Galán in Jaca (Aragón). The attempted coup fizzled quickly when military garrisons refused to join. The rebels were quickly rounded up and Galán was executed, thus becoming a martyr for the republicans. On April 12, 1931, Alfonso XIII called for municipal elections, and the results were that 46 out of 50 provincial capitals voted Republican. Having lost the support of the Army and his people, Alfonso abdicated and went into self-imposed exile. The Bourbon dynasty in Spain had come to an end, replaced by the Second Republic.[54]

From the ignominious end of the Spanish-American War in 1898 to the founding of the Second Republic in 1931, the Spanish Army underwent tremendous changes. Entering the twentieth century, the Army portrayed itself as the defenders of the fatherland and conservative values, while at the same time striving to maintain and promote its honor and status in society. However, the Army was severely weakened by its bloated ranks at the senior level, its antiquated equipment and poor training, and its dependence on seniority over merit when it came to promotions. The Moroccan War (1909–27) created further internal conflict and division when battlefield promotions based on merit was reintroduced, thus dividing the Army between the *peninsulares* (those who served in Spain) and the *Africanistas* (those who served in Morocco). In addition, the various branches of service began to unionize, thus creating further strife within the ranks. The *Africanistas* (mostly serving in the *Regulares* and/or the Legion) would quickly rise through the ranks and become the most professional and battle-tested officers in the Army. Overwhelmingly pro-monarchy and anti-Republican, these officers will go on to command the Nationalist armies during the Civil War. During the time of Miguel Primo de Rivera's dictatorship (1923–30), military reforms were carried out that modernized the Army. However, resentment for some of his reforms cost him his position, and eventually that of King Alfonso XIII as well.

CHAPTER **3**

World War I:
Unarmed Neutrality

Javier Ponce

The military history of Spain during World War I begs several crucial questions which we will consider in this chapter. We will begin by assessing the overall state of the Spanish military at the outset of the war. Its evident limitations explain why Spain remained neutral throughout the era. Furthermore, we need to determine whether the war brought about substantial changes in the organization, conditions, and status of the defense while the risks involved would increase considerably. Finally, if the existing military resources would allow involving itself in the main international challenge facing Spain at the time: respect for its rights and fulfillment of its responsibilities as a neutral nation which is always difficult to manage.

Military Might and Neutrality

A Starting Point

What was the military situation in Spain on the eve of World War I? The effects of the Spanish-American War of 1898 were still being felt; indeed those events were actually responsible for the lamentable state of the Spanish navy and army. The military problems included a lack of organization and manpower and poor status within Spanish society. If we take the model of the Prussian army, which in 1870 had defeated the French at Sedan, as a reference point for the Spanish military reform movement in the final thirty years of the nineteenth century, it would not bring on any substantial changes. Because compared to the Prussian army, formed by conscripted soldiers, in Spain the recruitment laws in the 1870s and 1880s filled the ranks with the poorest men who could not pay for their freedom. While Germany and other industrialized countries had an armaments industry to enhance their economies, with the army and navy forming a ready market, in Spain neither was a client, just a clumsy apparatus that, far from stimulating industrial development, bled the State coffers. Early twentieth–century reforms consolidated this situation in an effort to heal wounds caused by the disaster of 1898. As parliamentarianism weakened, in the face of rising social and regional conflict, the Law of Jurisdictions of 1906 came into effect entrusting the military with the custody of the freedom of expression, press, and assembly, forming an independent body from government authority. This would hinder any reform to make it more effective, such as the one carried out by José Canalejas in 1911, which included the Spanish version of the military service draft, although in peace time it could be replaced by the payment of state quotas.[1]

After the disaster of 1898, another colonial conflict in 1909, this time in Morocco, sapped Spain's military strength. Indeed, of the 140,000 forces listed in the army on the eve of the war, 76,000 were stationed in Morocco. Meanwhile the navy, decimated in 1898, had to wait until 1908 for the government to approve a program of naval construction, which although delayed several times, provided some improvements, although the general state remained precarious.[2] Thus, if we gauge a country's strength by its role on the international stage, in terms of military power, the first conclusion we can draw is that the Spanish military was in no state to participate in any alliances based on mutual commitment and even less so in a European conflict.

Having lost its last vestiges of colonial empire by the beginning of the twentieth century, Spain was considered a minor state perched on the southwest corner of Europe overlooking Africa, with its trade and interests serving only through the forbearance of France and Britain. Meanwhile, the governments of the major powers, pressured by their military staff, certain industrial groups, and some opinion sectors, strengthened an arms race which led to the clash of imperial ambitions that, precipitated by the power blocks, led to the fatal events that shook Europe from July 1914: the logical conclusion of the contentious armed peace.[3] Thus, World War I began, renowned for being the first *all-out war*, the massive use of new weaponry developed through industrial progress, used to bring about terrible destruction of both people and material goods.

Spain participated only marginally in the formation of the power blocks that would lead to war. This participation included the 1907 Cartagena Treaty, which hardly committed Spain to anything. Both the Entente powers and Spain considered this accord an instrument for safeguarding Spain's coastal and island possessions which were susceptible to foreign aggression.[4] In this respect, Spain, Great Britain, and France agreed that if any of their Atlantic or Mediterranean possessions were threatened, they would cooperate in their protection.

Nevertheless, when the events of the summer of 1914 augured war, Spain, more concerned with internal conflicts, was ignored and considered a nonentity by the Entente, which opposed dragging Spain into the confrontation. Britain and France felt they could win the war without Spain as an official supporter, believing that the participation of country with limited military potential would be of little assistance in a war which was not predicted to last long. The government of Spain, presided over by the conservative Eduardo Dato, published a decree on July 30, widely reported in the press, in which it declared strict Spanish neutrality. This official neutrality declaration was based on evident reasons: the division of the nation between those supporting the Allies and those who backed the Germans, Spain's lack of genuine interest in the conflict, the limited possible benefits derived from intervention, and the attitude of the French and British governments which opposed Spanish cooperation in the war effort.[5]

In his official meetings with the French President Raymond Poincaré in Paris in May and December 1913 and in Madrid in October of the same year, Alfonso XIII seemed to favor supporting France and Great Britain in a possible confrontation with the German Empire, as reported widely in Spanish and French press.[6] The king offered to make Spanish ports available to British and French squadrons. France could also make use of Spanish railroad lines to move its troops to Africa. In exchange, there were hopes of a united Iberia if—as royal prevision had it—anarchy reigned in Portugal and Spain was forced to intervene in the neighboring country. The French declined the offer of rail, as its military commanders considered transporting troops via Spanish rail lines to be too slow and precarious. Furthermore, the French ambassador in Madrid did not believe that most of the Spanish government would share the monarch's wishes and, most importantly, Great Britain would never accept any annexation of its ally Portugal by Spain.[7]

Once war broke out, the Spanish monarch chose to keep Spain out of the conflict, thus allowing himself to offer his services as mediator between the two sides in peace negotiations. In this way, Spain could once again participate actively in international politics and reinforce its stature. The candidacy of King Alfonso XIII was enhanced by the Spanish Crown's supposed loyalty toward two blocks, both explicable by virtue of the double influence of his immediate family surroundings. His mother was Austrian and his wife British.[8] But the neutrality of the Spanish government and its king was also a declaration of Spain's impotence, with a sluggish economy, an inoperative political system, an incompetent army—its presence in Morocco providing ample testimony—and an insufficient fleet to defend its extensive and undefended Atlantic and Mediterranean coastlines against any enemy assault.[9]

Neutrality in the Face of War

Furthermore, Spain's neutrality enhanced some parts of its foreign policy. Madrid became a favored center for certain negotiations. As the war dragged on, the Spanish diplomatic service began taking on a growing number of war causes and the king personally organized an office to war victims, mediating to obtain guarantees on military prisoners. Maintaining neutrality was not easy. In spite of increasingly aggressive warmongering by some Spanish factions and internal crises, Spain maintained official state neutrality throughout the four years of conflict. Among the factors that contributed most to this were the government's prudence, the peace movement within the working class, the king's action, Spain's diplomatic efforts, and the position of Madrid as the capital of European neutrality.[10] This took the form of wagers and hopes for victory in favor of one warring side or the other. Such bets constituted little more than desires, because the common platform that united the warmongering Spanish opinion was official neutrality, which aptly reflected the feeling of powerlessness and vulnerability that was behind Spain's "international option."

Nevertheless, it may seem difficult to accept that Spain remained strictly neutral, as the Dato government proclaimed. Certainly, if we take into account the imposed international direction, Spain's agreements with France and Great Britain in the years leading up to the war, and its geographic location and commercial interests, its freedom of movement in foreign policy was more reduced. Spain was firmly bound to the Entente and within this sphere of influence. That was the opinion of the most powerful men in the country, those who shaped Spain's international policy.

The Count of Romanones, President of the Cabinet during many of these years, responded to a request in the Senate, when the war was over, on the necessity that Spain's international policy leave off being undefined. The liberal leader confirmed that Spain had not been isolated prior to the conflict because the country had a clearly defined international policy dating back to 1902 with the projected agreements between France and Spain regarding Morocco. A similar policy had begun on a more permanent basis in 1904 with the Spanish-French accord, an agreement that originated the same year with the Anglo-French pact, in view of which France had come into dispute over Egypt, and Britain concerning Morocco. Romanones affirmed that the policy had been ratified in accordance with the 1906 Algeciras Conference, with its harshest statements concerning the Mediterranean in correspondence with London and Paris, which became known as the Agreement of Cartagena sanctioned in the 1912 treaty.[11] Romanones concluded that "when a nation has established bonds as strong as those described in the acts, when there have been intimate conversations with both the French and British, it cannot be considered isolated."[12]

Fernando León y Castillo, another important figure in Spanish foreign policy, was more explicit concerning the neutral path Spain should take in this era. In 1916, upon returning to the Spanish Embassy in Paris, which he had abandoned in 1910, the Spanish diplomat openly discussed the matter: "Let's get to the point. Does neutrality fit our foreign policy and what form or orientation should it take?" To answer these questions, León y Castillo then referred to the treaties of 1904 and 1907, which he supported, and concerning the last of these he added:

> Without losing sight of the agreements in that treaty, we remain neutral and retaining that neutrality should be the object of all our energies....
>
> But apart from the duty to ensure that our neutrality is respected, for which we should do whatever our Government instructs on this matter, we reserve the right to have certain inclinations...toward all that could be included in our preferences.
>
> ...We cannot set aside the 1907 agreement or what has been discussed in Paris, Madrid and London.
>
> These pacts and their predecessors among others signal our course; but they do not behoove us to intervene *manu militari* in the current struggle.
>
> We in the *Gaceta* are neutral; but not in spirit because no one can remain indifferent in the face of a war that affects our most vital interests.[13]

Though León y Castillo obviously harbored his own personal motives for defending a Spanish foreign policy that he had helped devise, his words summed up the way most of Spain's main liberal leaders understood neutrality throughout the war years.[14] While it is true that Spain remained officially neutral for the four years the war lasted, it should also be noted that the country's loyalty to the Entente powers increased as the war dragged on. The Allies intensified their economic pressure which, as the war seemed to move in their favor, brought the support of peripheral European countries who became *neutral allies.* The continuation of the war increased the importance of economic pressure and enhanced Spain's strategic situation with its French border and its Western Mediterranean and Eastern Atlantic position. Although Spain's Mediterranean location lost its value for the Entente from the spring of 1915, after Italy entered the conflict, in the economic war Spain offered France and Great Britain food and military provisions; in addition, Spaniards could work in French factories and thus freed military-age French workers to go to the front.[15]

For its part, Germany realized Spain had to appear friendly to France and Great Britain for economic and geographic reasons.[16] Commander Valdivia, military attaché of the Spanish Embassy in Berlin, expressed this sentiment in June 1914 to Arnold Kalle, German military attaché in Madrid; the Spanish attaché explained to the Germans the diplomatic maneuvers of Alfonso XIII, over the previous year, in recognition of the actual Spanish situation, too closely linked economically and physically to France and Great Britain to risk turning against them.[17] Spain's commitment to France and the significance of Poincaré's trip to Madrid in 1913 had also been taken up by the Central European press.[18] The attitude of the government and Spanish people, as well as the impartial way of observing the duties of the neutrality, once the war had begun, seemed quite extraordinary and had given rise to, according to the ambassador, fresh affection for Spain in both official spheres and public opinion. By extension, Polo de Bernabé had the satisfaction of hearing official praise for Spain and its Sovereign.[19] Furthermore, from the start of the war, the German leaders believed King Alfonso personally favored their cause, and the Emperor often made reference to royal solidarity between the two nations.[20] The friendship between Kaiser Wilhelm II and Alfonso XIII helped maintain Spanish-German diplomacy on a friendly basis, even when the war complicated matters. Emperor Wilhelm had written to the Spanish monarch via Valdivia, and this was the reply from Alfonso XIII, dated January 1918:

> Dear Wilhelm,
>   ...I am most pleased to learn that you have managed to undertake all the chores that, with my Government leaders, I too have carried out, so that Spain maintains its neutral policy which it has upheld since the outset of the war. In this I believe I have served my beloved country well interpreting its aspirations and I have helped avoid further bloody sacrifice for my people and other nations, as you well note in your letter....
>   I cannot hide that, given the special circumstances I have had to overcome a number of difficulties in upholding this neutrality policy. I hereby formally assure you that I must persevere in this endeavor as I feel it is the most favorable policy for Spanish interests, and for other nations. Only an act of aggression to our territorial integrity or an offense of our honorable flag could move us from this neutrality stance.
>   I feel cheered that your people recognize and appreciate the noble conduct of the Spanish people with relation to your country....
>   ...a fond embrace from your most loyal friend, brother and cousin
>   Alfonso XIII[21]

Strict Spanish neutrality had to be the German aim, as their Ambassador had indicated.[22] If it had joined the German cause, Spain would have immediately lost the Balearic and Canary Islands, all its important ports and links with its troops in Morocco, all of which Germany could not protect.[23] Furthermore, the Austro-Hungarian diplomatic corps in Berlin assumed that "if Spain wanted to break away totally with the allies it could mobilize an army of 500,000 men in six weeks. However, these would have to protect borders and coasts and Spain would lose its islands and

Moroccan territory."[24] As the Central European empires could not wait for the participation of Spain on their side, they considered its strict neutrality favorable. Therefore, the main task of Central European diplomacy involved resisting Entente influence and maintaining Spanish neutrality, for if Spain were to support the Allies too much it would become a "captive" of the Entente.

To carry out this aim, Berlin promised Spain economic aid and postwar political support, so that Madrid could free itself from Entente patronage. Germany prudently encouraged Alfonso XIII to carry on as mediator in the conflict, to maintain the hopes that Spain's international status could be reinforced, and also to prevent Spanish sympathies from growing too pro-Entente. At the same time, the *Auswärtiges Amt* (German Foreign Office) made vague promises that Spanish cooperation in the war would be rewarded by the annexation of territories and countries in an effort to stir outdated imperialist nostalgia—present at the most active international regeneration movement of Spain—which challenged Spanish foreign policy.[25] The most susceptible Spanish leaders—including Alfonso XIII—bought into the notion that Spain would take over Gibraltar, annex Tangier, have reign in Morocco and even, if Germany managed to defeat Britain at sea, obtain dominance over Portugal. With Spanish hopes for a close peninsular link, Portugal would become a constant object of foreign policy negotiations, an affirmative imperialist exponent that broke the mold of conservative and defensive strategies in the wake of the Cartagena Accords.[26]

In October 1914, German Ambassador Ratibor wrote encouragingly to the Spanish king, urging the monarch to annex Portugal. However grateful he might have been for this suggestion, Alfonso XIII could not act against Portugal, as he was well aware that, if he did so, France and Britain would occupy the Balearic and Canary Islands immediately, would shell Spanish ports, and would cut off Spanish communication with Morocco.[27] Therefore, in the face of their foreign interests and ambitions, such as controlling the entire Iberian Peninsula, the obligatory Spanish neutrality takes on more significance as the military impotence and implicit recognition of the frustration in the international sphere. Though Spain could not accept Germany's proposals, the Entente's knowledge of these propositions helped the king work the situation in favor of Spain. Thus, Alfonso XIII never ceased to encourage German maneuvers. In July 1915, he spoke with German military attaché Kalle about Spanish–German relations. The king emphasized the need for German economic assistance to help Spain shed the yoke of Britain and France. A month later, Kalle sent the monarch a memorandum in which nothing was promised directly, but favorable possibilities were mentioned if Spain followed a policy of neutrality and benevolence toward Germany.[28]

In August 1915, the German General Erich von Falkenhayn received a cousin of the king, Don Alfonso María de Borbón, in Teschen, where the latter was visiting the German front in Eastern Europe. Don Alfonso told the General that the republican parties in Spain were trying to push the country to join the war on the allied side. Germany would soon have to take measures against this, promising Spain that, during peacetime, it would support its territorial ambitions in Orán, Morocco, and Gibraltar. For his part, Don Alfonso would commission a person with a substantial sum of money, contributed by Germany, to foment a revolutionary movement in the French Midi, in the belief that then France would retaliate and occupy the Spanish islands, and in this way would give the king and conservatives a reason to initiate hostilities against their Gallic neighbor. Don Alfonso indicated he was acting by order of the king, telling Von Falkenhayn to pass the message on to the Chancellor Theobald von Bethmann-Hollweg, who would attempt to determine if Don Alfonso's suggestions represented the policy of the king and if Spain really was interested in going to war against France.[29] None of the channels confirmed this idea, since there was no evidence that Spain wished to participate in the conflict.

On September 14, 1915, in conversations with the German military attaché, King Alfonso said that his cousin did not have the authority to make any agreement with the Germans, although he left the possibility of later discussions open.[30] Alfonso XIII undoubtedly wanted to keep the German promises alive, despite the impossibility of Spain accepting them. This impossibility is evidenced in a letter sent by the Marquis of Lema, Minister of State in the Dato government, to the Spanish Ambassador in Berlin, in which he explained the reason for Spanish neutrality and also the tendency to side with the Allies despite German distrust:

> Let's not forget that, aside from our lack of military might to reject British or even French aggression, our commercial and industrial dependence and other matters is a widely recognized fact which perhaps Berlin does not accept, as I see it, but from Santa Cruz square [the Spanish Foreign Ministry] we see it all clearly. . .the amount of material that, if we do not receive it from Britain and even France, would cause considerable industry losses for ours and severely hinder our agriculture is enormous; and if we consider what we need to import from Germany, how will these products reach our ports if Great Britain, France and even Italy intervene? Also, if they oppose, how are we going to export our fruit and other products? And how are we going to get provisions to our troops in Africa?
>
> The old maxim "Primun vivere, deinde philosophari" still applies. Before we talk of grand ideals, which we keep in our hearts, we have to survive: we have to avoid the fire without getting burnt by falling embers and, if we cannot, the responsibility will not fall on the shoulders of the Prince of Ratibor, nor on another Ambassador, but on the President of the Cabinet and his

Minister of State who, blinded by dreams of future glories and influenced by partial counselors or that only see the one side of things, having put their country on the road to ruin or shameful humiliation.[31]

A month later, in December 1915, relations between Berlin and Madrid were further strained when Dato was forced to resign in the face of domestic problems caused by the war. The British and French exerted great pressure on the king to replace Dato with Romanones, whose favorable leanings toward the Entente were well known. At the behest of the king, Romanones then formed a new government, and introduced increasingly benevolent neutrality for the Entente. During the term of Romanones, Germany had to make concessions to resist the Spanish president's, whereas Alfonso XIII's mediating attitude, in spite of the inevitable concessions that came to the Entente, managed to avoid the open adhesion to the allied cause and to maintain the diplomatic flexibility inherent in considering by German proposals.

The visit to the port of Cartagena in June 1916 by a German submarine, bearing a personal message from Emperor Wilhelm to King Alfonso, came about thanks to the express wishes of the Spanish Monarch. This visit brought with it clear threats by the Entente to occupy Spanish ports, threats that led to the publication of a Spanish declaration negating the possibility of any further visits of this type. French and British pressure intensified throughout the summer of 1916. These actions of the Entente were paid by the German submarine war that caused important conflicts between Madrid and Berlin, since most of the German promises to respect Spanish ships and to facilitate Spanish commerce were not fulfilled.

On April 9, 1917, when, without previous warning, a German submarine torpedoed the Spanish steamer *San Fulgencio,* Romanones tried to get his government to break off relations with Germany, but failed because of resistance from both the king and his Cabinet, and he was forced to submit his resignation. The overthrow of Romanones, who the Germans considered a danger to Spanish neutrality, was fomented by an active journalistic campaign provoked by Ratibor, the German Ambassador in Madrid, who was keen to see the liberal leader fall.

Manuel García Prieto and Dato, successors to Romanones, tried to restore more or less strict neutrality. However, the 1918 German submarine campaign caused such a tense situation that Madrid almost broke off diplomatic relations with Berlin. The economic situation, worsened by the submarine warfare, induced Spain to lean more firmly toward the Entente,[32] and Germany threatened to cancel aid it had been providing to the Spanish fleet. Antonio Maura tried to lead the country back to neutrality, but it could not avoid deteriorating Spanish–German relations due to the submarine issue.

In August 1918, in a note to the German government, Maura declared that from that point onward for every Spanish ship sunk by submarines, Spain would have to seize German ships anchored in Spanish ports. Nevertheless, the Spanish government did not carry out this measure, since, according to diplomatic information, this would have shattered relations with Germany; in addition, Berlin decided to deliver six steamers to Spain as indemnification for the sunken ships, to calm the Cabinet in Madrid, because the war situation had gotten considerably worse for the Central Powers and Germany saw how Spain was being forced toward the Entente side. The end of the war, in November 1918, prevented Spain from joining the Allies' side in the struggle.

The Defense of Neutrality

Available Military and Naval Resources

The outbreak of hostilities that gave rise to World War I surprised Spain, so taken up with defending its own territory and coasts. This was due in part to an outdated communications system and old weaponry and also to the worrying state of its military, discouraged and divided into *peninsulares* and *Africanistas,* who needed a reform of the military institutions, a reform which World War I would make even more urgent.[33] Defending its coasts and island possessions required a naval policy that reorganized the navy, which in 1898 had seen the full extent and impact of its own decline. Nevertheless, the lack of a viable direction as well as effective operative means characterized the Spanish naval policy throughout these years.[34]

How then could Spanish coastal defense be approached, if it included islands located a considerable distance away and with insufficient Spanish naval bases, and whose waters were frequented by ships of the most powerful European naval powers? It would seem an impossible undertaking with Spanish naval means, thus Madrid had to look for the protection which the agreements with France and Britain provided. In this respect, we have the words of Ambassador Leon y Castillo, one of these agreements' signers, who posed this question during the war:

> If we were alone as in 1898 without the cooperation of Britain and France contained in the treaties of 1904 and 1907, for which Maura, Rodriguez San Pedro and Allendesalazar should be justly proud and which I had the honor to sign, what would happen in the Canary or Balearic Islands, in Vigo, in spite of our neutrality?...
>
> When it comes time to draw this matter to a close and reconstitute Europe, what would become of the Balearic and Canary Islands and our protectorate in Morocco...?[35]

Romanones also felt that the 1907 agreements enabled Spain to enjoy a period of relative calm as war was raging, "safe in the knowledge that parts of the Spanish territory, such as the Balearic and Canary Islands, were completely intangible and unquestionably respected."[36] This confidence in the security that the French and British naval fleets would provide reflected the distrust that he had of Spain's own resources.

In addition to limited material means, Spain's military also lacked direction and was unable to apply the existing position. A royal decree in March 1891 had established military zones on the coasts and borders of mainland Spain, and this was extended to include the Balearic and Canary Islands in September of that same year. Great tracts of land along coasts and borders were declared of military significance, so construction or changes to the land that might have an impact on defensive conditions could not be carried out without consulting the Ministry of War. However, the decree was never applied until two decades later, in April 1911.[37] The main problem was that by then some of the most important ports, such as La Luz which would be targeted in time of war because it was the first major port of call on the Eastern Atlantic, were largely owned by foreign companies, particularly British firms, who occupied areas which were essential for coastal control. Nevertheless, the lack of concern and incompetence of the different departments involved, together with the shortage of credit, kept these problems from being solved. In many of those places, the limited armed batteries did not have sufficient personnel to serve their needs in the event of war.

In February 1915, in the debate concerning a proposed law that would authorize the government to continue the construction and equipping of bases in military ports, it was noted that the government had set out to create an essentially defensive navy which would never be effective to operate or to prevent the blockade which would surely be set up in strategic Spanish enclaves in the event of war, given that the offensive power and operational range of that navy were very limited.[38] The concern over this lack of defense was a recurrent subject, so that, when in June 1918, months before the end of the war, an army reorganization project was discussed in the Congress, voices were raised again about the urgent necessity to ensure the defense of those enclaves.[39] The matter was also raised in the press, which included even the number of naval components that would guarantee proper defense.[40]

The lack of defense was a constant point of discussion throughout the entire war due to the limited measures taken to improve defensive means and conditions and funding needs. If a Spanish action against any military intervention or occupation was bound to fail, the best way to avoid such a scenario would be to ensure that Spanish neutrality was not violated by either side in the war, as this could cause the opponent to avenge such an act.

Thus, the scarce resources available to Spain were used to safeguard neutrality. However, it was important to ascertain the judicial framework in which neutrality could develop. The rules by which the neutral countries carried on their rights and responsibilities in relation to the warring sides were fixed by international treaties set down in the Second Peace Conference which took place in The Hague. The XIII Agreement of The Hague, on October 18, 1907, contained the precepts related to rights and responsibilities of the neutral powers in case of war at sea.[41] This agreement had not been accepted by Spain at the outset of World War I, with the expressed reason that advisability of subordinating that resolution to the 1909 London Declaration, which set out the rules for warfare at sea. This reason was more apparent than real and was consigned by the relationship between the material in the London Declaration and that of the XIII Agreement of The Hague.[42]

The XIII Agreement had not been accepted because the Naval Ministry had some reservations about several of the articles. However, when war broke out there was no sure way for Spain to invoke other principles of international law from those accepted by the majority of the countries at the Conference of The Hague, which had signed the agreement. Thus, for all intents and purposes, the Spanish government had to accept this agreement from the start of the war.[43] In early September 1914, the Navy Minister authorized the refueling of several British warships with coal so they could reach their country, advising them that for further provisions they would have to attend to the Agreement of The Hague regarding warships.[44]

To resolve the different incidents—which occurred from the outset of the war—regarding the right to dock foreign warships in wartime, a royal decree was drafted in November 1914 informing foreign nations that, while the conflict lasted, Spain put into effect the precepts of 1907 Agreement of The Hague, regarding rights and duties of neutral nations in sea warfare. A limit of three miles was set as Spanish area of jurisdiction, only for applying those precepts and to maintain Spanish neutrality during the war,[45] taking into account that rather than an area of rights and prerogatives, in the opinion of the Navy Ministry, it was an area of responsibilities and obligations.[46]

To ensure and maintain Spain's neutrality, the Ministries of War, Navy, and Interior took specific measures. Though these did not substantially ameliorate the country's lack of defense, they attempted to improve conditions and resources for defense and impede anyone breaking the country's neutral stance, guaranteeing, when possible, fulfillment of the precepts of the XIII Agreement of The Hague. Thus, in the first half of August 1914, the Minister of War informed his generals of the different nations that had entered the war and reminded them of their country's duty to remain strictly neutral.[47] The War Ministry also imposed new measures regarding military personnel. A royal mandate dated May 1915 stated that the generals, commanders, and officials were not to leave their posts while prevailing conditions continued.[48] Some days later, another order suspended all leaves granted by the recruitment law.[49] The course of the war seemed more unpredictable; in the weeks before Italy entered the conflict on the side of the Entente, creating a new allied-controlled Mediterranean sphere, the British transatlantic liner *Lusitania* was torpedoed—causing a worldwide outcry—due to the German submarine campaign started three months before.

Meanwhile, as the means of protecting ports from foreign warships was precarious, it became urgent to improve the defense conditions. Thus, a royal order of June 1915 arranged that the following measures were to be taken: first, military governors had to show to the local naval authorities the places of their ports where they would not permit foreign warships to anchor. Furthermore, any mooring for the servicing of foreign warships had to be reported beforehand to the naval commander. The number of crew who would disembark was also controlled, as well as the hours that they were going to remain on land, so that the naval authority could immediately warn local military and civil administrations to adopt appropriate security measures.[50]

Once these measures were applied, all the authorities under the Ministries of War, Navy, and Interior had to be coordinated, their actions within the directives of the Ministry of State established to maintain neutrality. Thus, in October 1915, the Ministry of War gave instructions to the commanders in chief so that, whenever foreign people or interests entered in their territory and they might be called upon to take part, they were required to report to the Ministry of War before adopting any resolution, so as to act in accordance with the Ministry of State.[51]

Naval authorities, on the other hand, took measures to try to counter any actions that infringed on neutrality in Spanish territorial waters: from the beginning of August 1914 radiotelegraph stations on foreign ships anchored at Spanish ports were made operable. Furthermore, boats that loaded cargo onto ships were inspected and these last were registered before departing to prevent the boarding of merchandise considered military contraband under The Hague Agreement. Spain also sought to control the escape of crews from the interned German steamers.[52] In this regard, naval authorities also had to monitor night traffic of any ship without official authorization, as well as the clandestine supplying or the escape[53] of the more than fifty interned or sheltered German and Austrian steamships in Spanish ports.[54]

However, the escape of the German steamer *Macedonia*—interned in Las Palmas—in March 1915 demonstrated the need to reinforce preventive measures and monitoring. The naval authorities ordered staff to take essential pieces of the machinery of all interned German ships in that

Spanish port to prevent them from setting out to sea, until the arrival of the 800-ton Spanish gunboat, the *Laya*. Although this ship was no match for any of those of the warring powers which frequented Spanish waters, it was a more effective means of monitoring. Nevertheless, not even in some of the ports with more German and Austrian ships anchored the permanent presence of the Spanish navy could be guaranteed. This became official in February 1916, when a British ship, the *Westburn*, was sunk in waters off the island of Tenerife by the German crew who had captured it on the high seas. The naval authority could not prevent its sinking as it lacked the means to carry out appropriate monitoring.[55] Therefore, although it is certain that all the measures adopted by the military administration were attempts to ensure Spanish neutrality, the course of the world war demonstrated that such measures were insufficient to avoid violations of neutrality by the two sides committed when their immediate interests demanded it.

Reforms Without Solutions

To guarantee national defense and reinforce respect for Spain's neutrality, the Spanish military had to be reformed so the army would cease to be a theoretical institution and become an effective body. The importance of this issue rose in 1914, when the outbreak of the Great War shocked the military. Nevertheless, the country's neutrality kept its army from benefiting from the military renovation taking place in warring Europe, since on the battlefield both sides were revolutionizing war, while in Spain the only military participation in the continental fight was the one that took place in public opinion, as lines were drawn between those supporting the Allies and those who sided with the German cause. Spanish officials' preference mainly for Germany did not come as a surprise, given that their training was based on the Prussian model. However, this was also questioned from the moment in which armies of the democratic countries were able to defeat the troops of the Central European authoritarian monarchies. This encouraged the liberal reforming policy, which tried to subordinate the officers to a control of their technical capacity.

Nevertheless, the reform projects had to handle the most immediate military needs, related to the social and economic consequences of the war in Spain. One was the rise in inflation, while all the State civil employees had their pay frozen from 1914. So in 1916 when attempts were made in Barcelona to control the Infantry's technical capacity to move up the scale that was smothered at that time and senior promotions were slowest in the peninsular garrisons, Barcelona's Infantry regiment officials formed defense *Juntas*, which spread across Spain. The *Juntas* delegates demanded economic and professional improvements and denounced merit raises for the military stationed in Morocco, as this was thought to hinder the bleak professional future even more. In the context of the 1917 national crisis, the military's influence in governmental affairs led to the imposition of a new Minister of War, who promised economic improvements and military reform. This took shape in the army reorganization law of 1918, which regulated how officials could advance in rank, without adapting the army to the new times. None of these laws—including the mentioned law of naval constructions in 1915—substantially transformed the military organization.

In conclusion, World War I served to contrast as well as accentuate some characteristics of the Spanish military reality which had become clear from 1898: the shortage of all types of resources and the country's very limited foreign involvement, with very little room to maneuver, even within the framework of neutrality that meant near total impotence. There was also limited possibility of military reforms—to create effective armed forces—which the war would make even more necessary and that clashed with a similar level of financial impotence, which led to Spain's outmoded military technology. Finally, the discovery that Spain's military forces could not contribute to the country's foreign projection, beyond Spanish African involvement, nor could it deal with the increasing demands brought on by war, would help the military fix its attention and action increasingly on national concerns, aggravated by the economic impact that World War I had in Spain.

CHAPTER **4**

Spanish Civil War:
Franco's Nationalist Army

George Esenwein

When a group of dissident senior officers declared a state of war (*estado de guerra*) against the Republic in July 1936, it was not the first time that the Army had intruded upon Spain's political stage. The tradition of military intervention in domestic affairs began in the early part of the nineteenth century and continued with only brief periods of interruption up to the time of the Second Spanish Republic (1931–36). Spain's experiment in democracy was short-lived above all because both left- and right-wing political parties proved incapable of reining in on the numerous centrifugal forces which were daily undermining the stability of the regime. It was against this background that a group of high-ranking military figures decided that it was necessary for the Army to impose its will on the Spanish nation. Their decision to overthrow the civilian government and establish a military directory on July 17, 1936, unleashed a civil war that would last for nearly three years. The process by which certain segments of the Army became politicized during the Second Republic and the nature and function of the Nationalist army which these rebel leaders forged during the Civil War are the themes which will be examined in this chapter.

Historical Background

The emergence of the military as a force for political change in Spain can be traced to the early decades of the nineteenth century. At that time, the army played a central role in establishing the character and content of liberal rule in Spain. The military continued to actively intervene in politics until 1876, when the main architect of the Restoration system, Antonio Cánovas del Castillo, sought to prevent the army from interfering with national affairs by greatly reducing their role in politics. During the early years of the Restoration (1876–96), the provisions of the

Constitution of 1876 that were aimed at excluding the military from the public sphere were largely effective. However, the persistence of electoral corruption (*caciquismo*); the failure of Spanish liberalism to respond effectively to the destabilizing effects of social change (regionalism), economic modernization (industrialization), and imperialism (colonialism in Morocco); and the inability of successive governments to develop the basis for professionalism among the officer corps, all contributed to a revival of the army's political activism.

The tensions between the military and the Spanish liberal system did not diminish with time, but rather were increasingly brought into sharper relief by a number of domestic and foreign issues. Perhaps more than any other, however, it was the government's disastrous colonial policy in Morocco that produced the greatest strains on civil–military relations.[1]

Though it had maintained a presence there since 1497, Spain's relationship with Morocco did not become a major concern until the early years of the twentieth century. Spurred on by the belief that Spain needed to recover its national prestige following its humiliating defeat by the United States in 1898 and partly to protect its own meager holdings against native rebellions and the intrusions of foreign powers, the government steadily expanded its involvement in Morocco. After 1904, the army was engaged in intermittent warfare in its occupied zones. This proved to be unpopular, not only because it stirred the anti-conscription feelings of the general population, but also because many liberal writers and politicians believed that such military action was a waste of money.

As far as the military was concerned, one of the most significant consequences of this imperial policy was the rapid expansion of the Spanish colonial forces. Between 1909 and 1926, the Army of Africa (as it came to be known) became the largest and most dynamic branch of the military. In addition to regular Spanish units, the army was composed of indigenous Moroccan troops (organized into four distinct groups), as well as foreign soldiers and Spanish volunteers who belonged to the legendary *Tercio de Extranjeros* or Foreign Legion.[2]

Despite its robust growth and despite some structural modifications which improved military operations on the battlefield, the Spanish Army's main problems—a bloated command structure, poorly trained and equipped military personnel, and low morale among the vast majority of troops sent to fight in Morocco—continued to fester. Moreover, this same period saw a dramatic increase in the resentment and dissatisfaction among junior and middle-ranking officers. Their efforts to address their economic and other grievances by forming pressure groups in 1916–17 known as *Juntas de Defensa* (military syndicates) not only undermined the unity of the army but also blurred the lines separating military and political activities.

The problems of the kind referred to here finally came to a head in 1923. A series of military disasters in Morocco between 1919 and 1921 gave rise to the widespread belief within the army that the civilian government was largely responsible for these failures. After the highly publicized Annual catastrophe of 1921, when some 8,600 Spaniards were killed during a confused and disorganized military campaign, the army was ready to save its own reputation by turning on the politicians in Madrid. Led by one of their own generals, Miguel Primo de Rivera, the army decided in September 1923 to revert to its nineteenth-century role as a vehicle for regime change.

Though he promised the Spanish people that his rule represented only a "brief parenthesis" in the constitutional life of his country, Primo de Rivera remained in power for the next six-and-a-half years (1923–30). Initially Primo de Rivera proved to be a popular dictator. After reining in on the centrifugal forces (regionalism and working-class radicalism) which had been gaining momentum up to this time, he turned his attention to the thorny Moroccan question. In contrast to the *Africanistas,* who were committed to a forward policy in the Protectorate, Primo de Rivera decided to pursue a strategy of retrenchment. Over time this cautious approach paid off. By 1927, Primo de Rivera had managed to reduce Spain's military operations in Morocco to a minimum.

One of the ironies of Primo de Rivera's rule was that, though he relied on the military's backing, his dictatorship eventually lost the support of key elements of the officer corps. His plan to modernize and professionalize the armed forces was one reason why this was the case. Rather than improving relations among the different branches, his reform policies— such as those aimed at standardizing promotions—nourished old rivalries and even drove some dissident officers to join the civilian opposition to his regime. The latter development eventually cost Primo de Rivera his post. The increasingly pro-Republican orientation embraced by the officer corps fatally undermined the support that both Primo de Rivera and the king (Alfonso XIII) needed to continue to rule. By 1931, major segments of the military were ready to back the establishment of a Republican form of government.

Military Reforms During the Second Republic

Not long after it came into being, the Republican government made clear its resolve to reform the military. Apart from its zealous efforts to determine the guilt of military officers who were corrupt or who had collaborated with Miguel Primo de Rivera's dictatorship, the government was anxious to implement a root and branch transformation of outdated military structures.

Within days after the Republic had been established, the new Minister of War, Manuel Azaña, set about drafting decrees aimed primarily at democratizing the army and keeping it out of politics. In order to diminish the size and influence of Spain's top-heavy command structures, he offered generous retirement terms to generals and officers. The result was that the officer corps was reduced by more than half in the first year of the Republic. In an attempt to create a new group of second echelon leaders and to reinforce the infrastructure of army leadership, Azaña's Ministry also established a special Corps of Sub-Officers composed of four ranks: first sergeant, brigade sergeant, sub-aide, and sub-lieutenant. Azaña also sought to "Republicanize" the military by fomenting a more progressive intellectual climate within the army. To this end, he ordered the closure of anti-Republican military institutions—such as the General Military Academy in Zaragoza—and military journals such as *La Correspondencia Militar.*

Although the Spanish Army was long overdue for reforms, Azaña's ambitious attempts to streamline the military bureaucracy and liberalize its culture by promoting a pro-Republican orientation of the officer corps were met with hostility by right-wing politicians and conservative military figures. They argued that Azaña's efforts to modernize and rationalize the organizational infrastructure of the armed forces only served to undermine morale and reduce the power and importance of military institutions. Not surprisingly, then, the army's loyalty to the new form of government was constantly being monitored, not least because the question as to whether the Republic was the same as the Spanish nation was answered in different ways by different sections of the military. For generals like Franco, who was representative of the old guard that was being targeted by Azaña's reforms, it was not.

Pro-monarchist figures like Franco were not alone in opposing the leftward direction the government took after 1932. In August 1932, for example, the pro-Republican, General José Sanjurjo, led an abortive coup attempt against the Azaña regime. Though it ended in failure, the *sanjurjada* inspired disenchanted elements of the military to engage in further conspiracies against the Republic. The following year saw the creation of the clandestine *Unión Militar Española,* UME. While its nominal goal was to protect the constitutional government from being overthrown by left-wing revolutionaries, some of its leading members increasingly saw the quasi-political organization as an instrument that could be used to spearhead a right-wing coup.

The reforming phase of the Republic effectively ended with the elections of November 1933, when a center-right led by the Radicals came into power. In May 1935, the leader of the right-wing *CEDA* (*Confederación Española de Derechas Autónoma*), José María Gil Robles, was appointed as Minister of War. During his brief tenure, relations between the government and the military improved. Besides rolling back the reform measures adopted during Azaña's tenure as Minister of War, Gil Robles was intent on reorganizing the military along more traditional lines. With this in mind, he made a series of personnel reassignments that placed known anti-Republican figures in the military hierarchy into key positions. Francisco Franco was recalled from Morocco and appointed Chief of the General Staff. General Emilio Mola replaced Franco in Morocco, while General Manuel Goded was elevated to several key posts, including Director General of the Customs Guards or *carabineros.*

Civil-Military Relations

During the so-called *bienio negro* or antiprogressive years of the Republic, two events, the Asturian uprising of October 1934 and the February national elections of 1936, served to reinforce the anti-Republican trajectory of the right-wing elements in the military. In October 1934, the country was convulsed by the most serious challenge to government rule since the establishment of the Republic. This was precipitated by President Niceto Alcalá Zamora's invitation to several members of the right-wing *CEDA* to participate in the national government. Confirmed in the belief that the *CEDA's* sole reason for entering the Cabinet was to lay the groundwork for a fascist regime, the Left responded on October 4–5 by launching a series of general strikes and protest movements. Nearly all of these, including the Esquerra's ill-conceived plan to establish an independent republic in Catalonia, were so poorly coordinated and supported that they had little chance of success. In fact, apart from a working-class uprising in Asturias, all of the leftist-inspired outbursts collapsed within a few days. United by a broadly based revolutionary pact or *Alianza Obrera,* some 20,000 anarchist, communist, and socialist workers from the Asturian mining areas managed to sustain their revolt for nearly two weeks.

Their initial successes—which included their occupation of the provincial capital of Oviedo—so alarmed the government that drastic measures were adopted to bring the revolutionary movement to an end. After placing the country under martial law, the Minister of War called on General Francisco Franco to use the might of the military to crush the rebellion. Showing no mercy to their adversaries, the expeditionary troops—accompanied by two *banderas* (battalions) of the Spanish Legion and one *tabor* (battalion) of Moorish *Regulares* under the command of Lieutenant Colonel Juan Yagüe Blanco—sent into the region quickly conquered the areas briefly dominated by revolutionary working-class committees. By the middle of October, the Asturian crisis had ended. As a result of the fighting, an estimated 1,000 civilians had been killed, while, according to an official government report issued at the end of October, the death toll among the army and various police forces was around 450.

A final blow against the radicalized working-class movement was dealt in the weeks following the uprising: some 30,000 workers were arrested and thrown into prison.[3]

On the Left, the Asturian rising quickly passed into legend as an example of the Spanish working-class movement's resolve to combat the oppression of the reactionary ruling classes. In the months to come, the initials of the Asturian workers' alliance, UHP (United Proletarian Brothers), became a rallying cry for the entire spectrum of Spain's left-wing radicals, most of who were now convinced that the day of an all-out confrontation with their class enemies was rapidly approaching. For the Right, the Asturian episode testified to the inherent weaknesses of the Republic. And despite the fact that the rebellion had been brutally suppressed, rightists were more fearful than ever that the government was losing its struggle to rein in the revolutionary Left.

The impact of the revolt and its aftermath on the military was no less profound. The incident not only served to strengthen the anti-Republican convictions of officers already convinced of the need to intervene in politics but also reinforced the belief held by Francisco Franco and other right-wing generals that parliamentary democracy was not an effective barrier against the threat of communist revolution. Without committing themselves to joining the circle of conspirators plotting to overthrow the government, this segment of the military was no longer content to stand by idly while the Republic unraveled under the pressures being brought to bear by the centrifugal forces in Spanish society.

Immediately following the leftist electoral victory in February 1936, Colonel José Varela and other senior officers of the UME sought to broaden the circle of their conspiracy by liaising with anti-Republican civilian organizations scattered across the country. They found a receptive audience among the three most important antigovernment forces on the Right, the Alfonsine Monarchists, the Falange, and the Carlists. Of the three, the Carlists were the most advanced in their preparations for overthrowing the Republic. Intractably opposed to the progressive politics of the 1931–36 period, the Carlists adopted a variety of tactics in pursuing their goal of overthrowing the Republic. They used their official organization, the Traditional Communion, as a vehicle for disseminating their ideas and forging alliances among right-wing parties that were equally determined to obstruct Republican policies. After 1934, Carlist leaders and their supporters began doubting the efficacy of legalist tactics and thus increasingly embraced violence as a means of achieving their goals. As a result, emphasis was placed on developing the size and effectiveness of the Carlist Youth organization, as well as the movement's armed militia, the *Requetés*. Under the guidance of José Varela, who by the end of the Civil War was promoted to general, the militia grew into a credible military organization which some saw as being capable of supporting a Carlist-led rebellion.[4]

But while they were seen as allies in their movement to overthrow the Republic, Mola and other ranking officers did not want to see their own troops being unduly influenced by the zealous adherents of a reactionary monarchist movement. They therefore insisted that these civilian militias play a subordinate role in the army's plans to establish a military-dominated Directorate.

Up to this point, the fascist Falange party had been neither a powerful nor a numerous body. Yet, the defeat of the legalist Right in the February elections attracted an ever-increasing number of recruits to their cause. In view of the movement's growing popularity, Mola and his fellow conspirators decided in June to inform José Antonio Primo de Rivera and other Falangist leaders that the decisive moment for their planned insurrection was rapidly approaching.

From Popular Front to Civil War

After becoming aware of the intrigues of the anti-Republican conspirators, the newly established Popular Front government took steps to break up the circle of plotters. High-ranking officers who were known to be hostile to the Republic were reassigned to command posts far away from the capital and other strategic locations. Franco was posted to the Canaries, Goded was moved to the Balearic Islands, and Mola was relieved of his duties as commander in chief of the Army of Africa in Morocco and transferred to Navarre, where he assumed command of the Pamplona garrison. On a more fundamental level, the government pursued a policy of neutralizing anti-Republican agitation among the rank-and-file by splitting up and transferring units from one garrison to another.

Despite these anticipatory measures, however, Mola and his fellow conspirators pressed forward with their plans. In April, the nominal head of the plot, General José Sanjurjo, appointed Mola as the "director" of the uprising. Given his aptitude for detailed planning and in view of his cautious temperament, Mola seemed a logical choice to act as the general coordinator of the conspiracy. His task was made that much easier by the fact that he was now based in Pamplona, the headquarters of the Carlist movement, where he could count on the assistance of fellow conspirators like the well-connected Lieutenant Colonel Valentín Galarza and other garrison officers who belonged to the clandestine UME.[5] Mola himself wasted little time in setting the plot into motion. His first directive, issued in May, outlined the main steps of the coup. In contrast to the vague preparations that went into the ill-fated *sanjurjada* of 1932, Mola's plan assumed that the success of a coup hinged in part on the support of right-wing civilian organizations. Participation of nonmilitary groups was intended to broaden the base of the conspiracy movement rather than to alter the role the army was to play in the insurrection itself.

Underscoring this point, Mola made it clear in his dealings with the Carlists and similar groups that all civilian militias would be placed under military control and that, once the rebellion had achieved its goals, a Directorate dominated by Mola and his fellow *Africanista* officers would initially run the country.[6]

Less than a month later, Mola met with other high-ranking officers who were to play a key role in the conspiracy and subsequent Civil War, the most notable being the head of the air force, Alfredo Kindelán, General Gonzalo Queipo de Llano, General Luis Orgaz y Yoldi, General Miguel Cabanellas, and General Joaquín Fanjul.[7] Noticeably absent from this widening circle of rebel generals was Francisco Franco. Though still reluctant to make a formal commitment to overthrowing the Republic, Francisco Franco nonetheless was seen by others and saw himself as a potentially key player should the army and their civilian allies decide to rise up against the Popular Front government. However, it was not until the coup was at the point of being launched in mid-July that Franco finally overcame his indecisiveness.[8]

Against the background of mounting violent public demonstrations, strikes, and skirmishes between rival ideological groups, politics was increasingly played out in the streets rather than in Parliament (*Cortes*). That the government was unable to rein in on the escalating incidents of violence was illustrated by the startling number of political killings (estimated to be around 270) and industrial disturbances (some 341 strikes and partial shutdowns), which occurred in the spate of less than six months. When, on the night of July 12–13, leftist police officers working in collusion with socialist gunmen murdered the right-wing politician José Calvo Sotelo, the final countdown to the military insurrection began. Now convinced that the Republic was rapidly descending into chaos, the conspirators, who were joined by Franco, scheduled the rising to begin on July 18.

Military Rising

The military rising that was launched in Morocco during the night of July 17 (a day earlier than planned) unleashed a series of similar actions on the mainland. Over the next forty-eight hours, garrisons scattered throughout the country rose up against the government and rebel leaders moved quickly to secure control of the provincial capitals and the major cities. By the 21st, however, it had become clear that the insurgents had failed to achieve their goal of seizing power quickly and painlessly. While the rebellion met little or no resistance in garrisons located in Spanish Morocco, the Navarre, and other conservative regions in the north and northwest, it was successful in only about one-third of the country. Apart from Seville, Valladolid, and Zaragoza, where enterprising rebel leaders overcame overwhelming odds, the revolt was put down in Spain's other major cities, Madrid, Barcelona, and Valencia. It was also apparent that, rather than being united in its opposition to the liberal Republic, the army was divided in its loyalties. The fact that most senior officers refused to join the insurrection demonstrated the extent to which Mola and his fellow conspirators had been exceedingly optimistic about the support they would receive from key segments of the military once the rebellion was underway. After the initial fighting died down, the insurgents (or Nationalists as they referred to themselves) controlled only 53% of the army—approximately 30,000 troops on the mainland and another 34,000 battle-trained officers and soldiers belonging to the Army of Africa— and around 35% of Spain's air force and navy.[9] The rebels' failure to secure the latter proved to be a major setback in their effort to link up the combat-ready forces in Morocco with the insurgency on the mainland.

Aware that the forward momentum of the insurrection depended on the support of the troops under his command, Francisco Franco wasted no time in appealing for outside assistance. Just a few days after the rebellion had begun, he dispatched emissaries to Hitler and Mussolini with requests for bomber-transports and fighter aircraft.[10] Their willingness to send planes to help Franco ferry his Moroccan troops across the straits would have far-reaching consequences.[11] Besides preventing the revolt from grinding to a standstill, this foreign assistance inevitably widened the dimensions of a conflict that had started out as a purely domestic affair. No less significant was the fact that German and Italian aid greatly enhanced Franco's status within the insurgent camp. From that point on, he saw himself, and was seen by others, as playing a leadership role in the anti-Republican struggle.

In addition to the men and officers drawn from the traditional military forces, the Nationalists could count on around 30,000 men coming out of Spain's three major national security organizations, the Customs Guards (*carabineros*), the Assault Guards (*Guardia de Asalto*), and the Civil Guard (*Guardia Civil*). The Nationalist army also drew strength in the first months of fighting from the support it received from the rapidly expanding para-militia formations of the *Falange Española* and the Carlists (*Requetés*). The latter, for example, were largely responsible for the rapid gains Mola's Army of the North achieved in the Basque region during the opening phases of the insurrection. While the ideological enthusiasm and indepen- dent spirit of these civilian forces posed a potential challenge to their authority, military leaders came to rely on the Falangists and Carlists to perform essential support tasks. Besides securing lines of communica- tion and imposing Nationalist rule in conquered areas by "cleaning up" (i.e., executing or sequestering) opponents of the Nationalists' *movimiento*, it fell to these civilian groups to maintain public order and security in the rearguard.

Nationalists at War

After Franco succeeded in transporting the bulk of his military units—
Moorish *Regulares,* the *Tercio* or Foreign Legion, and select units of the
army—over from Africa, the Nationalists relentlessly pursued their initial
goal of linking up their northern and southern armies. Advancing rapidly
northward from Seville, Franco's forces under the command of Colonel
Yagüe attacked Badajoz, the last town of any size separating the Nationalists' two military zones. Their hard-fought victory there on August 14–15,
which was overshadowed by widely reported accounts of atrocities committed against unarmed civilians, was followed up by further advances
into the Tagus Valley west of Madrid. Meanwhile, at the other end of the
country, communications between the Republic's northwestern region
and France had been cut off when Mola's troops captured the border town
of Irún on September 4.

The Nationalists' early and relatively easy victories in these regions
owed a great deal to the fact that their military formations met little
resistance from the opposing side. Poorly armed and unregimented, the
medley of popular militias (columns) and patchwork of regular army
units fighting on the Republican side during the first weeks of the conflict
were no match for the professional and disciplined paramilitary soldiers
confronting them. Moreover, in contrast to the Republican forces, the
Nationalist command structure was unified and generally supported by
well-trained lower-ranking (*alféreces provisionales*) and noncommissioned
officers.

It was not until the formation of a government-controlled Popular
or People's Army in late September that these major defects in the
Republican war effort were seriously addressed. The arrival of fresh
shipments of war materiel—rifles, planes, artillery, antiaircraft guns, and
tanks—from Russia and Mexico in this same period (late September) also
dramatically improved the Republicans' fighting capacity.

Although successful on every front, the Nationalists were convinced
that if they captured the capital city of Madrid the war would soon be over.
Their lightening quick and decisive victories during the summer of 1936
strengthened both their confidence as a fighting force and their resolve to
march on Madrid as soon as possible. By mid-September, they were at
the point of mounting such an offensive when Franco's attention was
diverted by a drama that was being played out in the Republican-held
city of Toledo. Shortly after the military rebellion had begun there, some
1,100 insurgents (mostly members of the Civil Guard and a few cadets)
had, along with several hundred women and children and approximately
100 Republican hostages, retreated to the Alcázar, a formidable structure
towering over the Tagus River which also served as training facility for
Spanish officers. Led by the indomitable Colonel José Moscardó, the

Nationalists demonstrated remarkable perseverance in the face of repeated Republican attempts to blast through the thick walls of the ancient fortress. By September, news of the siege had spread far and wide, and it was this publicity which convinced Franco of the need to send relief forces to the region.

This proved to be a calculated gamble on Franco's part. On the one hand, he must have known that such a diversionary move would inevitably dissipate the momentum of the Nationalists' advance on Madrid, thus allowing the Republicans more time to organize a proper defense of the capital. This is why Colonel Juan Yagüe Blanco, Franco's most successful field commander up to this point, adamantly opposed the decision. On the other hand, the political capital that could be gained from a dramatic rescue of the beleaguered insurgents in Toledo was too great to be ignored. At the time, the *Junta de Defensa Nacional* based in Burgos was at the point of selecting a supreme military leader of the Nationalist cause. A spectacular rescue operation in Toledo would therefore go a long way toward confirming Franco's chances of being chosen for this post. In the event, Franco's strategy produced both results. By diverting troops from the Madrid front, Franco had allowed the mostly pro-Republican *madrileños* the time they needed to shore up their defenses before the city was placed under siege. As we shall see, this meant that the Battle of Madrid would take a very different course than either side had anticipated. From a political standpoint, however, Franco's gamble had paid off. The troops he had dispatched to Toledo liberated the fortress on September 26, and their dramatic rescue efforts provided an enormous boost for the morale and image of the Nationalists in general, and of Franco in particular.

Franco's Rise to Power

The siege of the Alcázar did more than just expose Franco's pretensions to power, for it also revealed the extent to which politics was bound up with the Nationalists' military affairs. It will be remembered that Mola and his fellow conspirators lacked a blueprint for the government that would emerge following their insurrection. While all agreed that a military directory would be established to oversee the transition to another regime, they held differing views about the precise form and content of the new state system. For example, generals like Mola and Queipo de Llano were rebelling against what they saw as a dysfunctional liberal government, which had, through its misguided reforms, led the Spanish nation "to ruin." They were thus not opposed to the Republic as a form of government. For monarchists like Generals Varela and Kindelán, on the other hand, any type of Republican rule was unacceptable. They therefore promoted the idea of establishing a monarchical state organized along authoritarian lines.

Notwithstanding his own pro-monarchist sympathies, Franco rarely publicly revealed his political views. His strict military training had taught him to respect authority as long as it was legitimate, and, throughout the 1931–36 period, he chose to obey the laws of the legally constituted government. By joining the insurrection in July, however, Franco had taken sides with Mola and the others who felt that "indiscipline" against a failing government was justified.[12] During the insurrectionary phase of the Civil War, Franco preferred to concentrate on military matters—particularly on his role as the leader of the Army of Africa—rather than on the political future of the *movimiento*. But when the rebellion gave way to a more protracted struggle, Franco and other military figures recognized that a more coherent and concentrated form of authority was needed to coordinate and control the Nationalists' war effort.

By September, the military-directed governing body that Mola had set up in Burgos at the outset of the war (*Junta de Defensa Nacional*) sought to unify the disparate elements of their movement by selecting a commander in chief. Of those who would be considered for such a post, Franco stood out as the favorite candidate. This was true in part because of his superior military rank and well-established reputation as a battlefield commander and in part because Franco did not appear to be harboring any clearly defined political ambitions. Fate also intervened on Franco's behalf. General Sanjurjo, whom the chief conspirators had initially designated as the primary leader of the revolt, was killed in an airplane crash on July 20. His death opened the way for Franco to rise to the head of the rebel movement. The string of swift and resounding triumphs credited to Franco up to this point in the fighting (culminating with the widely publicized liberation of the Alcázar fortress) also helped to confirm his position as the first among equals within the military hierarchy.

Not surprisingly, then, when the rebel *junta* met for a second time in late September, it elevated Franco as commander (*Generalissimo*) of all rebel forces. What had not been anticipated by the members of the *Junta*, however, was Franco's insistence that he also be granted supreme political authority. Despite some opposition to this daring political maneuver, on September 29 Franco was proclaimed as the new head of the Spanish state (*El Caudillo*). A *Junta Técnica* (Technical Junta), which became the nucleus of Franco's regime, then replaced the Generals' Junta. In this way, Franco became more than just the person in charge of the Army's command structure, for he was now invested with the power to define and control the social and economic institutions of the new Spanish state.

While primarily preoccupied with winning the war, Franco's dual status fed his ambitions to exercise greater political power. Urged on by his more politically astute elder brother, Nicolás, and his pro-fascist brother-in-law, Ramón Serrano Suñer, Franco set about constructing the basis for a corporatist-authoritarian state system (*nuevo estado*), which he intended to rule after the war had ended. The Decree of Unification issued in April 1937—which abolished the fascist Falange and other political parties on the Right—was the first concrete step in this direction. Henceforth, only one party under Franco's control would represent the Nationalists: the *Falange Española Tradicionalista de las Jons* (*FET*).

The social and economic structures underpinning the emerging Francoist state were also modeled along fascist-corporatist lines. From 1937, all working-class groups in the Nationalist zone were forcibly consolidated into one monolithic organization, the *Organización Sindical Española*, which was to be completely subordinated to the *FET*. By so doing, Franco believed that it was possible to create the basis for a harmonious relationship between employers and employees. Finally, to foster social cohesion in the new state, Franco turned to the Catholic Church, whose tacit support of the Nationalist cause supplied his regime with a certain degree of legitimacy, as well as a much-needed moral basis of authority.

Early Military Engagements: 1936–37

When Franco's troops reached the outskirts of the capital in early November, everyone, including the Republican government, believed that the city would soon fall to the Nationalists. On November 6, Prime Minister Francisco Largo Caballero and his Cabinet transferred the Republican seat of government to Valencia, leaving the administration of the defense of the city in the hands of a provisional ruling body known as the Defense Council (*Junta de Defensa*). Meanwhile, the citizens of Madrid readied themselves for the inevitable attack. Overnight civilian groups were mobilized into work battalions used for digging trenches and fortifying the city's defenses. While the Nationalists attempted to undermine the morale of *madrileños* by circulating the rumor that a "fifth column" of their supporters would be waiting for Franco's troops to enter the city, the largely pro-Republican citizens thundered back with defiant slogans such as "Madrid will be the tomb of fascism" and "They shall not pass." The arrival on November 8 of the first shipments of Soviet arms and the newly formed units of the International Brigades reinforced the spirit of defiance among the besieged Republicans. The battle itself began a few days later. In their initial assault, the Nationalists sent some 4,500 troops into western Madrid. Arrayed against them were more than 18,000 armed defenders of the Republican army. Some of the fiercest fighting took place in and around University City, where Franco's men became pinned down in a bloody slogging match with mixed Republican militias and fresh units of the communist-led International Brigades. Unable to overcome the unexpected resistance it encountered in the first two weeks of fighting, the Nationalist offensive soon ground to a standstill.

When it became apparent in late December that he would have to abandon his frontal offensive, Franco sought to end the stalemate in Madrid by undertaking a series of flanking operations. On February 6, 1937, the Nationalists attempted to encircle the capital from the south by attacking Republican defenses along the Jarama River. But after only a few days of fierce fighting on the ground and in the air, this initiative had to be abandoned. The ferocity of the attack tested the mettle of the Republic's new army and the International Brigades, whose units were seriously demoralized by the staggering number of casualties (2,800) they suffered in combat. Yet because they had halted the Nationalists' advances and had for the first time in the war inflicted heavy casualties on their enemy (estimated to be between 6,400 and 10,500), the battle represented a "defensive victory" for the Republicans.

One month later, the Nationalists suffered another humiliating setback when Republican forces at Guadalajara repulsed an Italian-led offensive. This was the first major military operation involving the recently organized assault troops of the *Corpo Truppe Volontarie* (CTV), which was placed under the command of the inexperienced battlefield commander, Major General Mario Roatta. Partly because he was not ready to mount another offensive so soon after Jarama, Franco allowed the Italians to play a leading role in an attack aimed at cutting off Madrid from the northeast. However, far from becoming the *guerra di rapido corso* which he had hoped, Roatta's mechanized infantry units of the much-vaunted Black Flames and Littorio Divisions were halted by a combination of bad weather and the constant strafing by squadrons of Russian Polikarpov I-15 *Chato* fighter planes. The CTV's slow and hesitant offensive also bought the Republicans enough time to launch a stunning counterattack. While they incurred as many if not more casualties than the Italians did during the two-week battle, the Republicans successfully blocked another one of Franco's efforts to encircle Madrid. They thus viewed the Battle of Guadalajara as their first important victory against the Nationalists.

Above all, the difficulties the Nationalists experienced at Jarama and Guadalajara demonstrated that defeating the Republicans was not as easy as it had been during the first few months of the conflict. Better armed and organized than before, the formidable qualities of the Republican army forced Franco to reconsider his plans to cut short the war by conquering Madrid. Urged on by his German and Italian advisers (Generals Hugo Sperrle and Roatta), Franco decided to shift Nationalist military operations to the relatively quiet northern zone. Conquering this isolated sector of Republican territory would achieve two much-desired objectives: the Nationalists would gain control over the important coal and steel industries in the region, and Franco would be able to free up troops that could be used for more concentrated offensives in the Madrid area.

Backed by the Italians' esteemed Black Arrows Division, the German Condor Legion, four well-trained Carlist Navarrese Brigades (each numbering between 4,000 and 6,000 men), and some 50,000 Spanish troops, General Mola launched a major offensive in the Basque Country at the end of March. Warning the citizens of Vizcaya that he was prepared to conduct a total war against his enemies, Mola made full use of the foreign airpower at his disposal in the opening phases of the invasion. The undefended Basque towns of Elorrio and Durango were the first to be heavily bombarded by German Junkers Ju-52s and Italian Savoia-Marchetti SM.81s. Less than three weeks later one of the most politically controversial and emotionally stirring episodes of the war occurred. On the afternoon of April 26, a squadron of German bombers sent on orders of the Nationalist high command dropped high explosive and incendiary bombs over the small market town of Guernica. In the space of a few hours, the ancient capital of the Basque homeland was reduced to a heap of smoldering rubble. Equally shocking was the fact that an estimated 900 innocent civilians had been either killed or injured during the raid. News of the atrocity was soon broadcast around the world. In an effort to preserve their public image, the Nationalists denied that they were responsible for the attack, insisting that the "reds" had deliberately destroyed their own town. The scandal nevertheless refused to die down, not least because the renowned Spanish artist, Pablo Picasso, was inspired to immortalize Guernica's tragedy in his famous mural shown at the Paris Exhibition in June 1937.

Further Nationalist advances soon followed the destruction of Guernica into the Basque Country. In the course of the next few weeks, surviving sections of the relatively small (less than 30,000 troops) Army of Euzkadi took up positions behind the series of fortifications surrounding Bilbao known as the *Cinturón de Hierro* or Iron Ring. The Nationalist assault on these defenses began on June 12, and four days later the city of Bilbao was under siege. Yet, with the port to the city blockaded and supplies rapidly running out, the citizens of Bilbao were forced to capitulate on June 19. Not long afterwards, the rest of the Basque territory fell under Nationalist control. In the course of the next few months, the Nationalists launched further military operations aimed at conquering the remaining pockets of Republican territory in the north.

The Nationalist Army at War

Nationalist successes in their northern campaign were in part the result of major operational and structural changes to the army that had occurred in the previous months of fighting. As we have seen, in the early days of the conflict, the Nationalist army relied on the support they received from a variety of civilian militias. Both the Carlists and the Falangists proved to be indispensable allies, not least because they provided the enthusiasm and sheer numbers needed to overwhelm Republican resistance. As soon as possible, the volunteers from both movements were organized into fighting units—sections, companies, and *banderas* (battalions)—and most of these were incorporated into the ranks of the regular army. Though it reared its head from time to time, civilian opposition to being placed under the military's chain of command never became a major issue. This was made clear at different points during the war, such as when, in December 1936, the truculent Carlist leader Manuel Fal Conde sought to create a separate training facility for the *Requetés*. Because such a move challenged the supremacy of the army's control over military matters, Franco acted quickly to put a stop to this plan. He also sent a pointed message to anyone else with similar ambitions by banishing Fal Conde from the Nationalist camp.

Once it became apparent that the rebellion had evolved into a full-scale Civil War, Nationalist military leaders set about expanding their forces. Beginning in August 1936, conscription was imposed in the Nationalist zone, and, by the spring of 1937, the army had mobilized 350,000 recruits. Further call-ups in the following months added tens of thousands of more men to the Nationalists' rolls.[13]

In response to its growing numbers, the army greatly expanded its training programs. Following the creation of the MIR (Mobilization, Instruction, and Recuperation) bureau in March 1937, the army increased the number of its training schools to twenty-two, making use of German advisers whom Franco and the supervisory head of the MIR, General Orgaz y Yoldi, heavily relied upon to assist in instructing officer candidate courses. After Franco was named as commander in chief of the Nationalist army, a special effort was made to train junior officers or *alféreces provisionales*, who were desperately needed to provide internal cohesion to the lower-level command structures of the rapidly expanding armed forces.

In the first phase of the Civil War, the Nationalists used the independent battle-column formations—ranging in size from 200 to 2,000 men—with the battalion as the major unit. By the spring of 1937, however, the ever-evolving conditions of the war demanded a transition from column formations to that of mass movement. As a result, the Nationalists began to reorganize their columns into tactical divisions, many of which were commanded by lieutenant colonels who had seen service in Morocco as junior officers.

Foreign Contributions to the Nationalist Army

While it is true that Franco did not look to foreigners to supply the manpower he needed to wage war, his army, navy, and, above all, his air force relied on the military experience and technical knowledge provided by outsiders. This was particularly true after 1937, when it became apparent that the Nationalists were able to achieve air superiority thanks to the Germans and Italians, who were supplying him with aircraft that were superior to those that the Soviet Union was making available to the Republican side.

In addition to the transport planes and fighter aircraft they supplied over the course of the conflict, Italy and Germany contributed much-needed transportation vehicles, ammunition, armaments (including artillery and light tanks), military advisers used for training personnel, and, in the case of Italy, ground troops. The fact that both Germany and Italy were willing to act as allies rather than as rivals in Spain also redounded to the benefit of the Nationalists. Nevertheless, despite Franco's efforts to coordinate German and Italian assistance, the two "Axis" countries generally operated independently of one another. While the Italians saw their participation as a means to promote the prestige and effectiveness of Mussolini's military forces, the Germans were interested in exploiting their intervention for other purposes. Besides seeking mining concessions that could be used to subsidize Germany's rearmament plans, the Germans wanted to use the war in Spain as a training ground for their army and air force. The fact that all the important fighter planes—Messerschmitt Bf-109s and Junkers Ju-87s (Stuka)—the Luftwaffe put into action during Hitler's early *blitzkrieg* offensives had been introduced in the Spanish conflict attests to the extent to which the Germans used the Civil War as a laboratory for testing their aircraft.[14]

The quantity and quality of foreign assistance also deserves mention here. While the Italians sent some of their latest Fiat tanks and fighter planes, these were not always used to great effect during military operations. The former were considered too light—compared to the more heavily armored Russian "Vickers" medium tanks—and too unreliable to be battle worthy. In terms of their performance characteristics, Italian aircraft (Fiat CR.32 fighters and Savoia-Marchetti SM.81 bombers) were also of good quality and comparable to their German counterparts in the early phases of the conflict. However, the Italians' commitment to using bomber aircraft to terrorize the civilian population in the Republican camp proved to be a major miscalculation. This became apparent late in the war, when such bombing attacks stirred up negative publicity for the Nationalists both at home and abroad. A series of Italian bombing raids over Barcelona in March 1938, for example, provoked a storm of international protests against Franco's policy of bombing undefended cities. No less significant was the fact that growing numbers of Nationalists began to deeply resent the "foreigners" who, despite being under the command of Franco, were seen as butchering fellow Spaniards.[15]

Even though the Italians sent many more ground forces to fight for Franco (an estimated 72,000 over the course of the war) than the Germans did (approximately 19,000 military personnel), German contributions were viewed by both the Nationalists and the foreign observers as being of far greater value than that being offered by the Italians. This was partly because of the generally high quality of their military equipment—such as their state-of-the-art 88-mm guns—and partly because, unlike their Italian counterparts, German "instructors," pilots, and other military personnel tended to be both respected and well received by their Spanish hosts.

It should be emphasized that, however dependent he became on foreign assistance, Franco did not easily yield to German and Italian efforts to interfere with his command of Nationalist military operations. Thus, whenever it proved impossible for Franco and foreign military advisors to reach an agreement on planned operations—such as when he clashed with the Italians during the Nationalist offensive in the Basque region—the Generalissimo made certain he maintained the upper hand.

Foreign Volunteer Forces

In contrast to the men and women who enlisted in the International Brigades of the Republican army, foreign volunteers who went to fight for the Nationalist side have not received much publicity. This is partly due to the fact that the Nationalists themselves did not want to generate any diplomatic waves by drawing attention to outsiders who were fighting on their behalf. Because they wanted to avoid any "international complications," the Germans also tended to downplay the full extent of their military contributions.[16] It was also true that, unlike the Republicans, the Nationalists were either unwilling or unable to capitalize on the propaganda value of having foreigners join what was, according to their own rhetoric, a national crusade. In the event, several thousand anticommunist volunteers hailing from Portugal (who provided the largest foreign contingent of volunteers known as the *Viriatos*), France, Romania, Russia, the United Kingdom, and Ireland joined Franco's crusade against "red" Spain. The vast majority of these volunteers were organized into military units (*banderas*) that served in the Foreign Legion, though most did not see action throughout the war. Moreover, due in part to language and cultural barriers and in part to the uneven quality of their fighting abilities, most of the foreigners, like the some 700 blue shirts of Eoin O'Duffy's Irish Brigade, saw themselves and were widely seen by the Nationalists as outsiders.

Nationalist Military Engagements, 1937–38

Although the Nationalist army had, by the summer of 1937, developed into a fighting force that was capable of defeating its enemies, Franco's timetable for winning the war was no more definite than it had been at the outset of the conflict. This was due in part to Franco's belief that it was necessary to wage a war of attrition against the Republicans. In practice, this meant that Nationalist troops tended to move much more slowly and cautiously than they otherwise needed to given their superiority over the forces they were fighting. While this strategy caused his foreign military advisors to complain loudly that the Spaniards were squandering their many opportunities to defeat the Republicans, Franco himself was confident that, by taking its time, the Nationalist army would prepare the ground for an uncontested victor.[17]

Political developments in the Nationalist zone during the spring and summer of 1937 also contributed to a slow down in the progress of the war. We saw earlier that, after having been designated as both the military and the political leader of the Nationalist cause, Franco began laying the foundations for his new regime. As we have also seen, however, his early efforts to establish his absolute rule did not go unchallenged. Franco faced a particularly thorny situation when the Falangist leader, Manuel Hedilla, refused to relinquish control over his party and movement. After a brief and tense confrontation with him, Franco made it clear that he was prepared to deal swiftly and summarily with anyone who opposed him and his government. By acting in this way, he effectively eliminated future challenges to his authority. Above all, Franco's confrontations with Fal Conde and Hedilla illustrated that his role as commander in chief of the army could not be divorced from the political world to which he now belonged.

Meanwhile, Nationalist advances toward Santander and Asturias during the summer months were delayed by a series of unexpected Republican attacks along the Madrid front. In July 1937, the Republicans sought to relieve Nationalist pressure in the northern zone by mounting their first major offensive of the war. The Battle of Brunete, as this operation came to be known, began in the early hours of July 6 on a sparsely manned Nationalist front just fifteen miles west of Madrid. Unlike their ill-fated attacks at La Granja and Huesca a few months earlier, the Republicans' assault on Brunete was a well-guarded secret that enabled them to achieve complete surprise. Altogether, some 59,000 Republican troops organized into ten divisions and three army corps were thrown into the initial stage of fighting. Backed for the first time in the war by effective artillery, tank (Russian T-26), and aerial support, Republican forces were buoyed by the prospects of a great victory. After taking Brunete, Republican forces took only two days to occupy the nearby villages of Quijorna, Villanueva del Parillo, and Villanueva de la Cañada. The air superiority that the Republicans enjoyed during the opening phases of the assault helped to underscore their initial successes.

But it did not take long before the shortcomings of the Republican military organization were revealed. Their biggest challenge was how to exploit their early gains. Rather than pressing forward and broadening the scope of the offensive, field officers allowed their troops to be tied down by the vastly outnumbered Nationalists who were doggedly defending nearby villages. Above all, this allowed the defenders enough time to send in much-needed reinforcements.

From the beginning, the discipline and organization of the Republican troops were also put to the test. Apart from being exposed to the withering effects of a scorching summer heat, ground troops were subject day and night to unrelenting machine-gunning and shelling from artillery and air strikes. On top of all of this, Republican communications were so poor that soldiers often found themselves unable to communicate with each other or with their superior officers. In these appalling conditions, it was hardly surprising that many soldiers lost their will to fight and that the discipline of the frontline units began breaking down. Not surprisingly, the Republican offensive ground to a standstill.

Though initially caught off guard, the Nationalists moved rapidly and effectively to bring down reinforcements from the north. Bolstered by the arrival of a fresh shipment of German aircraft (including the formidable Messerschmitt Bf-109 fighters), the better-equipped and better-organized Nationalist forces took only a week to recover much of the territory that had been captured by the enemy. By July 25, the Republicans were in full retreat, and the battle itself ended a few days later.

Given the huge losses on both sides—some 25,000 Republican and 17,000 Nationalist casualties—neither side could claim victory. As far as the Republicans were concerned, the results of the campaign were not entirely negative. Primarily, the Republicans had forced Franco to transfer some of his best troops and most of his air units (Italian, German, and Spanish fighters, bombers, and reconnaissance aircraft) from the northern sector, which inevitably interrupted the Nationalists' preparations for their assault on Santander. No less significant was the fact that the Brunete campaign demonstrated that the Republicans were capable of going on the offensive. And, though their territorial gains had been rather small— they had only succeeded in lengthening the front by some twenty square miles—the hope was that the newly reorganized Popular Army would inspire Spaniards and foreigners alike to have faith in the fighting capacity of the Republican side.

With the return of some of their best troops to the northern zone, the Nationalists were able to renew their campaign to conquer Santander and Asturias. Commanded by General Fidel Dávila, who had replaced General Mola after he was killed in a plane crash in July, Nationalist forces began their attack on Santander in mid-August. Despite facing heavy resistance from around 80,000 Republican defenders, the Nationalists managed to take control of the city on August 24.

Defeating the remaining Republican strongholds in Asturias proved to be more problematic. Shielded by the natural defenses of the mountains of Asturias, Republican guerrilla forces scattered throughout the region were able to hold out against their enemies for several more months. Nationalist advances were also delayed by yet another spoiling offensive launched by the Republicans on the Aragon front in the northeast. Only two days before Santander fell to the Nationalists, some 75,000 Republican troops were sent into action on an 80–100 kilometer front. The heaviest fighting took place in and around the villages of Belchite and Quinto. In Belchite, fierce resistance from a small contingent of Nationalist troops (1,500) met Republican forces. The town fell on September 3, but at the cost of many casualties on both sides. Attacks in the direction of Zaragoza were even less successful. By early September, the campaign was already winding down, though sporadic fighting—including a concerted effort to take the town of Fuentes de Ebro—continued until October 24. In the meantime, the key Asturian cities of Gijón, Avilés, and Oviedo had fallen to the Nationalists. However, it was not until the end of October that the Nationalists could claim victory in their hard-fought seven-month campaign.

Though it had taken his army much longer to conquer the north than even he had anticipated, Franco was finally able to redeploy his troops to the main battlefronts in the center and the south. In addition to having built up his troop strength to the point that his army was now nearly equal in size to its Republican counterpart (approximately 600,000), Franco had successfully overseen both the reorganization of his forces into five army corps and the creation of the formidable Army of Maneuver. Confident that he could now take Madrid, Franco believed that the time had come to mount another major offensive.

Upon learning of the Nationalists' plan to attack in the Guadalajara region, the Republicans decided to undertake a preemptive strike in the provincial capital of Teruel. The surprise attack started on December 15, just as a particularly fierce winter storm began to blanket the region with a thick layer of snow. For the first week, the offensive went as planned, with the Republicans managing to capture the surrounding towns of Campillo, San Blas, and Muela de Teruel. Nevertheless, after having successfully navigated the harsh weather conditions and rocky terrain around Teruel itself, the Republicans faced stiff resistance from the contingent of Nationalists defending the town. It took nearly two weeks of heavy street fighting, from December 22 to January 7, before they finally conquered the city.

News of their sudden and unexpected victory immediately created a stir in both camps. From a political standpoint, the fall of Teruel caused Franco to lose face in front of his fascist allies. Overnight, their confidence in him and the Nationalists' fighting abilities had been badly shaken.

As one German diplomat put it at the time, "While before Teruel the end of the Spanish Civil War seemed to be in sight, today the end of the war seems once again to have moved into the far distant future."[18] Mussolini in particular was now threatening to cut off aid to the Nationalists if they did not bring a quick end to the conflict.

The Republicans' successful attack on Teruel disturbed Franco so much that he decided to postpone his assault on Madrid in order to launch a counteroffensive aimed at recapturing the town. On December 29, 1937, he ordered Generals Varela and Antonio Aranda to relieve the defenders holed up in the city, but appalling weather conditions prevented them from aiding their besieged comrades. For the next two weeks, the Republicans were subjected to heavy shelling from artillery and bombers, the latter of which began flying sorties as soon as weather conditions permitted. Inside Teruel, conditions were rapidly deteriorating for the Republican troops, most of whom were cold and hungry and desperately short of supplies. By February 20, 1938, the Republicans faced certain encirclement and were thus forced to abandon the town. A few days later, their forces were in full retreat.

Undeterred by the humiliating setback he suffered at Teruel, Franco began massing his troops along the entire Aragon front in preparation for a major offensive. Just two weeks after reconquering Teruel, the Nationalists smashed through Republican lines as part of a large-scale operation along a sixty-mile front that involved over 100,000 troops, 200 tanks, and some 1,000 aircraft. Meeting only nominal resistance from the other side (disorganized and demoralized Republican forces had not anticipated such a sweeping attack), it took them only six weeks to reach the Mediterranean. Republican Spain was now split in two. For the Nationalists, it appeared as though the war would soon be over. However, as events would soon show, their hopes for an imminent victory were premature.

With the Nationalists closing in on Valencia, the Republicans decided that the only chance they had of forestalling their defeat was to mount another offensive. Hoping once again to achieve complete tactical surprise, Republican commandos crossed the Ebro River (between Mequinenza and Tortosa) on the night of July 24–25, 1938. Catching Yagüe's Moroccan army completely by surprise, the leading units of Juan Modesto's Army of the Ebro first cut Nationalist communication lines and then proceeded to occupy a wide bridgehead, which they used to drive deeper into Nationalist territory. By the end of the week, they had advanced nearly 40 kilometers and were at the point of taking Gandesa, the center of an important network of roads and communications. However, it was at this stage of the attack that the offensive began bogging down. Instead of moving forward and exploiting their initial successes, a small but determined group of Nationalists tied down Republican forces. The defenders managed to hold on long enough for Yagüe's troops to stabilize their lines. In the following weeks, the battle was transformed into a war of attrition.

The initial phase of the Ebro campaign had achieved its desired goal, namely, to take pressure off Franco's drive toward Valencia. The scale of the Republicans early successes had also forced Franco to suspend his offensive operations in Estremadura. Furthermore, the offensive had once again undermined the confidence of the Nationalists, who, only a few weeks earlier, were convinced that the end of the war was in sight. Now it was the Republicans' turn to be lifted by a surge of optimism. Nevertheless, while Republican propagandists were declaring Ebro to be another turning point in the war, Franco began concentrating his forces for a major counterattack. As he had done throughout the war, Franco was prepared to abandon his own military objectives in order to prevent the Republicans from gaining ground in Nationalist territory.

From August until the end of October, the two sides were locked in a series of bloody confrontations. The tide of battle finally turned when the Nationalists launched an offensive into the Sierra de Pandols on October 30. By November 16, the Republicans had been driven back from all the territory they had conquered since July 25. The longest and most grueling contest of the war was finally over.

Dissension in the Nationalist Camp

In spite of the fact that few believed in the spring of 1938 that the Republic would survive another Nationalist offensive, victory continued to elude Franco. As we have seen, his slow and tedious conduct of the war was not popular among his fascist military advisers, who were critical of Franco's slavish commitment to a strategy of attrition. When, after the division of Republican Spain, it appeared to most senior military strategists on both sides as though the Republic could be defeated rapidly by an offensive in Catalonia, Franco once again defied conventional military logic by launching an attack toward Valencia. In this instance, however, his decision nearly provoked a minor rebellion among his own commanders.

Franco's questionable military decisions were not the only source of problems developing in the Nationalist camp.[19] Ever since 1937, news of disaffection among Franco's troops—particularly among Carlists, Moorish, and Foreign Legionaries—began making their way into the foreign press reports and diplomatic dispatches emanating from Nationalist Spain.

After 1937, there were also signs, if not of dissatisfaction, of growing war-weariness among the rank-and-file soldiers. This most likely accounted for the inconsistent performance of Nationalist units on the battlefield. While they were better-equipped and fed than their

Republican counterparts, the morale of Franco's soldiers was daily being undermined by several factors. The unexpected setbacks they experienced when the Republicans struck an offensive blow was one source of declining morale as was the high casualty rates that invariably accompanied these bloody slogging matches. While there was no way of knowing for certain how far this particular malaise had advanced among Nationalist troops, there was the ever-present danger that it could spread as long as the war continued.

By the spring of 1938, the generally optimistic mood of the population in Nationalist territory was increasingly being tested. Ironically, this might have owed something to the triumphal rhetoric underpinning Franco's regime. The accuracy of the regime's indulgent predictions of the imminent demise of the Republic was called into question every time the Republican army forestalled defeat. As a result, disillusionment began to sink in among those who were beginning to believe that the end of the war was not forthcoming. The mounting number of civilian casualties late in the war also generated rumblings of discontent, particularly among the die-hard Nationalists. This was particularly evident in the period when the Nationalists were conducting heavy bombing attacks against the civilian populations on the other side. Though Nationalist censors suppressed accurate news of these raids, rumors of the carnage they were causing circulated more freely.

The fact that Franco's fascist allies (particularly the Italians) were largely responsible for these bombing missions caused a certain number of Falangists and Carlists to begin calling for "Spain for the Spaniards," a subversive refrain that echoed the Republican view that the Germans and Italians were acting like foreign invaders. The problems referred to here were serious, but they were not major impediments to Franco's rule. For the most part, the authoritarian state apparatus he was constructing withstood the challenges of dissent and disillusionment. Franco himself managed to weather each crisis with characteristic aplomb—such as his clash with Yagüe over the Caudillo's decision not to advance on Catalonia—and his grip on power remained firm throughout his frustratingly slow and deliberate march to total victory.

The Fall of Barcelona and Madrid

The Republicans' defeat at Ebro paved the way for the Nationalists' final offensive. Toward the end of December, some 300,000 of Franco's troops attacked all along the Catalonia front. Although the tattered remains of the Republican defense forces put up a spirited fight, their resistance was in vain. By January 3, 1939, the Nationalists were well on their way to victory. Their primary target, Barcelona, held out until January 25 and was occupied by General Yagüe's troops the following day. The collapse of the regional capital sparked off one of the greatest mass exoduses of modern times. Behind the fleeing members of the Republican government, who had just days before taken refuge near the French border in the small town of Figueras, there followed tens of thousands of civilians and soldiers.

With the fall of Catalonia, the last Republican stronghold, Madrid, was now surrounded by a sea of Nationalists. Short on ammunition and weapons and with their food supplies running out, it is hardly surprising that the Republicans' will to continue resisting was rapidly dissipating. The faint hope that Spain's conflict could be drawn out until the outbreak of a general European war was extinguished in early March, when a mini-Civil War between anti- and pro-communist elements erupted in the Republican zone. The establishment of an anticommunist *junta* (Defense Council) was seen by some as the only chance the Republicans had of negotiating a peace settlement with Franco. By this point, however, Franco's quest for a total victory was now within his grasp. He, therefore, felt no need to reach an understanding with anyone or any group on the opposing side. A few days after the fighting between the communists and their leftist enemies ended, Franco gave the order for his troops to occupy Madrid. On March 27, Nationalist troops began slowly marching into the capital, and four days later, Franco declared that the war was over.

CHAPTER **5**

The Popular Army of the Spanish Republic, 1936–39

Michael Alpert

In the press of the wartime Republic, the Popular Army (the Spanish adjective *popular* means "of the people" but to call it "People's Army" would suggest a similarity to forces which did not exist at the time, as well as begging the question of communist influence) was often called the *Spanish* army, to underline that Franco's forces were foreign, as indeed they were to a greater extent than those of the Republic.[1] The Popular Army consisted of the remains of those parts of the Spanish Army, its war materiel, and its professional and noncommissioned officers, who had not rebelled and in some cases had taken part in the crushing of the rebellion of their fellow officers on the weekend of July 18–19, 1936. From these the Republic created a military force that fought the war that arose from the coup launched by the larger part of the officers and the garrisons and led by General Francisco Franco. The Popular Army became a full-size force of several hundred thousand men, who fought for two years and eight months in particular conditions of inferiority.

Its interest for historians and Hispanists in general lies in the issues that arose during the Civil War from arguments about the nature of the army and from the political tensions suffered at the time as they affected the character of a national army fighting a civil war, together with questions of armament and politico-military issues regarding appropriate strategy. For military, social, and political historians, the significant questions lie in the area of the extent to which an army can be "revolutionary," how this term is interpreted, and how far discussion of the nature of the Spanish Popular Army can be understood and assessed against the criteria of successful forces created in comparable situations elsewhere. The Soviet Russian advisers of the Popular Army inevitably thought in terms of their experience of the Russian Civil War of 1918–20. In historical terms, references were made to the armies of the French Revolution of the late eighteenth century and even to the New Model Army in the English

Civil War of the seventeenth century.[2] In their turn, historians of the future may perhaps look at the Spanish Popular Army against the model of the People's Army of China or Vietnam.

First Reactions

Once the immediate crisis caused by the uprisings of the military garrisons all over Spain was over and the approximate extent of success of the coup was known, the Republic's new government, under José Giral, had to decide how to tackle the threat posed by the advance on Madrid by insurrectionary troops from garrisons to the north of the capital and from Andalusia. These units were composed largely of young men undergoing their compulsory military service, together with volunteers from right-wing political movements. The authorities in Madrid, Barcelona, Valencia, and the other cities where the coup had been defeated could probably have faced the insurgent columns successfully even though the former had released the conscripts from their oaths of obedience to their rebellious officers and were issuing arms to undisciplined and disorderly militias. The greatest threat, however, came from the forces in Spanish Morocco, which were professional and experienced in colonial warfare and which soon managed, with German and Italian naval and air support, to cross the Strait of Gibraltar and begin to march toward Madrid. The Republican or Loyalist—as they were called in the United States at the time—columns of labor union and left-wing militia, mixed with small army forces and units of the National Assault Police, Carabineers (customs police), and the Civil Guard (renamed National Republican Guard), were unable to resist the professional ruthlessness of the Foreign (though mostly Spanish) Legion and the native Moroccan troops at the service of the Insurgents. By early autumn, the latter were advancing swiftly toward Madrid, while other insurgents were either holding an unbroken line in eastern Spain, which militias from Barcelona and Valencia could not penetrate, or defending positions won in the north of Spain and cutting the Republic off from France at the western end of the frontier. It seemed as if the Francoist insurgents, soon well equipped, particularly in the air, by Italy and Germany, would take Madrid and end the war by the fall of 1936.

The Creation of an Army

By the time the battle for the capital began, however, on November 6, 1936, considerable progress was being made in the construction of the new Popular Army of the Republic. By this date, the Giral government had been replaced by a widely based administration headed by the veteran socialist Francisco Largo Caballero. This government would soon include representatives of the anarchist movement. Given that the anarchists, of great importance in the Spanish working-class movement, were hostile to the formation of a traditional-style army, their agreement to take part in a government that proposed creating a new regular-style army rather than the loose guerrilla style warfare that anarchists favored indicated that the steady militarization of the undisciplined militias was going to continue.

The governments of the Spanish Republic during the Civil War were hardly revolutionary. All of them worked hard to restore law and order, to put an end to murders and robbery that had occurred, particularly in the early weeks of the war, and to establish the Republic as an internationally respected State. Creating a disciplined army echoed the urge to present Republican Spain as a bourgeois, liberal State threatened by foreign-aided rebels. This in turn reflected the stance of the Soviet Union and the Comintern, whose Popular Front policy was to hold back revolution and to defend liberal parliamentary regimes against the fascist threat. Indeed, the communist ministers who joined the Largo Caballero government did so even though the Comintern had tried to prevent Largo Caballero from heading an administration because of his recent revolutionary record which would make the Democracies suspicious.[3] The communists took portfolios because they recognized that unless they did so they would be unable to impose their views of the type of army that was appropriate in the circumstances. The Comintern representatives and the few hundred Soviet military advisers, who arrived following the establishment of diplomatic relations with the USSR at the end of August 1936 and in October once the Soviet Union was sure that Germany and Italy were ignoring the European agreement not to sell arms to either side in the Spanish war, were convinced that only a unified command and a conservatively structured army would have a chance of successfully resisting the rebel forces, who insisted on being called Nationalists in the foreign press rather than Insurgents or Rebels. From mid-October 1936 onward the USSR sent substantial quantities of war materiel, almost certainly saving Madrid, but this had to be done clandestinely and, as will be seen, not with the regularity or in the quantities which Germany and Italy supplied to Franco.[4]

The Question of Officers

The view of the approximately 2000 prewar professional officers who served in the Popular Army was that many more would have been willing to do so had their loyalty not been unjustly suspected. This may be so even though only a small number were members of the loyally Republican *Unión Militar Republicana y Antifascista* or *UMRA*, which took over the War Ministry in the first chaotic days.[5] Very frequently, as new units of the Popular Army were being formed, their training was entrusted to a professional officer, either retired or on the active list, but who had not taken part in the coup.[6] Yet when the new unit was ready for active service, the field commander appointed was a war-temporary officer from the political or labor union militias. On the other hand, the uprising of March 6, 1939, led by professional officers against the Republican government of Dr. Juan Negrín, and the surrender of Republican forces to Franco at the end of that month may throw some doubt on the loyalties of those who did serve the Republic in the war. Besides, the Russian advisers, looking at the Popular Army from outside and with fixed ideas of the role of professional officers based on their experience with Tsarist ones, frequently accused many of them not so much of treason, but of sabotage, an accusation which in Soviet terms can better be interpreted as idleness and incompetence.[7] Without proso-pographical studies of the several thousand officers who were living or stationed in the cities of the Republican zone and had not taken a part in the failed uprisings but were nevertheless rejected by the new Army, counterfactual history of what might have been is impossible. In contrast, however, the Franco or Nationalist army rejected only those officers who had opposed the coup or were known to have strong Republican or left-wing sympathies.

By the time both armies had constructed divisions, army corps, and armies, it was obvious, as command lists reveal, that the Nationalists had an adequate professional officer corps to lead units down to the level of companies. They were able to organize an efficient program to train new junior officers—the *alféreces provisionales*. In the Popular Army, how-ever, commanders at every level were too low ranking and inexperienced for their commands. Ex-captains were leading divisions and ex-majors were army corps commanders. Most commanders at brigade level and below were not professionals. Franco's corps and army commanders were mostly young lieutenant colonels and colonels of infantry on the active list, who had enjoyed fast promotion during the Moroccan campaigns of the 1920s. Few such *Africanistas* served in the Popular Army where senior commanders might well be from the Artillery or Engineers, branches that in the Spanish military tradition had a very different military education from infantrymen.[8]

The process of forming the Popular Army implied militarization of the militias and the creation of a new corps of junior officers up to the rank of major or *comandante*. Later in the war militia, officers often led divisions and, by the latter part of the war, even army corps. While these were often outstanding men, it is noticeable that many who carried the responsibility of serving as chiefs of staff, particularly at brigade level, had not had the training or experience that was enjoyed by their Nationalist equivalents. A small number of these militia leaders were allowed to rise to the rank of lieutenant colonel, but the militia officers remained on a separate seniority list, as did the several thousand war-temporary officers selected for brief training in officers' schools and commissioned as *tenientes en campaña* or temporary lieutenants. Only a few of these obtained promotion to captain's rank.[9]

Militia

The social and political circumstances of Spain in 1936 created a revolution, indeed on both sides of the lines of battle. In Insurgent Spain, however, all political and military power was centralized and soon put into the hands of General Franco although, paradoxically, it seems that a larger element of autonomy of command decision was given to his commanders than to those of the Republic. Any argument or attempt to organize some form of structural autonomy in Franco Spain, however, was crushed, so that the militia volunteers of the Fascist *Falange* and the Traditionalists or Carlists were rapidly brought at once under military authority. In the government zone, in contrast, militia columns characterized the early months of war. They lasted until the end of 1936 in central Spain, but in Catalonia, where the anarchists dominated until May 1937, some consequences of the militia epoch, such as the indiscipline, the disorganization, and the political infighting, continued until the end of the war.

Observers of the first few months of the Spanish war transmitted their pictures of the immensely newsworthy militias, the disorganized, untrained, and barely armed defenders of the Republic against Fascism, who were at the same time carrying out a revolution. The militias wore overalls and miscellaneous items of military uniform and carried the weapons that they had managed to seize when they had sacked the barracks after defeating the rebellious officers. Later, after some hesitation, the government had ordered the arsenals to be opened and rifles to be issued to the militias.

The militias were not, however, totally disorganized. In August 1936, the Ministry of War set up the Militia Command (*Comandancia Militar de Milicias*). This institution continued its functions until all the militia units were formed into units of the army. The units or columns of militia bore sonorous and revolutionary names such as "Lions of the Republic" (*Leones de la República*) or titles originating from the occupation of the men: printers, steelworkers, railway employees, and even bullfighters. They might bear the name of a politician or a political party. Professional officers, noncommissioned officers, or anyone who was trusted and had some military experience commanded some. The new heroes who came from the labor unions, men who had led strikes, and members of political committees led others. None of these militias could compete with the Moroccans or legionaries of Franco's African Army, who were trained and ruthless though often fewer in number, and infinitely more skillfully led, which accounts for the retreats of the Republican militia all through the late summer and autumn of 1936 and the loss of substantial amounts of equipment.

In August 1936, the Republican militias were militarized and, in theory at least, made subject to military law.[10] Regulations were issued for appointing officers, confirming the commanders who up to then had been elected by the militia columns themselves. The carefully kept registers of the *Comandancia Militar de Milicias* list the militia columns. At their height, in mid-October 1936, in central Spain the militias totaled somewhat over 85,000 men. The Militia Command did not register lists of anarchist militias operating in Aragon and the Levant, but other calculations would estimate these at about 30,000. There was also a sizeable number of men enrolled in militia battalions in the northern zone of the Republic, the Basque Country, Santander, and Asturias. To receive finance, equipment, ammunition, and orders and be recognized as a battalion by the Ministry of War, a militia column had to have a properly enrolled minimum of 300 men. Altogether, there were about 150 of such units in the lists of the *Comandancia Militar de Milicias.* Since each column was required to have a paymaster and the senior major of a regular Spanish battalion had this responsibility, the latter's title of *mayor* was given to militia officers holding that rank. The disintegration of the Republican zone caused by the insurrection itself led to a situation not foreseen by the framers of the Catalan Statute of Autonomy of 1932 and the Basque one of October 1936. Although these charters reserved matters of Defense and War to the central government, nevertheless, until the crushing of the disturbances of 1937 in Barcelona, the Catalan government, the *Generalitat,* ran its own militarized militias as the Army of Catalonia (*L'Exercit de Catalunya*), based on divisions rather than the brigade as the basic unit. The Basques also ran their forces with little reference to the general sent to command them from the central government.[11]

The Fifth Regiment

Many, if not most of the militia columns, were substantially larger than the minimum stipulated of 300 men, especially the communist-organized *Quinto Regimiento* or Fifth Regiment, so-called probably because the government asked five loyal officers to organize a volunteer battalion each.[12] The fifth battalion became linked with a communist-organized recruitment drive. It took over an abandoned convent in the working-class suburb of Cuatro Caminos in Madrid and used it as a training depot. Because of its propaganda but also to a considerable extent because of its merits, the Fifth Regiment came to occupy an important place in the left-wing historiography of the Spanish Civil War. The *Quinto Regimiento* was the pride of the Spanish Communist Party and nursery of many of the later militia commanders. It trained many thousands of men, though one may doubt the propagandist figure of 70,000 and perhaps reduce it to a still very substantial 40,000 who passed through the building in Cuatro Caminos, and in branches in the Calles Hortaleza and Lista.

Communist Views on the Army

From the first week of the war, the need to organize proper regular-style nonrevolutionary military forces was recognized by the Communist Party and proclaimed in its newspaper *Mundo Obrero* and in *Milicia Popular,* the brilliantly edited newspaper of the Fifth Regiment, through whose pages one can trace the early careers of future leaders of the Popular Army who emerged from the Fifth Regiment, such as Juan Guilloto León, known as "Modesto," and Enrique Líster.[13]

Both Modesto and Líster, having had some training at the Soviet Frunze Academy in 1935 while political refugees, would occupy very high positions in the new Popular Army, Modesto becoming a general and Líster a corps-commanding colonel, and both would hold ranks in the Soviet Army after going into exile in 1939. The recruits of the Fifth Regiment received the best training possible and the best weapons and uniforms. Unlike the situation in other militias, men in the Fifth Regiment were trained not to question orders and to respect and salute professional officers. The Fifth Regiment introduced the Political Commissar, an institution which soon became common to all units of the Popular Army down to the level of company. It was the communists, probably because of their political education and the history of the Russian Civil War, who understood that, while the new army had to use professional officers so long as they were loyal, even if they were conservatively inclined, and while absolute obedience was essential, raw new recruits, often illiterate, had to be taught as well as ordered to obey. It had to be explained to them that war required discipline, cleanliness, and the proper care of weapons. They had to receive political education and to understand why the war was being fought. A corps of officers to be mentors and guides was necessary for this. Because the communists understood this better than other political bodies, who looked on the Commissar merely as a method of controlling the professional officer, it was the former who would predominate in the Corps of Political Commissars established in October 1936, at least in central Spain. Alternatively, one might say that the type of young man who would be suitable as a Commissar or a political and educational or welfare officer would be attracted to the Communist Party because its leaders were young, because its thinking was clear, and, most of all, because from October 1936 onward the Soviet Union was the only country save Mexico to dispatch war materiel to the Republic.

The Anarchists and the Army

The problem for the anarchists and their organization, the National Confederation of Labor, or CNT, lays in the circumstance that their long history of hostility to the bourgeois State and particularly to the Spanish Army, to hierarchy and to authority in general, made it difficult for them to accept that, while a new army to defend the Republic against the insurgents was needed, this new army, if it had any chance of being victorious, would have to have a regular structure, with ranks, uniform badges, and salutes, and be authoritarian rather than one where every order or decision was subjected to democratic vote. Nevertheless, in central Spain, the leader of the anarchist militias, a construction worker called Cipriano Mera, would, like a small number of other anarchist figures, become a lieutenant colonel and head an army corps. He and a few other leaders from their movement came to realize that anarchist principles would not function in a war situation.[14]

The Mixed Brigades

From October 1936, at the height of the militia period, the government began to organize an army by forming Mixed Brigades. These were soon linked into divisions, the latter into army corps and these into armies. After Franco's advance had split the Republic into two in April 1938, the armies would be organized as the Army Group of the East (*Grupo de Ejércitos de la Región Oriental*) and the Army Group of the Centre (*Grupo de Ejércitos de la Región Central*), the former covering Catalonia and the latter an approximate triangle with its apex in Madrid and its other angles at Valencia and the sea between Cartagena and Málaga.

The basic unit of the new army was the mixed brigade, so-called because its four infantry battalions were, at least in theory, supported by detachments of artillery, engineers, signals, and other units, as well as a staff, with the aim of making it a small self-contained autonomous tactical force. Generally speaking, however, the Spanish prewar army was based on regiments and divisions. It may be, as some insisted, that the mixed brigade was advocated by the Soviet advisers who came to Spain during the Civil War, but it was also similar to the column which was the traditional way the army had fought in the Moroccan wars, as well as being the easiest way to militarize the militia battalions.

Franco's army was in many ways more responsive to the changed situation of real war. It was not subject to the bureaucracy of a War Ministry nor the control of a civilian government, and of course, not the targets of any press criticism or political pressure. Paradoxically, the Popular Army of the Republic was less flexible than Franco's army in many ways, not the least in its attachment to military structures of the past. In the case of the organizational tables of units, structures were minutely laid down for the new mixed brigades and down to the level of battalions, companies, platoons, and sections. The mixed brigades consisted of four infantry battalions, each with three companies of riflemen and one of machine guns, together with units of mortars, light artillery, signals, engineers, and medical personnel. Unfortunately, what was complete on paper was not always so in fact. From the beginning, it was rarely possible to launch a complete brigade into combat. After major battles, brigades were often undermanned, dissolved, or merged with others.

The first six mixed brigades were created in October 1936 in various cities of the Republican zone such as Ciudad Real, Alcázar de San Juan, and Albacete. The speed with which the columns of militia were organized into brigades, provided with at least a rudimentary military structure and supplied as far as possible with uniforms, weapons, and military impedimenta in general, despite the apparent collapse of the State in the summer of 1936, the shortage of suitable military personnel for organization and training purposes, and the chaos of the War Ministry, is a reflection of the intense work put in by the new General Staff, a creation of Largo Caballero.[15] That Largo Caballero was defenestrated in May 1937, among other reasons for his possibly misplaced loyalty to senior officers who could not accept the new type of army, who were inefficient or idle, or who were uncertain of their loyalties, ought not to ignore the credit due to him for reconstructing the War Ministry, which he headed as well as the government, and for identifying and appointing officers of great capacity. Among these was Major Vicente Rojo, Professor of Tactics for many years at the Military Academy of Toledo, who became Chief of Staff in the defense of Madrid and then overall Chief of Staff of the entire Popular Army. Rojo would go into exile at the end of the war and return in later years, to be tried for his responsibilities in leading what the court-martials called "Marxist" forces. While the thirty-year sentence handed down was suspended, Rojo neither recovered his rank nor his pension rights. Despite his great personal prestige as a strategist and despite his fervent Catholicism, Rojo was ignored by the Francoist military establishment.[16]

By spring of 1937, eighty to ninety mixed brigades had been constituted. Sometimes the numbers allocated to new brigades were transferred from brigades that had been destroyed earlier in battle. Sometimes the brigade was never actually formed, particularly toward the end of the conflict, but the total of functioning brigades created during the war was about 150. The mixed brigade was, however, probably not the best tactical unit in the circumstances. It needed a large number of trained junior officers and noncommissioned officers, which was precisely what the Popular Army lacked. The mixed brigade was not the ideal unit for poorly trained soldiers. It suited a hardened professional and independent group of men. Furthermore, the theoretical artillery, engineers, and other services that the tables of organization required were in reality lacking. In contrast, Nationalist army did not use the brigade as a unit of organization and merely formed a brigade where necessary, from battalions and accompanying artillery and engineers, rather like the columns of the Moroccan war. Once the particular operation was over, the brigade was dissolved. This could not happen in the Popular Army precisely because the War Ministry rigidly laid down military structures. Franco's army, in contrast, used its units in the form demanded by military requirements at the given moment. It published no fixed establishments for its battalions and companies, and even its divisions might vary greatly in composition. The Republican Army suffered from bureaucracy of the prewar type, a lack of professional junior and noncommissioned officers, an irregular and always insufficient supply of war materiel, and, despite all efforts, over-politicization.[17]

Despite the theoretical concept of independent mixed brigades, those of the new army were soon grouped into divisions (three brigades per division). This process was more rapid in central Spain where eight divisions were formed by December 1936. Successive numbers were allocated to Andalusia. The numbering of divisions in Catalonia and the Levante started in the twenties because in those areas militarization was slower. It is significant that there were more divisions in the Popular Army than in the Franco army even though the latter, at least toward the latter part of the war, had more men. Yet these divisions all required staffs and the various divisional units of artillery, engineers, etc. Yet these were the elements in which the Popular Army was often deficient. Soon afterwards, the divisions were grouped in army corps, first in central Spain, then a corps in Andalusia, and another in Extremadura. Further numbers were allocated to corps formed in Catalonia and to the Basque Country, Santander, and Asturias.[18]

The Popular Army, for the reasons already suggested, created units rapidly, but lacked the infrastructure of a professional officer and noncommissioned officer body, as well as the superstructure of a professional leadership except at the highest levels of command. It may well be described as a army on paper.[19] At its height, in October 1938, as the Popular Army of the Republic was fighting its last great battle on the River Ebro but had been divided into two by Franco's successful offensives of that spring, it consisted of two army groups, six armies, twenty-three corps, seventy divisions, two hundred brigades, and several other groups and units. Where had all these men come from?

The Draft

At the beginning of the Civil War both Spanish armies were composed of the professional forces, police forces, volunteers, and the conscripts who were undergoing their compulsory year of military service. As has been seen, the insurgent Nationalists had the advantage of being able to use the Legion and the Moroccan troops. The Republic, while it had the conscripts and the various police forces of its zone, was immensely weakened militarily because most of the professional officers had rebelled or were suspected of sympathy with the insurgents and had hidden from the hostility of murderous militias bent on killing all representatives of Spanish militarism. In the insurgent area, however, the military columns were able very soon to take the field, with almost all their own officers and noncommissioned officers and with their equipment. The militias that accompanied them were brought under strict military discipline. On the government side, however, the militia that accompanied troops in the heterogeneous columns marching out of cities such as Madrid, Barcelona, and Valencia was not disciplined; the professional officers were apprehensive of them. While the militia constituted the popular strength of the insurgents, they were a source of disorder and chaos for the Republic.

Nevertheless, on both sides, the bulk of manpower came from drafting the reserves, that is those men who had completed or were still to complete their military service. Because the Popular Army steadily lost ground, it had to draft more and more classes. In September 1936, men of the classes of 1932 to 1935 were called; in 1937 even older men, many married and with families, going back to 1931. The class of 1938 was called before its time. After the battle of Teruel in early 1938, the classes of 1929 and 1930 were called, and after the great rout of April 1938, several more years were called, including boys who were not due for service until 1941. During the Ebro offensive, in September 1938 two more older classes were called, and in desperation, in the midst of the retreat through Catalonia in January 1939, the authorities drafted men of the classes of 1919 through 1922, who were in their forties, and boys, known as the *Quinta del Biberón* or the "baby's bottle class," who were not due for service until 1942. In all, men between the ages of seventeen and forty-five were called to the Popular Army. Communist opinion was that such total mobilization should have been undertaken long before. Yet, without sufficient equipment and commanders for them, the wisdom of such a procedure would have been doubtful. The Nationalists did not draft so many classes of reserves as the Republic because they had more volunteers in the Moroccan units, the Legion and the battalions of *Falange* and Carlists. In any case, the Republican territory which they overran provided, if not large numbers of recruits for the Army, at least a conscript labor force. The two armies, Popular and Nationalist, approached a total of not far short of two million men, a colossal figure for a population of under twenty-five million.

The International Brigades[20]

The contribution of the Popular Army's International Brigades, one of its best-known features, should be considered. By mid-October 1936, in the provincial capital of Albacete and surrounding villages, the foreign volunteers for the Republic were being formed into International Brigades. Part of the first International Brigade went into combat on November 8 and 9 facing an imminent assault on Madrid by the enemy. By this time, however, several more Spanish mixed brigades had been formed. Thus, the first International Brigade was allocated the number eleven and the others were numbered successively up to fifteen. Statistics have varied enormously, but present-day calculations suggest a maximum of about 35,000–40,000 foreign volunteers, but not more than perhaps 15,000 at any given moment. The formation of the International Brigades represented a decision by the Comintern to do something concrete for the Republic and to direct the flood of volunteers and prospective volunteers for Spain so that they would offer an example of international left-wing solidarity.[21] As channeled through the French Communist Party, controlled and led by French and Italian communists, including some who had had training and experience in the USSR, the Internationals would be controllable in the context of the Soviet need to prevent the Democracies thinking that a major social revolution was taking place in Spain. Moreover, the crushing of the revisionist anti-Stalinist revolutionary communist party, the *Partido Obrero de Unificación Marxista* or *POUM*, in June 1937 was accompanied by the dissolution of its unit, the 29th Division, in which many foreign volunteers fought.[22]

The International Brigades were seen as an example of proletarian solidarity with the Republic. Because it was also thought that they were more militarily skilled than the Spaniards, more experienced in war, and more disciplined than their hosts, the Internationals were used as shock troops. However, the records of the Internationals and the memoirs of men who participated in the International Brigades reveal that the amount of chaos and unskilled leadership that they suffered was at least as great as among Spanish units. It is inexact also to claim that any significant number of Internationals had had experience of the 1914–18 war except their commanders, which is why they were appointed. Probably only among the French volunteers, who admittedly formed the greatest individual number of Internationals, had most men completed military service. The Italians were refugees from their country, as were many of the Eastern Europeans. The Germans had come to military age during the Weimar Republic when Germany had no compulsory military service. Neither the United States nor the United Kingdom had obligatory service. In any case, the Internationals cannot be fairly compared for experience, training, discipline, or leadership with Franco's shock troops, the Legion and the Moroccan troops. Losses among the Internationals, who were thrown against the Legion and the Moroccans, were thus very heavy, and by the time of the Battle of Brunete in July 1937, the International Brigades, reinforced already many times by new volunteers, included many Spaniards. By the time of the Ebro battle (July–November 1938), at least two-thirds of the troops of the International units that took part were Spaniards.[23]

Soviet Arms Shipments

Once the Soviet Union decided that propaganda, nonmilitary aid, and the advisers who arrived in the train of the Soviet ambassador at the end of August 1936 were insufficient, given Franco's successful advance and the abundant supplies he was receiving from Germany and Italy, it began a program of arms shipments. This subject has been closely examined, especially since the opening of Soviet archives.[24] While unknown areas remain, and others are in dispute, it seems that in general Soviet military hardware totaled quantitatively markedly less than what Franco received. By 1938 the Spanish gold reserve, which had been shipped to the USSR to be sold on the international market to pay for armaments, was exhausted. Franco, in contrast, received his German and Italian supply on credit. The USSR provided a credit for the Spanish Republic. It did so again when a massive shipment was sent in early 1939.[25]

The problem was that Soviet aid was less specifically directed toward Spanish needs than German and Italian supplies. Franco could request particular materiel, ammunition, spares, and so on by cable to Berlin and Rome and could expect an instant and complete response, while the Republic could not obtain that level of immediate reaction. The armament of the Popular Army was always heterogeneous, with rifles and artillery of a wide variety of calibers. Some Soviet equipment was first-class, particularly the aircraft which dominated the skies over central Spain over the winter and spring of 1936–37 and the USSR's T-26 and BT-5 tanks. Other items, such as the rifles sent in the autumn of 1936, were in bad condition or out-of-date.[26] The European nonintervention agreement and the United States' embargo on selling weaponry to Spain meant that the Republican Army had to look for war materiel in the murkier areas of the arms-dealing market, and was very often cheated financially and in the quality of what it received.

Russian Participation

The extent of Soviet influence in the Popular Army is difficult to measure. The few hundred Russian tank drivers and pilots who came with the first shipment of tanks and aircraft were highly valued by the

Spaniards, and the reports on them that were sent back to Russia were generally favorable, though pointing out that some men lacked discipline, and drank or womanized too much.[27] High-ranking Soviet officers were attached to Spanish units, but not in sufficient numbers to make any considerable difference to the efficiency of the leadership of the Popular Army. Anarchist memoirs understandably scorn both the skill and the influence of Soviet officers, while communist ones praise them highly, while at the same time insisting that the Russians did not really interfere with command decisions. The Russians did indeed have very strict orders limiting their function, orders which some of them realized were contradictory if they were to give the advice that was needed by inexperienced Spanish militia commanders. At the highest army, corps and general staff level, it is hard to imagine senior Spanish officers taking any notice at all of Soviet advice. Such lack of cooperation was marked in the air force that appears to have been controlled by Soviet officers and sometimes simply not to have appeared when it was most needed. It remains a mystery why the USSR did not imitate the German practice of using Spain to try out newly developed aircraft, such as the German Bf-109. Russian aircraft, supreme in 1936, were greatly out of date by the end of the war. Possibly the Russians did not want to run the risk of loss of aircraft and secrets, or they preferred not to risk the death or capture of their pilots. The fact is that by the end of the war the Popular Army was fighting largely without air cover.[28]

The Russians seem to have lacked confidence, which is hardly surprising considering the decimation of the Soviet officer corps that was taking place at the time. No Russian officer would dare, for example, to support the views on the use of tanks advanced by the now disgraced Marshal Mikhail Tukhachevsky. Indeed, Soviet tanks sent to Spain were very advanced, but coordination between them and the infantry was not developed. Consequently, many of the massive T-26 machines were captured.[29]

Generally speaking, Soviet reports from the first few months of the war underline the contribution of communist-led militia units. For the Russians, learning from their own experience in the Russian Civil War, anarchist indiscipline was intolerable. The problem in Spain, however, was that large sections of the population saw the anarchist, rather than the socialist and still less the communist, movement as their ideal. It was possible to persuade the Spanish authorities in 1937 to crush the dissident communist *POUM* but not the huge anarchist *Confederación Nacional de Trabajo* or *CNT*. Prime Minister Largo Caballero was difficult to deal with, in the Russian view, because he suspected the communists of muscling in on his own socialist movement, and, more importantly from the military point of view, because he was fiercely loyal to senior officers whom the Russian advisers despised as bureaucratic, old-fashioned, idle, and possible traitorous. The Russians blamed the loss of Málaga in

February 1937, and with some justification, on these senior generals.[30] Largo Caballero was forced to resign in May 1937 and replaced by Juan Negrín. For another eleven months, the socialist Indalecio Prieto served as War Minister, but he himself was forced out by communist pressure, largely because he objected to what he saw as growing communist hegemony in the army and air force of the Republic and in particular in the Corps of Political Commissars.

A definite conclusion on this entire issue is difficult. It may be that, as the Soviet officers and the Spanish communists believed, they were doing no more than striving to create an army that would win the war. Juan Negrín, Prime Minister for the last two years of the war, held this view, which is why he was accused of handing Spain over to communism. Nevertheless, there is a valid view that crushing a revolution as the communists tried to do, and dragooning thousands of men into a fiercely disciplined army, was a recipe for disaster, and that a guerrilla-type strategy might have been more successful. All the same, although occasional guerrilla activity was indeed productive and caused considerable alarm in the Nationalist rear, it may be doubted whether a strategy based entirely on guerrillas in territory that was not necessarily supportive of that kind of activity would have produced favorable results.[31]

The Casado Uprising

Communist influence was strongest in the Army of the Ebro commanded by militia Colonel Juan Modesto. This army crossed into France in February 1939 after Franco had overrun Catalonia. Communist power in central and southern Spain must have been much weaker, for, when Colonel Segismundo Casado and the professional officers rebelled against the Negrín government, which they considered without authority once the President of the Republic had resigned, the Spanish communists and the foreign Comintern delegates flew out of Spain and into exile. Resistance to Casado by some communist-led units was crushed.[32]

Casado and his colleagues had been in touch for some time with Franco's agents in Madrid. The concern of the anti-Negrín conspirators was to achieve a reasonable peace settlement, to save what could be preserved and to allow time for those in peril to escape. The professional officers seem to have believed, naively, that their colleagues on the other side, men whom many of them knew as friends and old colleagues, would welcome them back into the military family. After all, the professional officers of the Popular Army had obeyed their oaths of loyalty and had done their duty. They had not been guilty of any criminal acts, and many of them were socially conservative and Catholic. The Republican professional officers were, in the event, misled. Every officer was court-martialed after the war by Francoist tribunals. At the present stage of research, it seems that sentence of execution was confirmed only against those officers who were seen, because of their rank, to have been responsible for the deaths of their fellow officers sentenced by court-martial for their rebellion in 1936 and perhaps against others who were strongly associated with political forces of the Left. Many officers, nevertheless, spent years in prison, or purging their sentence in labor camps. Most were expelled from the Army and eked out difficult lives in postwar Spain.[33]

Strategy

The question of strategy may be more a matter of political rather than military decision. Proactive attacks by the Republican Army, such as those at Teruel in December 1937 and on the Ebro in July 1938, may have corresponded more to political decisions than to military appropriateness. The problem with major surprise assaults such as the crossing of the Ebro on the night of July 25–26 was that, as the Italians learnt to their cost at Guadalajara in March 1937, such movements needed air cover. They also required a clear view of what had to be done once the initial gains had been made. On the Ebro, air cover was scarcely present, so that advancing Republican troops and the pontoon bridges over which all their materiel had to come and their wounded evacuated were constantly bombed by the enemy. Advancing Republican troops, whose inexperienced commanders lacked initiative, allowed themselves to be held up by strongpoints of lesser importance. They thus lost the element of surprise. Furthermore, Franco's logistics were of an extremely high order, which allowed him to bring up reinforcements before the Army of the Ebro, the best trained and equipped of all the Republican forces, could take full advantage of its initial success.

On a more theoretical point, it seems arguable that, although officers on both sides had imbibed the same military ideas because they had attended the same military academy, on the Republican side it was French defensive concepts, highly respected in the Spanish military academy, personified in confidence in the Maginot Line, and encouraged by the communist view that even an unskilled army could force a favorable decision by resistance, that seemed to predominate, while few shared the more aggressive concepts of colonial warfare. Did this contrast arise because *Africanistas,* many of whom had taught at the General Military Academy that he himself had commanded in the 1920s, commanded Franco's armies?

Perhaps such contrasts were more applicable to tactics. Were company and platoon movements taught better in Franco's army than in the Popular Army of the Republic? If this was not so, can the clearly better infantry performance of Franco's army, even excepting the Moroccans and the highly trained Legionaries, be explained in terms of better officer and noncommissioned officer training, an absence of revolutionary rhetoric or better morale? Alternatively, was it all merely a matter of more arms, better discipline, and greater confidence in the professional quality of commanders at all levels?[34]

Once the Republic, because of its inner political chaos, had made a number of incoherent and mistaken strategic decisions, such as abandoning the blockade of the Moroccan coast and not backing the initiative by militia from Valencia to recapture the port and naval base of Palma de Mallorca, its inability to defeat Franco's insurrection was probably inevitable. Nevertheless, without the refusal of foreign countries to supply arms to the Republic, in contrast to the regular supplies that Franco received from Germany and Italy, a stalemate might have been possible. The construction of a new army in such a situation can be seen, in retrospect, to have been a substantial achievement.

CHAPTER **6**

The Spanish Military During World War II

Wayne H. Bowen

Spain was not an official belligerent during World War II, but its military was deeply affected by the conflict. Born in the Spanish Civil War, the victorious armed forces of Nationalist Spain emerged in 1939 with an austere Catholic and authoritarian ethos. Partly out of necessity and partly out of the ideological preference of its master, the Spanish military maintained these principles of self-abnegation and Spartan existence for many years after the end of the Civil War. Despite the close ties of the Spanish military to the Axis, and the similarities between Spain's Falangist Party and the fascist parties of Germany and Italy, the Spanish Army remained on its bases during the broader European war that began the year Spain's Civil War ended. Many observers expected General Francisco Franco's army, which had been trained and equipped by Germany, to enter World War II on the Axis side. Despite negotiations to this end, Spain did not join Nazi Germany in its war or undertake any major military operations during the conflict.

Nevertheless, some elements of his army and air force saw combat during the conflict. The Spanish Blue Division, a volunteer unit in the Germany army, served on the Eastern Front from 1941 to 1943, as did the Blue Squadron from the Spanish Air Force. Sent at the initiative of Franco, these forces demonstrated Spain's solidarity with the Axis, without a declaration of war. Other smaller units, without authorization from the Franco regime, served in the German military and SS. The Spanish Army and security forces also fought on Spanish territory against communist-led guerrillas, the *maquis,* who invaded Spain from France beginning in late 1944.

The vast majority of the Spanish armed forces, however, remained in their barracks during World War II. Although its public image was one of heroism and glory, and on paper, its divisions seemed formidable, the Spanish military suffered from severe financial neglect, even as the Spanish state trumpeted the institution as the key to the Civil War victory and the foundation of the regime. Poorly equipped, so badly paid that even officers had to hold outside employment to survive, the Spanish military would have been hard pressed to defend against even a half-hearted invasion of the peninsula by the Axis or the Allies. This paper will demonstrate the weakness of Franco's military during this critical time in the regime's history. Although the military served as one of the key pillars of the regime, the weakness of Spain's armed forces illustrates the overall fragility of the dictatorship of General Francisco Franco. Despite an outward appearance of total unity, the Spanish government during World War II was divided between hostile factions, notoriously incompetent in almost all areas, and characterized by an ambivalent authoritarianism that reflected the broader disagreements within the government and in society at large. The armed forces echoed these divisions and magnified them at the level of general officers.[1]

On April 1, 1939, General Francisco Franco, sick in bed with fever, issued this statement: "On this day, with the Red Army captive and disarmed, the Nationalist troops have reached their final military objectives. The war has ended."[2] The Spanish Civil War, which had begun almost three years earlier, ended with a Nationalist victory, leaving the nation in the hands of General Franco and his supporters. The Nationalists won because they had internal unity, a more cohesive and better-led army, and consistent foreign support from Nazi Germany and Fascist Italy. The defeated Republicans, surrendered or fled into exile to France, Mexico, or the Soviet Union, the latter being the only nation to provide substantial military assistance to the Republic of the Popular Front. The war was over, with the Republican army in prisoner of war camps or huddled in refugee camps in southern France.

Even though the Nationalist armed forces had won the Civil War, within a few months of the end of the conflict its readiness and strength had declined precipitously. In a rush to demobilize large numbers of soldiers, the army retained far too many officers and lost its base of enlisted combat veterans. German and Italian military aid, which had provided the bulk of Spain's modern weapons and training, ended suddenly with the victory. As a result, by the end of 1939, even as World War II was beginning on the continent, Franco's armed forces, so recently arrayed in triumph and effectiveness, were in no condition to fight a protracted war. The Spanish Army was large, over 500,000 when mobilized, but had no oil, little ammunition, and only two under equipped motorized divisions. The rest of the divisions marched on foot and were perpetually short of food, uniforms, boots, and rifles, most of which were from World War I anyway. Even after several years of attempting to purchase arms from the Axis and the Allies, Spain was woefully short in almost every category. The air force had only a few modern fighter aircraft, mostly German Messerschmitt Bf-109s left over from the Civil War or purchased in small numbers thereafter. Most of the navy had been sunk during the Civil War, with one heavy cruiser, one light cruiser, one seaworthy submarine, and a handful of destroyers able to defend Spain's coast and maritime interests. The army had almost no tanks, trucks, or modern artillery. This weakness came despite the high percentage of the national budget which went to the military: 45% in 1941 and as high as 34% even in 1945.[3]

This was not the face of a nation prepared for modern war or even minor offensive operations against Gibraltar or French North Africa, both of which were seriously considered by Franco during World War II. Even with an Axis victory, Spain would have suffered yet another blow to its fragile economy, leaving even more of its citizens hungry and desperate. While new territories in North Africa would have helped with food supplies, the costs would have been high, as France, even after being defeated by Germany, was more than a match for Spain's weak military. In the case of Spanish entry into the war, it seems likely that Hitler would eventually have sought to replace Franco with a more pliable leader, as happened in Hungary in 1944. Even facing an imminent Soviet invasion of Germany, Nazi leaders maintained the wherewithal to overthrow the aged Admiral Miklós Horthy, who had dared to open peace negotiations with the Allies, and gave power to the fascist Arrow Cross Party in Hungary.[4]

Despite its penury, the military remained a powerful force within Spain's borders. The most important interest groups working within the Spanish government were the military, the Catholic Church and its lay organizations, Bourbon monarchists, the Falange, and Carlist monarchists. Of these groups, the first three were the most consistently influential over the life of the regime, with the earlier influence of the Falange fading with the defeat of the Axis during World War II. During World War II, "the Falange, Church and army shared power, with clear pre-eminence to the military."[5]

The military was the essential foundation of the regime and provided the most consistent support for the personal rule of Francisco Franco. Essentially created by Franco during the Civil War, the new army of the Nationalist state was more loyal to the Caudillo than any other institution. This was true despite the neglect and underfunding of the armed forces that characterized World War II. The army underwent significant restructuring in the months following the Civil War. In July 1939, Franco ordered Spain divided into eight military regions, each led by a lieutenant general appointed to be "Captain General." The metropolitan districts were Madrid, Seville, Valencia, Barcelona, Zaragoza, Burgos, Valladolid, and La Coruña, with an additional two regions in Spanish Morocco, headquartered in Ceuta and Melilla. The Balearic and Canary Islands continued as autonomous districts, with much smaller forces than on the mainland. In each peninsular military region was a corps of two or three infantry divisions, plus a small mobile reserve of armor and artillery.

Franco remained supreme military commander and made sure the best funding, equipment, and officers went to the forces in Spanish Morocco, the border regions, and near urban centers, to forestall domestic unrest.[6]

Primary responsibility for internal security, however, was the responsibility of two law enforcement agencies: the *Guardia Civil* and *Policía Armada*. Although martial law and military tribunals remained in force until 1948, serving as the primary means to judge and punish those accused of political crimes, the military played only a limited direct role in maintaining law and order in Spain after 1939. Although as an institution the army did not serve as a law enforcement or internal security arm of the government, many of its high-ranking officers, especially from the infantry, held dual roles as commanders in the *Guardia Civil* or as high-ranking bureaucrats in the Ministry of Interior. The army also remained responsible for the "discipline and internal order" in the *Guardia Civil*, while the Interior Ministry funded and directed the force's activities and operations.[7]

Along with restructuring of its forces, the military also undertook a program of education among its officers, many of whom had received temporary commissions during the Civil War and lacked formal military education. One of the key forums for this education was the official magazine *Ejército* (Army) that debuted in February 1940 and published monthly during World War II and beyond. Despite its title, it included significant material about the army but also the navy and air force. Subtitled as the "Illustrated Magazine of the Arms and Services," it featured articles on strategy, tactics, field services (such as medicine, transportation, and logistics), fortifications, engineering, geography, and training. Reflecting views common among Spanish officers that moral strength and inspiration could defeat material superiority, the largest number of articles during World War II covered the subjects of "Psychology and Military Morale" and "Military History."[8]

In January 1941, the navy resumed its traditional journal, *Revista General de Marina* (General Naval Review), a publication dating to 1877, but interrupted in 1936 by the Civil War. Issued every six months, in January and June, it covered a wide range of naval topics, from tactics at sea to developments in World War II. Unlike *Ejército*, which was intended for the broad audience of all officers, the naval journal focused exclusively on the navy, with a large percentage of its articles on naval history and technical questions, unlike the more philosophical and political tone of the army review. Given the modest size of the navy, the circulation of the *Revista* was much more limited.[9]

The armed forces were perhaps the only internal Spanish institution capable of overthrowing Franco. As the source of the Caudillo's initial legitimacy in 1936, when a gathering of Nationalist generals had endorsed Franco as the absolute commander of their forces, the military also presumably had the power to reverse this decision, especially since the initial reason—fighting a Civil War—was no longer relevant. More generals in 1939 were monarchist than anything else, but there was no clear consensus, as some were Falangists, Carlists, or just generally supportive of military government and authoritarianism. In some ways, it was easier to identify what officers opposed: democracy, communism, socialism, anarchism, and separatism.[10] Tensions between monarchists and pro-German Falangists in the armed forces, especially in the army, persisted throughout World War II.[11]

These political and personal rivalries between generals and the lack of any figures with charisma, with the possible exception of Blue Division commander Agustín Muñoz Grandes, made it more difficult for senior officers to promote alternatives to Franco.[12] In this final regard, the military had reason to be satisfied, as it retained emergency powers from 1936 to 1948, was able to try civilians in military courts, and had a privileged legal and political status.[13] Franco also made sure to give his personal attention to the armed forces, attending military maneuvers and praising the services in many of his public speeches.[14]

Franco moved quickly to silence, demote, or retire those officers who proved difficult. General Gonzalo Queipo de Llano, who had ensured that Seville rallied early to the Nationalist rebellion in July 1936, was perhaps the most significant threat to Franco within the armed forces. For a few months after the end of the Civil War, Queipo de Llano remained commander of the Seville District, even after the reorganization of July 1939, and the press even had to dismiss rumors that Queipo de Llano had been sacked. By August, however, Franco appointed the general to head the Spanish military mission to Italy—a delegation which did not exist.[15]

During the first year of peace, Franco dramatically reduced the size of the Spanish Army, from almost one million at the end of the Civil War to 250,000 in early 1940, with most soldiers two-year conscripts. Concern about the international situation, Spain's possible entry into the war, and threats of invasion led him to restore some of these reductions, leaving Spain with almost double the 1940 figure for the remainder of World War II. In November 1942, with the Allied landings in North Africa and the German occupation of Vichy France bringing the war closer than ever to Spain's border, Franco ordered a partial mobilization, bringing the army to over 750,000. The air force and navy also grew in numbers and in budgets, to 35,000 airmen and 25,000 sailors by 1945, although for fiscal reasons Franco had to restrain attempts by both services to undertake dramatic expansions.[16]

With the end of the Civil War, the Nationalist army demobilized most of its soldiers, but the internal and international situations required the maintenance of a large army. Conscription, revised in August 1940 to include all able-bodied males, provided the vast majority of enlisted soldiers, but the officer corps remained not only a volunteer force but also one that was oversubscribed by young men hoping for a military career. For every place in the *Academia General Militar* (General Military Academy, GMA), the service school that trained most Spanish cadets destined for military service during World War II, there were at least two applicants, a ratio rising to 4.3:1 in 1945.[17]

Even though the armed forces consumed 35–45% of all government expenditures, figures that remained constant as the overall budget rose, procurement was very limited during World War II. One of the reasons the navy, air force, and even army had to limit construction and acquisition of new weapons systems, despite the weakness of the armed forces to cope with any external threat, was that the vast majority of their budgets, at least 49% and as much as 80%, went toward salaries. The bulk of this went to the Spanish Army's "bloated officer corps," which included both generals over the age of seventy and thousands of provisional lieutenants (*alféreces provisionales*) commissioned during the Civil War and kept on active duty for political reasons, even though their services were no longer needed in a smaller military.[18] Additionally, many of the mid-level officers—majors and lieutenant colonels—had been Franco's infantry cadets when he had been director of the GMA in Zaragoza, 1927–31, and retained loyalty for the former teacher.[19]

Thus, the Spanish Army entered the period of World War II "with a great mass of soldiers poorly fed, clothed and shod, supplied with antiquated weapons and equipment, practically without any automobiles and using obsolete tanks and aircraft."[20] There were so few tanks in the army that many cavalry officers argued that Spain should ignore the tank and keep cavalry units on horseback. The military, especially the army, suffered from poor equipment and a lack of standardization. Even with the most basic kinds of military equipment, Spain was unable to afford one system. Instead of one type of rifle, which would have improved readiness and made training and logistics easier, the army had to rely on domestic weapons from the Spanish-American War, World War I, and eight other foreign variants. Even at the end of World War II, after six years of peace, the army still had ten different kinds of machine guns.[21]

Despite his extensive battlefield and administrative experience, "the problem of military efficiency never seriously preoccupied General Franco."[22] Franco even argued that Spanish soldiers could make up through strength of will what they lacked in war materiel. Spain's international defiance of Allied demands to lessen German ties also had a negative impact on readiness. For example, the British and U.S. oil embargo in early 1944 was so catastrophic that military aircraft and armored vehicles did not have sufficient fuel to participate in the victory parade on April 1, commemorating the fifth anniversary of the Nationalist triumph in the Spanish Civil War.[23]

In some ways, the large officer corps provided political benefits to Franco. Of the 29,000 *alféreces*, provisional lieutenants commissioned during the Civil War, only 3,000 returned to civilian life after the end of the Civil War, leaving Franco with a strong and loyal base at the lower rungs of the officer corps. Even if the majority of army careerists above the rank of colonel were monarchists who preferred a restoration, below that rank the officer corps was enthusiastically Francoist, especially the *alféreces provisionales*, who owed their status and improved prospects to the Caudillo's wartime leadership.[24] Salaries were low, but officers could supplement their income by selling on the black market, especially food which was available to them in special stores. Housing subsidies and other benefits also made conditions for officers better than for the majority of Spaniards. Officer salaries were also raised on July 1, 1940, by as much as 40%.[25]

Another way Franco held on to the loyalty of the army, despite low salaries for most ranks, was through offering additional remunerative positions. Senior officers could hold salaried positions in the Falange or state, wages which would be in addition to their military income. Accepting these sinecures often meant ending an officer's chances of being promoted to general, unless the officer was already at flag rank, but in the top heavy Spanish Army promotion to this grade was not a realistic option for most anyway. Colonels and generals often had two salaries, one from the military and one from the state. As many as one-third of all senior civil service and security positions were held by military officers. Junior officers without independent means often took jobs in the private sector, taking time away from their military careers to earn enough to provide for their families. In any case, promotions came only on the basis of seniority, not merit, so it made little career sense to be an aggressive and overachieving performer.[26]

There were other reasons for the loyalty of the Spanish Army to their commander in chief. In a Spain which was suffering so much poverty and hunger, army officers received a guaranteed salary, housing supplements, and access to food which was unavailable to the general public. These modest conditions were enough to keep most officers content, even if the majority had to hold second jobs to earn a living wage. For good reason, Franco was able to refer to the Army and Falange as "the two pillars of the Nation," by which he meant his regime. This contentedness also continued despite the inactivity of the armed forces during World War II. Aside from the Blue Division, Blue Legion, and Blue Squadron, which fought on the Eastern Front as late as 1944, and the few units involved in fighting communist guerrillas in northern Spain, 1944–45, the Spanish military did not gain any experience, or even participate in any major military exercises, during World War II.[27]

The only significant domestic use of the military, against the *maquis* guerrillas beginning in 1944, also had a consolidating impact on the regime. Faced with such an obvious threat to national security, the military rallied to Franco. In October 1944, the first insurgents entered Navarre, Spain, from France. This geographic choice, attempting to seize the Valley of Inclan, was a serious mistake, as it brought the communists into the Carlist heartland, surrounded by tens of thousands of conservative and Catholic peasants who had been nearly unanimous in their support of the 1936 Nationalist uprising. Still, several thousand rebels infiltrated and remained in the region for up to ten days before being crushed by the army and *Guardia Civil*. From Navarre, the communists spread throughout many of the mountainous areas of Spain, committing over 300 armed attacks on Spanish military, police, and civilian targets. The invasion had the effect of rallying the military around Franco, through raising fears of another Civil War. With the failure of the *maquis* on the battlefield, the French ended their tolerance for these incursions and closed the Spanish border on March 1, 1945.[28]

At the same time, Franco demonstrated his desire to prevent any rivals from establishing firm power bases. For this reason, there was no unity of command in the military. In August 1939, the Ministry of National Defense, which had been created in January 1938 to improve joint operations, was replaced by three separate ministries for each service. This was "largely an exercise in divide and rule," because only Franco, as the commander in chief, could arbitrate between the services and balance the institutional demands of the army, navy, and air force.[29] The official doctrine of the Spanish military was that of the "*mando único*" (single command), which exalted Franco as the sole leader of the armed forces. In practice, this meant that during World War II and beyond the service chiefs reported directly to Francisco Franco, rather than to a uniformed chief of staff or civilian war minister.[30]

For example, in the August 1939 Cabinet reshuffle, he dismissed the monarchist general Alfredo Kindelán, the commander of the Spanish air forces during the Civil War. Without warning or any expression of gratitude for his creation of Franco's air force from nothing during the Civil War, Kindelán was removed from office and sent to the Balearic Islands. Despite his proven expertise in aviation, the general was perhaps becoming too popular and expert in his position for Franco's comfort. The following year, however, Franco promoted Kindelán to lieutenant general and gave him command over the Barcelona Military District, one of the most prestigious in Spain.[31]

In Kindelán's place as Minister of the Air Force, Franco appointed the Naziphile general, Juan Yagüe Blanco, an excellent battlefield commander who had played a key role in the uprising of July 1936 and led a column of Moroccan soldiers for much of the Civil War. Unlike Kindelán, however, he had absolutely no experience with aircraft, aerospace, or managing a large bureaucracy. One virtue of Yagüe's, however, was that his Falangist credentials—he was perhaps the general most sympathetic to calls for revolution—convinced radical Naziphiles that they had a comrade in the Cabinet. Rather than giving him command of a military district, corps, or other unit, where he might have become a focal point for opposition, Franco appointed him to the Cabinet in the hopes of keeping him busy with the administrative minutiae of starting a new ministry, and therefore less able to meddle in politics or give support to Falangist schemes.[32] As both of these cases illustrated, whenever Franco feared that an officer was a potential threat, he was ready with demotions, awards, and promotions to bring him to heel.[33]

In the summer and fall of 1940 Spain came closest to entering the war, with the Falange and military in ascendancy over more moderate monarchists, the Church, and business interests. Uncertainty pervaded the mood of Spain during those months, with Spain's edging closer to war coinciding with the heights of the black market and corruption in postwar Spain.[34] Most of the military believed that a Nazi victory was imminent and that Spain needed to affiliate quickly with the Axis to take its proper share of the spoils of war.[35] Franco was still hesitant to embrace belligerency on the side of the Axis, barring financial and military guarantees from Hitler and Mussolini. When Air Force Minister Yagüe proposed at a cabinet meeting that Spain should immediately enter the war on the side of Germany, Franco told him to keep quiet and dismissed him from office shortly thereafter.[36] The Caudillo also fired General José López Pinto, the Captain General of the frontier Sixth Military District, after allowing excessive Hispano-German fraternization at the border.[37]

The German attack on the USSR transformed Spanish politics overnight and genuinely stimulated "a patriotic clamor" and anticommunist demonstrations throughout Spain. While Falangists, Alfonsin monarchists, Carlists, Catholics, and business interests may have had significant political differences, they coincided in their hatred of communism and anger at the Soviet Union for having assisting the Second Republic and prolonging the war.[38] Franco appears to have briefly considered declaring war, as requested by Nazi Germany, but his nation's economic dependence on Great Britain prevented this from being possible.[39]

Instead, following the suggestion of Ramón Serrano Suñer, his foreign minister and brother-in-law, Franco offered to send a volunteer division of Spaniards to serve in the German army, a proposal accepted immediately by Nazi leaders. Recruiting began with a massive demonstration in central Madrid, during which Serrano Suñer declared: "Russia is guilty" of beginning the Spanish Civil War, murdering José Antonio Primo de Rivera (the founder of the Falange), and otherwise contributing to the destruction of Spain's economy and prospects. Within a few weeks, tens of thousands of Falangists, Carlists, and other anticommunist Spanish youth had volunteered for the unit, leaving it oversubscribed several times over.[40]

The Spanish Volunteer Division, its official name, left Spain for Germany in mid-July 1941, witnessed in Madrid by four cabinet ministers and most of the leading Falangist leaders, with the noted exception of Franco, who perhaps wanted to maintain some official distance from such an obvious breach of neutral behavior. Serrano Suñer, even though Foreign Minister, felt no such hindrance, declaring to the Nazi newspaper *Deutsche Allgemeine Zeitung* that the creation of the Blue Division signaled Spain's position as one of "moral belligerency on the side of our friends and against the most hated of all the enemies of the Spaniards," the Soviet Union.[41]

The Blue Division received the official support of the government for its first two years on the Eastern Front. Newspapers contained frequent mentions of the heroism of the unit, memorializing fallen soldiers and denouncing the evils of communism. The Falange opened a special office in Madrid to assist families of the division and sponsored radio broadcasts featuring soldiers calling back to their friends and relatives in Spain. Congregations throughout Spain held special masses in honor of the troops, attended by prominent figures in the Falange and government, and the Women's Section of the Falange organized drives to collect winter clothing and other gifts for the unit, especially around Christmas. Upon their return from battle, Blue Division veterans gained the same hiring preferences as those who had fought in the Civil War, and one year of service in the unit credited a soldier with two in the regular Spanish Army.[42]

One result of the dispatch of the Blue Division was the rise of General Agustín Muñoz Grandes, the unit commander, as a popular figure. As a young officer, he had served with distinction in Morocco and had held key positions during the monarchy and republic. During the Spanish Civil War, after making a daring escape from the Republican zone, he had been a skilled Nationalist commander. With his army background, experience as Secretary General of the Falange, and proven battlefield leadership, he became the focus of a tremendous amount of attention. The Spanish press covered his speeches, which were also broadcast over Spanish radio hailing the courage of his soldiers.

> Hard is the enemy, and harder still is the Russian winter. But it does not matter: even harder is my race, supported by reason and the courage of its sons who, embracing their heroic German comrades, will in the end achieve the victory, towards which we fight without ceasing.[43]

In addition to the Spaniards who followed his exploits, Muñoz Grandes also garnered the attention of Hitler, who saw in him a potential replacement for Franco. The German leader met several times with the Spanish general, awarding him the highest military decoration and encouraging him to remain involved in politics. Franco heard about these discussions, and replaced Muñoz Grandes as commander of the division, a replacement delayed several months at the insistence of the Nazis. Hitler wanted to ensure that the Blue Division's commander gained sufficient victories to become even more popular in Spain. Upon his eventual return, to a hero's welcome, Franco promoted Muñoz Grandes to the rank of lieutenant general—too high to command an army division again—and appointed the general in March 1943 to head his military household. Despite the celebrations and banquets in his honor, it would not be until March 1945—just before the end of World War II—that Franco would trust Muñoz Grandes with troops, giving him command of the prestigious Madrid Military District.[44]

The summer of 1942 saw another major political crisis. On August 16, Carlists gathered at the basilica of the Virgin of Begoña, in Bilbao, to commemorate their Civil War dead. Among the 5,000 in attendance at the church in the Basque Country was Army chief General José Enrique Varela. Several Falangists outside the church, after a confrontation with the Carlists, threw grenades at the crowd, injuring several dozen worshippers. Varela immediately accused the Falange of attacking the army, sent telegrams to the commanders of Spain's military districts, ordered the guilty to be executed, and demanded that Franco punish the party. Franco refused to do so, but did use the crisis to reorganize his Cabinet once again. Among the surprises were the dismissals of Varela, who had been too aggressive in his anti-Falangism, and Franco's brother-in-law Serrano Suñer, identified with the Naziphile faction of the party, and therefore an increasing political liability. Interior Minister Valentín Galarza, who had been the focal point of the May Crisis, also lost his position, as one who had agreed with Varela that the Falange needed to be punished.[45]

Much as it had during the May Crisis, the Spanish press attempted to downplay the Begoña incident, even in an editorial titled "Changing of the Guard."

> It is unnecessary to repeat again that the substitutions of some persons in Government or party offices does not produce nor will it produce the least variation in domestic or international politics. It would be another thing entirely to deny the incidental meaning of the changing names of men, which does not change the permanent nature and the service of the Totalitarian State. The experience has been repeated frequently in nations of a similar structure and with the same nature. In reality, all of this obeys vital laws, common to all healthy organisms, subject to wear and tear and fatigue, but suitable for the quick reestablishment of normal forces.[46]

The army, in particular, was delighted at the sacking of Serrano Suñer, and this change quieted much of the grumbling among senior officers through the rest of 1942 and into 1943.[47]

Bad feelings remained between the Falange and the Carlists, however, and so in one measure to calm the conflict, Franco delayed the opening of universities until November 1 to avoid confrontations between rival student groups.[48] To prevent more armed confrontations and appease the army, Franco also dissolved the Falangist militia. The end result of the Begoña affair was to convince the army and the Falange that they could not exercise independently of Franco. He was the final arbiter of Spain's destiny and the master of its internal politics, for good or ill.[49]

The army remained the key to the survival of the Franco regime, and its dependence on the dictator characterized its existence during World War II. Poorly funded, badly equipped, and deprived of a unified command structure, the military was also in conflict with the other important political forces in regime. Defined by the Civil War struggle against communism and the Popular Front, the Spanish armed forces persisted in this fight through its only two opportunities for battle: the fight of the Blue Division on the Eastern Front, and against the communist-led *maquis* in the rugged terrain of northern Spain. Had Franco decided to enter the war on the side of the Axis, as he considered during the early phase of the war, his military would have struggled to fulfill its primary mandate: the defense of the nation. Fortunately, for the officers and conscripts who served during World War II, Spain's military never faced a serious test of its capabilities. After winning a Civil War against a determined opponent, the Nationalist army of the Franco regime stagnated during World War II, reflecting the weakness and fragility of the state it purported to defend.

CHAPTER 7

Decolonization and the Spanish Army, 1940–76

Shannon E. Fleming

The Colonies Defined and the Role of the Spanish Army

While Spain lost the remainder of its Caribbean and Far East colonies during the 1898 Spanish-American War, this event did not signal the end of Spanish colonialism. In fact, it might be argued that the 1898 defeat gave new impetus to Spain's late nineteenth– and early twentieth–century participation in the "scramble for Africa." By the mid-1930s, this more contemporary empire was composed of protectorates in northern and southern Morocco, the enclave of Ifni on Morocco's southern coast, the Spanish Sahara, and the central African territories known collectively as Spanish Guinea. While not the equal in territory or significance to the west European empires or even the Portuguese colonies, by 1950 the Spanish controlled or laid claim to 340,700 square kilometers in northwest and equatorial Africa, managed the destiny of approximately 1,300,000 north and sub-Saharan Africans, and occupied some strategic coastal areas, particularly along the southern Mediterranean.

A common thread in Spain's "new imperialism" was that it was undertaken exclusively in Africa, particularly in Northwest Africa, and involved territories with which Spain had a long historical connection. Another common thread was that with the notable exception of Spanish Guinea, the task of occupying, pacifying, and administering these colonies was given to the Spanish Army. This was mainly due to the fact that these areas had never really been subjected to a centralized authority, and thus, from the European perspective, first needed to be controlled and then organized and administered. Accordingly, army personnel found themselves engaged not only in military actions, particularly in Spain's Moroccan Protectorate, but also in ongoing administrative, legal, and security roles. This placed added responsibilities on the Spanish

Army which in many ways was unprepared, in terms of structure, resources, and training, for them.[1]

Spanish Morocco, 1940–56

This was especially the case in Spanish Morocco, Spain's principal twentieth-century colonial possession. From 1912 through 1931, the Protectorate administration was basically the responsibility of the Spanish Army. From the High Commissioner down to the local tribal and clan *interventores*, Spanish Army officers played a pivotal role in imposing and then maintaining law and order, administering justice, and managing the Protectorate's limited economic, social, and cultural initiatives. The Second Republic's efforts to "civilianize" the Protectorate proved only partially successful as evidenced by the events of July 17–18, 1936, and the rapid subjugation of the Protectorate by the so-called Army of Africa for the Nationalist cause.[2]

Under the control of the Franco government, the Protectorate reverted once again to an administration run by the Spanish Army. From 1940 until Moroccan independence in April 1956, the ultimate authority in the Zone—the High Commissioner—was a Spanish Army lieutenant general, and while his staff might by necessity include civilian personnel, the important liaison positions with the sixty-six Berber tribes were occupied exclusively by military officers. The High Commissioner's role was further amplified and strengthened by the Protectorate's administrative reorganization of November 8, 1941. The intent of this restructuring was to unify and broaden the High Commissioner's powers and to provide for the better coordination of Protectorate responsibilities and services under a Secretary General and five delegations: indigenous affairs; education and culture; public works and communications; economy, industry, and commerce; and finance.[3]

As might be anticipated, the Spanish Army's role in the Protectorate in the early 1940s was also conditioned by the European war. Based on estimates provided in the spring of 1940 by French Resident, General Charles Nogues, to the French government, the Army of Africa's troop strength exceeded 100,000 men: two corps in the Tetuán sector and one in the Melilla sector. Víctor Morales Lezcano has suggested that this figure was in fact closer to 150,000 men, counting both European and indigenous troops.[4] The Franco government, through both its neutral and its nonbelligerent phases in the early 1940s, probably had three objectives for keeping a substantial force in the Protectorate. The first was to forestall any resistance to its occupation on June 14, 1940, of the international city and territorial enclave of Tangier. This was carried out significantly by 4,000 indigenous troops the day after Paris fell to the Germans and justified on the grounds that Spain was ensuring Tangier's neutrality in light of the general conflagration. The second was to furnish a force to support Franco's apparent, and ultimately frustrated, willingness in late 1940 to enter the war on the Axis side in exchange for, among other concessions, much of France's northwest African territories. The third, especially into 1942, was to plan for the defense of Spanish Morocco in anticipation of an Allied invasion. This occurred on November 8, 1942, when, as President Franklin Roosevelt warned Francisco Franco, "a powerful American military force" disembarked at various points on French Morocco's Atlantic coast. The Spanish perhaps judged their sizeable military presence in Spanish Morocco as a possible deterrent to Allied incursions into their Protectorate.[5] However, given the Spanish military's less than cutting edge state in the 1940s and 1950s in terms of equipment, artillery, armor, and air and sea power, it is doubtful that they would have been particularly effective against the fewer but better-equipped Allied forces.

Franco's post-1940 deftness at keeping Spain out of the war also extended to its North African colonies. While General Luis Orgaz y Yoldi, the Spanish High Commissioner from May 1941 to his death in January 1945, followed the Franco government's pro-Axis stance and allowed German commercial and espionage activities in Spanish Morocco, he also cultivated stable relations with Nogues, Vichy's Resident General in French Morocco, and later the Americans and the Free French Resident General, Gabriel Paux. By late 1944 the Spanish felt secure enough in their neutrality and the Protectorate's internal security to reduce the army staffing level in the Protectorate to about 60,000 men. This represented two corps: one based in Tetuán and another in Melilla.[6]

Along with its staffing reductions, the Army's role in the Protectorate also shifted. While the basic missions were still those of security and administration, as the war threat eased the latter duty became more notable. Under Orgaz y Yoldi, the Protectorate's military-based bureaucracy initiated a number of reforms and projects that, as Juan Vilar observed, accelerated a "modernization rhythm" in the Protectorate from the mid-1940s until Moroccan independence in 1956. This included such initiatives as the reorganization and expansion of the Protectorate's primary, secondary, technical, and religious schools; the establishment of the *Caja General de Creditores* to finance public and private initiatives; and the creation of *Juntas Rurales* which furnished a mechanism for directing funds into rural public works and development. The apotheosis of these activities were the five-year economic plans of 1946 and 1952 which pumped 520 million *pesetas* into the Protectorate's infrastructure, social services, and general development. These not only demonstrated the military's paternalistic *Africanista* ethos but reflected Francoist colonial policy, which, unlike the French, emphasized public expenditure over private development.[7]

Orgaz y Yoldi's successor, General José Enrique Varela Iglesias, who served as High Commissioner from March 1945 until his death in March 1951, continued, within Spain's postwar economic realities, to support developmental initiatives. However, in the mid-1940s these were circumscribed by a severe drought which resulted in a series of bad harvests that dramatically reduced cultivated lands from 319,416 hectares in 1944 to 211,671 hectares in 1947 and dropped the Protectorate's overall population by over 17,000 or 6.6% between 1945 and 1950.[8] In addition to this human and economic crisis, Varela was also confronted with an upsurge in Moroccan nationalist activities which emanated from the French Protectorate and from outside Morocco. In an April 1947 speech in Tangier, Sultan Mohammed V generated a negative reaction from the French Resident General, Alphonse Juin, influential French *colons*, and pro-French indigenous elites when he aligned his throne with the *Istiqlal* Party's pro-independence goals. The following year Varela faced a similar experience in the Spanish Protectorate when Abd el Jalek Torres, the Spanish Moroccan head of the Tetuán-based Reform Party, made a pro-independence speech in Tangier. Varela immediately forbade Torres from entering the Protectorate and clamped down on both the indigenous press and the indigenous political activity.[9]

Despite these difficulties, Varela was genuinely popular with the Protectorate's rural Berber tribesmen whom he had fought against in the Rif War of 1920s and then led in battles against the Second Republic in the Spanish Civil War. As with a number of other career *Africanista* army officers, Varela understood and spoke some Arabic and Moroccan Berber and had a knowledge and respect for the local culture and customs. Where Varela was not entirely in accord as High Commissioner was with Franco's and, his Foreign Minister, Alberto Martín Artajo's Arab policy. This policy looked to garner conservative Arab support by emphasizing Spain's unique political, cultural, and diplomatic relationship with the Arab world; its refusal to recognize Israel; and, most important, its developmental programs and political/social tolerance and flexibility in Spanish Morocco.[10]

When Varela died suddenly in March 1951, Franco replaced him with yet another Civil War veteran and *Africanista* officer, General Rafael García Valiño. García Valiño's concept of Spain's role in Spanish Morocco was considerably different from Varela's and more in tune with the Francoist Arab policy. Within a month after taking office, he facilitated the visit of the Arab League's Secretary General to Spanish Morocco and Tangier. He championed a more liberal and accommodating policy toward the indigenous political parties and media. In early 1952 he allowed Torres to return to the Protectorate and resume his political activities and then induced him to head one of the Caliph's governmental ministries. During a speech marking the twenty-fifth anniversary of the

Rif War's conclusion, he forthrightly declared that he would recognize the "freedom of the press and the political parties" in Spanish Morocco. On the economic and social fronts, García Valiño and his second in command, Tomás García Figueras, pushed forward with a variety of projects. According to María Ybarra, while García Valiño extended existing public works programs, his administration also undertook "the development of inexpensive homes, libraries, sports camps, orphanages, old peoples' homes, hospitals, and rural dispensaries." Under García Valiño, the yearly Protectorate budgets increased from 872,000 *pesetas* in 1950 to over 1,100,000 *pesetas* in 1955.[11]

In comparison with the Spanish Protectorate, in the early 1950s the French Zone seethed with nationalist agitation and popular discontent caused, to some degree, by Sultan Mohammed V's pro-independence declarations and the *Istiqlal* Party's nationalist activities. As a reaction to and further stimulating this situation, the French Resident General, Augustin Guillaume, with the support of the French *colons* and the traditional conservative Moroccan elites, convinced the French government on August 20, 1953, to dethrone and exile Mohammed V and replace him with his more compliant uncle, Muley Arafa. Moroccan reaction to this internal coup d'etat was immediate, negative, and in some cases, violent. The Spanish reaction was, as Martín Artajo stated to the French Ambassador, one of both genuine "surprise" and "sincere reservations."[12] In the next two years, García Valiño's responses, conditioned by his more liberal policies and anti-French sentiments, were even more pronounced. He refused to recognize the new Sultan and ordered that Friday prayers continue to be made in Mohammed V's name. He permitted controlled demonstrations and print and radio propaganda in support of the dethroned Sultan. More significantly, he provided a haven in Spanish Morocco for the southern nationalists and the Liberation Army, a semi-clandestine military force that espoused Mohammed V's return and ultimately Moroccan independence. From 1953 through early 1956 these policies, as the French suggested, probably helped encourage the 6,700 terrorist incidents and the 2,700 resulting deaths in their Protectorate. At the same time, Spanish forces, which in late 1953 numbered approximately 58,000 men, assumed a more passive role in terms of border security. This may have been due as much to the "lamentable condition of the Spanish Army" in terms of its aging equipment, artillery, ordinance, and intelligence gathering as it was to a policy decision. By mid-1955, with the tacit approval of García Valiño's colonial administration, Spanish Morocco became the staging area and entrepôt for arms and men into the French Protectorate. This placed the French in an untenable situation. Faced with the prospect of a drawn-out guerrilla war in their Protectorate, they ultimately choose in August 1955, again without consulting the Spanish, to restore Mohammed V to the throne, and in an even more significant policy change, to move rapidly toward full Moroccan independence.[13]

The French decision to move their Protectorate toward full independence stimulated the inevitable call, backed by demonstrations and other pro-independence activities in Tetuán, for a similar course of action in Spanish Morocco. The Spanish were caught off guard by these developments, feeling that their paternalist rapport with the Moroccans and their recent support of the Sultan and the Moroccan nationalists would somehow preserve the status quo in their Protectorate. These events generated at least three different perspectives at the highest Spanish policy levels. García Valiño advocated that Spain start quickly to negotiate with the French, the Sultan, and the Moroccan nationalists to preserve their security and economic interests in what he concluded was the pending fact of Moroccan independence. Franco was less enthusiastic about moving precipitously on the issue and felt that the whole process needed to be slowed down, reflecting his, as well as his *Africanista* comrades', nostalgia for a Spanish North African empire and his apprehension about "judeo-masonic-communist" influences in Morocco. In January 1956, Franco confided to his cousin and private secretary, Francisco Franco Salgado, that he was "a supporter of Moroccan independence conceded in stages, little by little, without a great deal of haste." Lastly, the Foreign Minister, Martín Artajo, seemed more concerned about the impact of Spanish actions in Morocco on its international relations, particularly those with the French, the Arab world, and especially the United States. He was more inclined to follow the French lead and to bow to American pressure to support the transfer of power to a basically conservative monarchist regime that would not rock the boat in a strategic part of the world. At this point, therefore, Spain's policy toward the rapidly unfolding events in Morocco lacked a focus and was essentially reactive.[14] Further, as Franco Salgado noted, Spanish public opinion and, more significantly, the Spanish Army were not inclined to support another colonial war in Spanish Morocco. Memories of the long, bloody, and expensive struggle from 1912 to 1927 to pacify the Protectorate were still part of the collective consciousness of many Spaniards.

Consequently, as the French moved unilaterally toward the formation of a national Moroccan government, the restoration of Mohammed V to his throne, and the eventual abrogation of the Protectorate on March 2, 1956, the Spanish found themselves essentially presented with a *fait accompli*. Franco finally bowed to the inevitable on March 15, 1956, inviting Mohammed V to Madrid to negotiate Spain's recognition of Moroccan independence. In accepting Franco's invitation, the Sultan came to Spain "not as a friend but as a winner."[15] The negotiations were indeed tense. The Sultan was "reticent, distant and almost discourteous."[16] On April 6, 1956, in the middle of the talks, Franco pointed out to his cousin that "the

Moors plainly want the total independence of the Zone and the end of the Protectorate without any concessions on their part and without furnishing us with what they have conceded to the French."[17] The end result on April 7, 1956, after three days of difficult discussions, was a brief Spanish-Moroccan accord which recognized Moroccan independence. An additional protocol offered Morocco Spanish military assistance, put off a change in the Protectorate's monetary situation for later negotiation, suspended the need for interzonal visas, and guaranteed that Spain would continue to represent individual Moroccan interests overseas. What the Spanish did not get was recognition of its existing possessions in the Sahara area, an accord concerning Spanish fishing rights off the Moroccan coast, and a convention of military cooperation that would ensure at least some Spanish influence over the Royal Moroccan Army.[18]

Unlike the imperial demise of 1898, which generated an unprecedented level of national breast beating and introspection, the loss of Spanish Morocco was met with a sense of resignation. Franco subsequently blamed the French and especially García Valiño for the events of 1955–56, telling his cousin that "Valiño was trying to incite the rebellion in the French camp without taking into account that once it was burning in that Zone the fire would reach ours."[19] Such a reaction was curious given the Franco government's apparent support of García Valiño's policies through late 1955.

The Protectorate's Spanish administrators and the Army faced a number of difficulties given the rapidity of event in early 1956. Spanish forces numbered some 70,800 men—approximately 44,200 in the Protectorate and a combined 26,600 in Ceuta and Melilla.[20] Given these staffing numbers and the necessary equipment and support logistics, there had been little time to plan a smooth transition. In the months following Moroccan independence, the Spanish Army in particular continued to exercise administrative and public order functions in a territory that was no longer Spanish. To many Moroccans, this smacked of a foreign occupation and the situation continued to exacerbate tensions between the two countries. Even as late as June 1958, the Spanish felt the need to maintain a detachment of troops in bases near Tetuán, Larache, and Alcázarquivir to protect the persons and property of Spanish nationals who still remained in Morocco. In December 1958, the French estimated that Spain still had 30,000 troops on Moroccan territory stationed proximate to the Spanish *presidios* of Ceuta and Melilla. These were not totally withdrawn until August 1961, reflecting the Spanish concerns that these settlements were vulnerable to attacks from the Liberation Army.[21]

Spanish West Africa, 1956–76

These tensions were compounded by the fact that Spain still controlled territories that many Moroccans considered part of what the *Istiqlal* Party defined as "Greater Morocco." These included Ceuta and Melilla, and Spanish West Africa, which was composed of the small Ifni enclave along Morocco's southern coast, the so-called Southern Protectorate (the region between the Draa River and Parallel 27° 40′) and Spanish Sahara. With the exception of Ceuta and Melilla, these were isolated and underpopulated areas administered almost exclusively by the Spanish Army. Until Spanish West Africa was reorganized in January 1958 into two Spanish provinces (Ifni and Spanish Sahara), it was commanded by a governor, a brigadier general based in Ifni's primary city, Sidi Ifni. Before April 1956, this individual was subordinate to the Spanish Moroccan High Commission. After Moroccan independence, he reported administratively to the *Dirección General de Promoción del Sahara,* which in turn reported to Franco's Undersecretary, Luis Carrero Blanco, and militarily to the Captain General of the Canary Islands. Given their remoteness and isolation, the Franco government elected to keep a low military profile in these territories. In Ifni the Army garrisoned about 3,200 troops, most of them in Sidi Ifni and some 600 more assigned to fourteen outlying posts. In the more extensive areas of the Southern Protectorate and Spanish Sahara, Spanish forces numbered about 3,100 men assigned to a number of small outposts from Villa Bens (Tarafaya) in the north to La Güera on Spanish Sahara's southwest coast.[22]

The lack of military strength in Spanish West Africa did not go unnoticed by the Moroccans. In a May 1956 speech, Mohammed V laid claim to the Ifni enclave. That same year, in an article published in *Al-Alam,* the official newspaper of the *Istiqlal* Party, the *Istiqlal* leader, Allal al-Fassi, defined "Greater Morocco" to include most of western Algeria, large portions of French West Africa (all of Mauritania and most of northern Mali), and all of Spanish West Africa. These irredentist claims were followed in August 1956 by the first clashes between the Liberation Army and the French forces in French West Africa. Spain initially declared its neutrality in this conflict and acquiesced to the Liberation Army's use of the Spanish Sahara as an access point into French territory. At the same time, the Spanish also saw the need to collaborate clandestinely with the French against what they realistically judged to be a common threat. General Ramón Pardo de Santayana, Spanish West Africa's governor, met with his French counterpart, General Gabriel Bourgund, in February 1957 to establish a designated radio link between commands and to allow French forces to undertake "hot pursuit" of Liberation Army forces both on the ground and in the air into Spanish Sahara. Spanish neutrality was further compromised by General Mariano Gómez Zamalloa who replaced Pardo de Santayana in May 1957. He held a second meeting with the French in July 1957, accelerated defensive measures in both Ifni and Spanish Sahara, and called upon his superiors to increase his forces. A third and more substantive conference was held

with the French on September 20–24, 1957, which led to specific commitments regarding information sharing and the development of plans for
potential military operations.[23]

By September 1957, Ben Hammú, leader of the southern branch of the
Liberation Army, assembled some 5,000 men and stockpiled considerable
artillery and equipment on Morocco's southern border. This buildup
was in preparation for the expansion of Liberation Army activities.
In mid-1957 the Spanish started to experience sporadic attacks against
their isolated Ifni and West Saharan outposts, minor incidents of urban
terrorism in Sidi Ifni and the murder of indigenous troops or their deser-
tion to the Moroccan cause. These incidents were in fact the prelude to
the main Liberation Army assault on Sidi Ifni and its outposts on the
morning of November 23, 1957. Some 2,000 Moroccans invaded the
enclave cutting communication lines, attacking various garrisons and
armories, and laying siege to a number of the outlying posts. Smaller scale
attacks were also initiated in Spanish Sahara. In a blunt November 26
message, Franco's recently appointed Foreign Minister, Fernando María
Castiella, charged that "sovereign Spanish territory" had been attacked
and that the Spanish response would be "rapid and energetic." What
was missing from this message was an acknowledgment that the Spanish
Army had been ill staffed, ill prepared, and ill equipped to defend itself
against what purported to be an ad hoc indigenous army.[24]

This situation put the Franco government in a difficult position.
Morocco's official and disingenuous position was that these attacks were
being undertaken by forces over which it had no control. Mohammed V
and his government disclaimed any responsibility for an aggression that
involved their nationals and emanated from their territory. Concomitantly,
the United States was pressuring Spain to work with Morocco toward a
diplomatic settlement of the latter's irredentist demands. As a negative
incentive to this end, the Eisenhower administration strictly defined what
American military hardware the Spanish could and could not use against
the Liberation Army. While the Spanish public was provided with very
little balanced information about what would be labeled the "Ifni War,"
Franco and his *Africanista* army comrades knew that they could not allow
either the reality or the perception of a Moroccan military victory. Not only
would this call into question the regime's viability—which, after all, was
led by Spain's most illustrious *Africanista*—but it would unalterably
tarnish the glory of the Spanish Army and its legendary *Africanista* officer
corps which had triumphed over the Moroccans in the 1920s. Thus while
most Spaniards, including Franco and his immediate circle, probably had
little desire for a prolonged colonial war, Franco's reaction to the conflict,
as he stated to his cousin, was that "come what comes" Spain was going
to maintain its West Saharan territories. When Mohammed V's son, Muley
Hassan, the future Hassan II, offered to mediate the crisis in exchange for

the recognition of Moroccan sovereignty over Ifni and the Southern Protectorate, Franco rejected this out of hand and, on January 10, 1958, signed an emergency decree which officially made Ifni and Spanish Sahara Spanish provinces.[25]

As during the Rif War of the 1920s, the Spanish chose the inevitable course of uniting with the French in joint military actions against the common enemy. Generals Bourgund and Gómez Zamalloa finalized this collaboration in December 1957 and by January 1958 had agreed to a three-phase military strategy. The first phase had the Spanish undertaking offensive operations in Ifni in late December 1957 using, for the first time, paratroopers. The second and third phases had them aligning with French forces to drive the Liberation Army out of the northern half of Spanish Sahara (January 16–24) and then out of its southern half (February 20–24). The French committed 5,000 troops to this effort, a considerable quantity of artillery and supplies, and a squadron of fifty planes that not only strafed and bombed the enemy but also employed a new weapon against them—napalm. By early February, the Spanish had over 14,500 troops in Ifni and the Sahara. In the process of this buildup, the Spanish were circumscribed by logistical problems and insufficient or antiquated equipment. They lacked adequate harbor and airport facilities in Sidi Ifni and Spanish Sahara to handle sufficient shipments of equipment and supplies. Their weaponry and equipment were also in some cases inadequate. Most Spanish rifles dated from the early 1940s. Spanish aircraft was Civil War vintage: Junkers-52 for transport and Heinkels-111 and Messerschmitts Bf-109 for offensive operations. Naval transports were leftovers from the 1920s and 1930s. The French were especially critical of Spanish preparedness and logistics. In some instances, they noted that the Spanish lacked functioning tanks; had not armor-plated their vehicles, trucks, and ambulances; had inadequate radio transmission with their aircraft and ground forces; and failed to supply their troops with sufficient ammunition and appropriate desert uniforms and footwear, acceptable rations, and even goggles to protect them from the sun and the fierce desert winds.[26]

Despite these shortcomings, the joint Spanish-French operations were ultimately successful. The Liberation Army was soundly defeated and forced back into Morocco. Their dream of a successful guerrilla war to incorporate French and Spanish West Africa into Greater Morocco encountered the realities of modern warfare and the difficult Saharan environment. The combined Spanish-French forces were simply too numerous and advanced in terms of military technology, airpower, and maneuverability to defeat. Further, the natural obstacles of distance, topography, and climate; an indigenous nomadic population that was mostly unsympathetic to their cause; and the lack of significant urban centers to mount a disabling terrorist campaign all worked against the Liberation Army's operations. Nonetheless, Morocco did realize a territorial benefit from this campaign. Between March 31 and April 1, 1958, the Spanish and Moroccan foreign ministers conducted secret negotiations in Cintra Bay south of Villa Cisneros on the Saharan coast during which Spain agreed to return the Southern Protectorate—the Tekna Zone—to Morocco in exchange for controlling the activities of the Liberation Army and the recognition of Spain's Saharan rights. Furthermore, Spain recognized Moroccan eminence in Ifni by abandoning most of the enclave and pulling its administrative and military functions into Sidi Ifni. Eleven years later in the Fez Treaty of January 4, 1969, Spain ceded the truncated and increasingly expensive enclave to the Moroccans in exchange for a fishing agreement.[27]

In the mid-1960s, Spain's remaining colonial possessions, Equatorial Guinea and Spanish Sahara, while not the epicenter of international attention, were from time to time the focus of United Nations interest and calls for independence. In terms of military significance, Equatorial Guinea was of secondary importance. It included the islands of Fernando Poo, Annobon, Corisco, and the more substantial mainland territory of Río Muni. Equatorial Guinea was noted for its robust economy based on cocoa and hardwood production, its internal tranquility, and the lack of irredentist claims against it. According to data that the Spanish provided the United Nations in the early 1960s, the colony maintained a combined *Guardia Civil* and indigenous police force of some 14,000 men. As the Spanish gradually acceded to UN and international pressure to move Equatorial Guinea toward independence after 1965, the issues they encountered had more to do with local ethnic and political rivalries than with anything that required a significant military presence. Unlike other cases of decolonization, armed militia groups either inside or outside the colony simply did not exist. This allowed the Spanish to adopt the British approach to decolonization. In 1963, they granted autonomy status to the colony, which permitted the development of a number of political parties. In late 1967 and early 1968, they organized and hosted two constitutional conferences in Madrid for these political factions who, after much squabbling, crafted a constitution. Independence was eventually granted on October 12, 1968, and Francisco Macías Nguema, a mid-level bureaucrat in the Spanish colonial administration, was elected the first president. Within a year he created one of the most horrific dictatorships in sub-Saharan Africa compelling the Spanish in March 1969 to evacuate some 7,000 of their nationals and *Guardia Civiles* from the former colony in an operation that involved both the Spanish navy and air force.[28]

The decolonization of Spanish Sahara was a more complex affair that eventually placed the Spanish military at the center of a domestic and international crisis. With the defeat of the Liberation Army in 1958, the colony reverted once again to a state of quiescence remaining, from the Francoist viewpoint, "as much a territory of Spain as the province of

Cuenca."[29] At the same time, the colony was modernized and urbanized by three noteworthy events during the early 1960s. The first was the severe drought of 1959–60 which decimated at least 60% of the area's livestock, accelerating the urbanization of the nomadic population. The second was the Spanish exploitation of extensive phosphate reserves in Bu Craa in the north of the colony which provided significant indigenous employment and further undermined the nomadic lifestyle. The third was the expansion of public works undertaken, as in the Spanish Moroccan case, by military personnel. The 1960s witnessed, for example, the construction of 105 elementary schools, two upper-level trade schools, two new hospitals and twenty dispensaries, and over 5,000 kilometers of paved roads and the construction of three new seaports and significant airport expansions in Spanish Sahara's capital, El Aaiún, and Villa Cisneros.[30]

With urbanization came increased politicization of the Saharawi population that Spain attempted to channel in the mid-1960s into the *Djemaa*, a conservative, traditional consultative assembly that was closely monitored by the Army and the colonial bureaucracy. Saharan politicization took a more activist turn in the late 1960s and early 1970s, stimulated ironically by better-educated Saharawi youth and by the increasing interest of the United Nations and the developing world, especially the three North African countries of Morocco, Mauritania, and Algeria. The most notable manifestation of this increased politicization was the organization of a shadowy nationalist movement in the late 1960s which organized a pro-independence demonstration in El Aaiún in June 1970. This was harshly suppressed by the Spanish Army resulting in the death of three Saharawis and the arrest of hundreds more. This event was one factor in stimulating the founding of the *Frente Popular para la Liberación de Seguia el-Hamra y Rio de Oro (Polisario)* by a small group of left-leaning Saharawi university students in May 1973. Supported increasingly by a majority of the Saharawi population, Algeria, and eventually Muammer al-Gaddafi's Libya, the *Polisario's* primary objective was the creation of an independent Saharan Arab Democratic Republic.

In pursuit of this goal, the *Polisario* organized a series of small-scale guerrilla attacks against Spanish military outposts and other political and economic targets. Over the next two years these attacks, usually undertaken at night, increased appreciably. The most spectacular occurred on October 26, 1974, when the *Polisario* sabotaged two conveyor belt control stations of the Fosbucrá company that transported phosphates from the Bu Craa mines to the coast. On May 10, 1975, in another notable incident, units of the Saharan *Tropas Nomadas* mutinied taking fifteen Spanish officers and soldiers hostage and joining the *Polisario* with their arms and equipment.[31] Given the increased level of *Polisario* activity and bowing to repeated UN calls for Saharan independence, in July–August 1974 the Franco government formally announced plans for granting real internal autonomy to the Saharawi people and scheduling an independence referendum in Spanish Sahara. These were to be the first steps in a measured Spanish exit from the colony, which would, it was assumed, ensure Spanish political and economic preeminence in the area.

Despite their recent calls and support for Saharan self-determination in September 1970, the Moroccan and Mauritanian governments categorically opposed the Spanish plans. Morocco, in particular, harkened back to its "Greater Morocco" policy. In a August 20, 1975, speech Moroccan King Hassan II rejected the concept of a popular Saharan referendum that included an independence option and pledged that Morocco would "liberate its Sahara region, whatever the price."[32] At the same time, Spanish Foreign Minister, Pedro Cortina y Mauri met with *Polisario* representatives in Algiers to start the process of transferring Saharan sovereignty to the Saharawis.

In mid-1975, the Spanish military forces in the colony were caught between a radicalized and intransigent *Polisario* that was totally committed to a fully independent Sahara, and a determined Morocco, and a more reluctant Mauritania, which claimed unequal portions of the Spanish colony as their own. Added to the external challenges, the recently appointed Spanish Saharan governor, General Federico Gómez de Salazar, also faced a major crisis in Spain. On October 17, 1975, Francisco Franco began his long final illness, which was to last more than a month. With Franco incapacitated and factions within his last government in fundamental disagreement over what course to follow in Spanish Sahara, Gómez de Salazar's dilemma was whether to deal with the *Polisario* in terms of an eventual transfer of political authority or to focus on placing his force of 5,000 elite legionnaires and 16,000 combined regular Army and indigenous troops on offensive alert against 20,000 Moroccan troops that Hassan had now stationed on Morocco's southern border. In this instance not only were many Spanish lives in potential jeopardy but also the reputation of the Spanish Army. Not since the Moroccan independence crisis in early 1956 and the Ifni War of 1957–58 had the Spanish military faced such a predicament. Gómez de Salazar started the sensible process of withdrawing his troops from small outlying posts and focusing them on Spanish Sahara's urban settlements and its northern border with Morocco. And in *Operación Golondrina* on November 3, 1975, his forces also assisted in the compulsory evacuation of all Spanish civilians from the colony.[33]

Hassan brought the crisis to a climax on November 6, 1975, by rejecting the UN and International Court of Justice mandates for Saharan self-determination and ordering the so-called "Green March" of 350,000 "peaceful civilians" a few kilometers into Spanish Morocco.[34] This piece of political theatre forced Spain's hand, and with Franco at the point of death, the Arias Navarro Cabinet acquiesced to the Moroccan threat and

agreed to negotiate the colony's status with the Moroccans and Maurita-
nians. These negotiations took place in Madrid, November 12–14, 1975,
and resulted in the "Madrid Accords" in which Spain agreed to transfer
"all responsibilities and powers," but not sovereignty, in Spanish Sahara
to Morocco and Mauritania. By January 12, 1976, Spain withdrew the last
of its troops from El Aaiún and on February 26, 1976, officially ended its
administration in the former colony.[35]

Conclusion

With the exception of Equatorial Guinea, the Spanish Army played a
pivotal role in the establishment, pacification, and security of Spain's
twentieth-century colonial empire. Beyond that, it also had key administrative responsibilities, particularly during the Franco era. Either directly
or indirectly, Spanish Army personnel oversaw the day-to-day administration of the protectorates and colonies and had ultimate responsibility
for managing a variety of public works and developmental projects. While
the Spanish Army was not entirely unfamiliar with such responsibilities,
their degree of involvement was perhaps heightened by a combination of
deep-rooted paternalism (the so-called *Africanista* ethos), increased
government investment in the colonies, and a Francoist predisposition
that colonial administration, at least in Spain's North African territories,
be mainly a military responsibility.

The Spanish Army's role in the decolonization process was perhaps
equally as complex. Not only did Army leaders such as García Valiño,
Gómez Zamalloa, and Gómez de Salazar have to deal with rapidly changing events in the field, but they also had to be aware of policy shifts and/
or lack of policy emanating from Madrid. The Franco regime's strategies
in the decolonization process were not always clear and direct. In fact,
they were invariably premised on a variety of geopolitical issues and
pressures that did not necessarily place military considerations in the
forefront. Further, until the late 1960s, Spain's colonial forces seemed to
be consistently shortchanged in terms of equipment, supplies, logistical
support, and training. This was especially the case during the Ifni War of
1957–58. That the Spanish Army sustained only 198 deaths and 654
additional causalities in that combat had probably more to do with the
professionalism of local commanders and French assistance than with
the support the troops received from Madrid.[36]

CHAPTER **8**

Rejoining Europe:
From Isolation to Integration, 1945–2006

Kenneth W. Estes and José M. Serrano

Upon the end of World War II in Europe, the Spanish armed forces faced enormous difficulties in strategic position, resources, organization, and modernization that for the most part remained well beyond their capacity to correct. Strategically, Spain faced isolation at least as grave as that of the war, in which Spain had exceeded a strictly neutral position in favor of a "nonbelligerency" tilted toward the Axis powers, Germany and Italy. As a result, Spain already faced the prospect of sanctions in the newly founded United Nations (spurred by a naturally hostile USSR), a dearth of allies of any sort, a growing nuisance in the form of Franco-Spanish resistance fighters crossing the Pyrenees, and severe problems of a backward and obsolete military establishment.[1]

Postwar Spain thus remained a pariah state in Europe and maintained conscription and extensive defenses into the 1990s, although any invasion threat faded with the coming of the Cold War. The army fought the last insurrections in North Africa and departed its last African colony in 1975.

Spanish forces modernized in the 1950s with military assistance from the United States in return for bases and garrison privileges, and again in the 1960s with the beginning of the Spanish economic recovery. NATO membership in 1982 introduced the last phase, by which Spain converted to a modern, all-professional force by the turn of the century. The army has trimmed down to a mechanized division, aviation squadrons, and several handy rapid deployment brigades; the air force has squadrons of interceptors and fighter-bombers with supporting echelons; and the navy maintains modern sea control, minesweeping, and amphibious and submarine squadrons. Spain has participated actively in interventions and peacekeeping actions of NATO, the United Nations, and the Western European Union since 1991.

For this important period, we assess the military establishment's development in terms of several major themes:

1. The threat, resources, and political-diplomatic position
2. Strategy, force structure, and organization
3. Personnel, defense spending, and other administrative issues
4. Impacts of diplomacy, military alliances
5. Army, Navy, and Air Force issues
6. Development of new arms and capabilities

Post–World War II, 1945–54

France closed the Pyrenees border temporarily in June 1945 and definitely on March 1, 1946. Although the dangers of outright invasion by the victors of World War II subsided, the strategic priority for Spain clearly remained in the defense of the Peninsula, with colonial affairs a distant second. The defense of the peninsula fell mainly upon the Spanish Army, for the air and naval services remained too weak and obsolete after the tumult of the Civil War and Spain continued to lack resources for modernization and other reforms. The army thus reinforced its existing coast defense arm, maintained a large conscript (18–24 month service) force of mostly foot infantry formations, and expanded its antiaircraft artillery arm.

Spain already had many coastal defense sectors, chiefly ports, featuring powerful coast defense artillery works, topped by eighteen 15-inch and fifty-two 6-inch Vickers pattern guns purchased and installed in the 1930s, augmenting older guns dating from the turn of the century. After the Civil War, these were reinforced with another sixteen 12-inch cannon salvaged from battleships lost in 1923 and 1937, the last being installed in the 1950s at Mallorca and on the Straits. Light antiaircraft guns of various wartime marks augmented the 4-inch antiaircraft guns (forty-eight installed). Although most works were closed in the 1990s, several remained operational and the last 15-inch training shoot took place in 2007. Two coast defense forts used their fire control equipment to track and report the advancing oil slick from the tanker *Prestige* in November 2002.[2] On the landward defenses, a comparable effort consisted of several thousand blockhouses and related installations incorporated in Line P across the Pyrenees mountains. This series of numerous minor works ranks as both the last great belt of fortifications of World War II and the first of the postwar period.[3]

Spain already was under attack in a minor way at wars' end, as Spanish communists and anarchists, many being members of the French *Maquis,* attempted their own version of the 1944 liberation across the Pyrenees.

The Spanish Republicans fighting on the side of the Allied forces during World War II may have exceeded 30,000 men in total, including 10,000–15,000 in the French Resistance. The first incursions into Navarre and Basque regions gained little support but a major effort at Vall d'Aran aimed at Lerida may have totaled 4,000 guerrilla fighters. This incursion required the intervention of military as well as police forces, and General José Moscardó, the military governor of Barcelona, lent his prestige to the effort. Most of these guerillas fled back to France, but numbers remained in the mountains and the interior, where anarchist bands also roamed as late as 1952, with some isolated incidents extending to 1963. Atrocities committed by both sides recalled the Civil War and some banditry typical of earlier epochs also occurred. The Spanish government declared an official end to the Guerrilla War in 1949. By then, the last efforts of the USSR to rally support in the UN Security Council against the Franco regime had failed and France reopened her border with Spain on February 10, 1948.[4]

World War II put paid to expansion and modernization plans for the forces, as the war soon overtaxed the economies of the powers that could supply the necessary know-how and materials, leaving only the very inadequate indigenous industry to try to take up the slack. The continuing crisis meant for Spain that manning levels for the Army had to be kept high, though that was eased by an overabundance of officers as a result of the war (academies were set up to incorporate in the regular army the provisional officers that fed the Nationalist army lower ranks) and by incorporating members of the former Republican army that were of military age. Since materiel could not be renewed, the armed forces as a whole were condemned to progressive obsolescence, with weapons being repaired and used until they were so worn out that they had to be scrapped.

The lack of a technological base meant that little got beyond the drawing table and when it did it suffered from chronic unreliability to the point of being rendered useless. Aircraft produced under license from Germany stagnated for lack of engines when the local alternatives failed. Warships had to make do with technologies dating to World War I. A typical attempt to take account of new forms of warfare, such as the conversion of light cruiser *Mendez Nuñez* into an antiaircraft cruiser, failed when the lack of suitable fire directors rendered it useless. More critical than that was the shortage of fuel, which left much of the air force on the ground during 1943 and 1944 with deleterious effects on training and operational readiness. Fuel supplies remained controlled by the Allies and also served as a powerful diplomatic weapon influencing the Franco regime.

The postwar Spanish Army remained as reorganized in 1943. A general reserve contained most of the modern equipment and the rest remained a foot infantry and artillery force largely unchanged since the Civil War.

Integrated infantry–artillery units were raised to defend the naval bases at Bilbao, El Ferrol (del Caudillo), Vigo, Cádiz, and Cartagena. In 1945, the army included some 250,000 men, 25,000 NCOs, and 26,000 officers, organized in nine military regions and ten army corps that contained the major formations: one armored division, one cavalry division, twelve infantry divisions, four mountain divisions, twenty-five separate infantry regiments, and eight cavalry regiments (two motorized).

By the end of World War II, the Spanish air force could only line up among its eight fighter and seven bomber regiments:

- 125 Fiat CR.32
- 32 early Messerschmitt Bf-109 (11 B, the rest E models)
- 27 Polikarpov I-16
- 15 Messerschmitt Bf-109F
- 13 Polikarpov I-15 (plus five used for spares)
- 9 Heinkel He-112E
- 5 Fiat G.50

With 4,000 officers and 31,000 enlisted men, it briefly occupied a post as the second largest service.

The Navy fared just as poorly as it had added by the end of the war only two mine laying sloops, one ex-German U-boat (damaged, not operational until 1947), and six motor torpedo boats, German S-types bought in 1943. Many older units were relegated to service as floating schools and other hulks. The existing six cruisers, twenty destroyers, and six submarines could only be characterized as dilapidated. Several warships, including an entire class of destroyers, remained on the ways many years before they could be completed with modern equipment. The weak personnel establishment of 2,600 officers and 23,000 enlisted men reflected the ravages of Civil War purges and later decay.[5]

Postwar diplomatic isolation eclipsed the limited collaboration enjoyed with the Western Allies during the war, ensuring another decade of stagnation for the armed forces. Some surplus equipment, such as antiaircraft artillery and associated fire control equipment, was rounded up from the burgeoning international used arms market, but these provided only stopgaps in an increasingly obsolete force. Licenses for construction of German equipment obtained during the war continued in use, but these constituted mere stopgap measures in the losing struggle against obsolescence.

Materiel was used until it fell apart, and then was used for spares while the officer corps was isolated from technological and doctrinal developments elsewhere, including technologies that were becoming as commonplace as radar or reliable radios. In spite of this, the professional journals copied articles from foreign publications, and developments out-side of Spain were given at least some attention. It was not until 1953, however, with the signature of the cooperation agreements with the United States that development of the armed forces resumed, with new weaponry, equipment, and doctrine being received and with moderniza-tion programs being set up for whatever remained. One notes that these agreements did not solve all problems, as they came with significant strings in relation to the use of the new weapons, including the prohibition of using them in colonial wars. Not only that but also the equipment ceded by the United States was eminently defensive—F-86 fighters, *Fletcher* class destroyers, and antiaircraft guns—being of limited use for the kind of warfare that loomed on the horizon. Still, the 1953–54 agreements provoked a significant modernization of the armed forces incorporating all the lessons learned in World War II and the Korean War as well as introducing electronics and doctrines for their use.

Of no small importance to Spain was the huge number of officers retained on active duty during the emergency years of World War II, including almost 11,000 new subalterns. The "bubble" of officers thus cre-ated, augmented by over 200–300 new cadets admitted annually to the General Military Academy through the 1970s, placed a heavy personnel burden on governments well after the demise of General Francisco Franco in rationalizing the force.[6]

Initial Modernization and Alliance Politics, 1954–65

Beginning with the signing in Madrid of the U.S.-Spanish Mutual Defense Agreement of September 26, 1953, a series of supplementary accords extended U.S. military assistance to Spain and conceded base rights to the naval base and air station at Rota (near Cádiz) and air force bases at Morón de la Frontera (near Seville), Torrejón de Ardóz (Madrid), and Zaragoza, with attendant extraterritoriality and status of forces agree-ments for U.S. personnel stationed there and elsewhere in Spain (such as radar sites, communications stations, a naval support center at Cartagena, and a seismic survey site at Sonseca). The United States undertook con-struction of these facilities as well as a petroleum pipeline connecting the naval petroleum receiving depot and the air force bases. The United States gave up extraterritoriality in 1970, but the U.S. forces remained as tenants of the Spanish bases with little change until 1988.

The American use of Spanish bases never matched the original inten-tion, which was to place bombers of SAC (Strategic Air Command) within range of the USSR in the event of a thermonuclear war. SAC's 65th Air Division departed Spain in 1960, and the air force facilities devolved upon the tactical 16th Air Force in support of NATO air training and deploy-ments. The naval base at Rota became a base for U.S. ballistic missile submarines operating in the Eastern Atlantic and a major support facility for the U.S. Sixth Fleet in the Mediterranean. In addition to outright military assistance and bilateral training benefits, the U.S. forces also engaged the Spanish defense industry, first to maintain F-102 air defense fighters stationed in Spain, Germany, and the Netherlands. CASA has continued to work such contracts almost to the present day. Similar agreements affected Spanish industry through ship, aircraft engine, and automotive maintenance activities.

With American assistance, the reforming of Spanish forces gained momentum. Additional bilateral cooperation and exercises with other NATO countries such as Portugal, France, and Great Britain chiefly benefited the air and naval services, although the army experienced a "French" period in the 1960–80s. The U.S.-built air defense command system, manned largely by Spaniards, integrated into the NATO system, a typical example of ad hoc NATO collaboration that Spain began to enjoy. Long before its incorporation into NATO, Spain had become a de facto member of the alliance.

The Spanish reorganization and reforms had begun before the treaty and their later appearance sometimes gave a false effect of deep American influence. The army regrouped its mechanized cavalry into five brigades, formed its first battalion (*bandera*) of paratroops, and began to form new communications support units. In 1958, under the "Barroso Reform," the older corps headquarters and four of the eighteen divisions disappeared.

One clear example of U.S. influence did appear at this juncture. In 1958, three divisions converted to the new U.S. "Pentomic" organization with evaluation exercises in the following year. The Barroso program anticipated another five divisions to be so transformed, but only after the first three had been reequipped. The end of the Barroso reform came with the communication in 1962 from the military attaché at Washington that the U.S. Army was abandoning the pentomic organization. In 1963, the divisions had been reset, but the way had been paved for the 1965 reform and the beginnings of the "French" period. The general reserve reformed with the armored division, a mechanized division, and an airborne regiment (*agrupación*), and three new corps headquarters emerged each with a base of a field artillery brigade; an engineer regiment; a communications regiment; and groups of transport, medical, and support units. Army level units included machine gun regiments, antitank battalions, special operations companies (the first to be organized), and artillery rocket and antiaircraft regiments.[7]

The 1965 reorganization "Plan Menéndez Tolosa" governed the force structure until 1984, reflecting new French influences. The army divided into FII (Forces of Immediate Intervention) and FDOT (Forces for Territorial Operational Defense).[8]

Although the duties of the Army of Africa fell considerably when Spain gave up its Protectorate in Morocco and later Tangier, it maintained garrisons in the two Spanish cities of Ceuta and Melilla and continued its colonial rule in Ifni and Sahara. The Spanish Legion had returned entirely to North African garrisons after the Civil War with a peacetime establishment of three *tercios* (regiments) stationed at Ceuta, Melilla, and Larache with a total of eleven *banderas*, down from its wartime peak of eighteen *banderas* and a regimental tank group. The Legion Inspectorate was located at Ceuta, with the commander of the Army of Morocco, a lieutenant general, as the titular head. In late 1943, the three *tercios* received traditional names associated with the heyday of Spanish arms of the sixteenth century, in order: "Gran Capitán" (Gonzalo de Córdoba), "Duque de Alba," and "Don Juan de Austria." In 1950, the Legion staff became a sub-inspectorate and a 4th *Tercio* "Alejandro Farnesio" stood up. The 3rd and 4th *Tercios* deployed to Sahara in 1958 and for the second time the legion established light tank units, one company for each Saharan *Tercio*, and added organic artillery for the first time in the form of two air-transportable batteries. Between nine and thirteen *banderas* operated in North Africa and Spanish Sahara through the end of the Spanish colonial era in 1975. A legionnaire and his platoon sergeant posthumously earned the Legion's (and Spain's) last two Laureate Crosses of St. Ferdinand in a single action in 1958.[9]

As Spain ended her colonial presence in North Africa, the Legion disbanded its tank and artillery units and withdrew to its old garrisons in Ceuta and Melilla, and new bases on the island of Fuerteventura in the Canary archipelago, and in the peninsula city of Ronda. The Legion's inspectorate and recruiting office first located in Leganés, on the outskirts of Madrid, later moved to Málaga. Foreign recruitment ended in 1986, leaving only 109 foreign citizens still in service with the Legion. Despite its heritage as a foreign legion, the Spanish Legion only recruited 17.5% of its ranks from foreigners in its first decade of existence, over half of these hailing from Portugal, Germany, and Cuba.[10]

The garrisons of Ceuta and Melilla each received not only their usual *tercio* of legionnaires but also two regimental groups of *Regulares*, a light cavalry group, mixed regiments of artillery (field, antiair, and coastal), engineers, and infantry and various support groups.

The end of colonial rule in Morocco also allowed the 38,000-man air force to discard the obsolete aircraft it retained there because of restrictions on use of U.S. materiel. The two ground support fighter squadrons of HA-1112-MIL ("Buchón," a Bf-109G license-built after the war) and two medium bomber and reconnaissance squadrons with CASA 2.111-D (He-111H-16, also postwar license built) left active service in 1965 in favor of the F-86F and F-5 fighter-bombers, refurbished and license built, respectively, by CASA. However, the venerable Junkers 52 (CASA 352L) transports and Dornier Do-24 flying boat continued to soldier on, the latter until 1970 with the air-sea rescue service. The air force operated its F-86s as Air Defense Command interceptors in concert with U.S. counterparts beginning in 1956.

The Spanish Navy continued to operate its obsolete prewar ships, while adding U.S. ships generally dedicated to antisubmarine warfare. Thus, alongside the 1936 flagship, heavy cruiser *Canary,* one found twenty-nine destroyers and frigates, four submarines, and auxiliaries, including two LSTs from France and two LCTs from the United Kingdom. Personnel totaled 42,000 men including 10,000 naval infantry. Although heavily committed to supporting the colonial war in Ifni-Sahara, the navy continued to reconfigure itself for antisubmarine warfare, a mission for which it lacked any previous experience.[11]

Doldrums of the Regime, 1965–75

In the last decade of the Franco regime, Spanish military strategy began to evolve beyond territorial defense as a priority and consider problems posed by reunified and independent Morocco and its potential threat to the remaining Spanish overseas territory in North Africa. In addition, the position of Spain in the Cold War became somewhat less ambiguous with the drawdown of French and British naval forces from the Mediterranean, leaving the Spanish navy and supporting forces clearly in the front rank of navies facing the burgeoning Soviet navy and potential client states in the Mediterranean. Resources remained slim and the distraction of a new internal threat of insurrectionist groups such as the Basque Nationalist ETA and the anarchistic GRAPO further stressed the military establishment at a delicate and rather lackluster period of Spanish history. The January 17, 1966, "Palomares Incident" further clouded the period when a U.S. B-52 bomber crashed near the coast with its payload of four hydrogen bombs, accompanied by some plutonium contamination and requiring an extensive deep surveillance search in the sea to recover the last bomb. The United States agreed not to fly such armed missions in the future over Spanish territory.

The Army's Menéndez Toloso reform lasted for twenty years, until superseded in 1983 by the META plan. The immediate intervention forces were to be available for action in the shortest time possible at any point of the national territory, including the islands and colonies. These formed as parts of a mechanized army corps of one armored, one mechanized, and one motorized division, one mechanized cavalry brigade and corps troops of communications, artillery, aviation, and engineers in at least regimental strength. They were to receive the latest equipment, be fully motorized, and be at least at 70% strength in the higher levels and fully manned at brigade and below level.

The components of the DOT, chiefly an infantry brigade per region but also including the two mountain divisions and a high mountain brigade, reported to the captain general or military governor of each military region, with the mission of providing cover for the deployment of the FII, defending the borders and coasts, counterinsurgency warfare, defending critical points, and fighting off subversion, as well as supporting civil power. In the event of a successful invasion of Spanish territory, they would provide the nucleus of guerrilla forces. The DOT were not intended for deployment beyond their military region, a fact underlined by having all support and logistic functions provided by the rear services of each region: logistic groups, regional transportation companies, and ordnance parks and depots. In peacetime, they were to be at 40–50% strength, with the exception of special units deployed to Africa, which were to be kept at full strength. Armament and materiel were to be provided by the armament programs developed under the aegis of Law 85/65; however, budget limitations meant that in reality its equipment frequently was limited to hand-me-downs from first-line units.

However, at the same time, Law 85/65 ordered the minimization of defense expenditures by accepting multiyear programs but was critical in creating the bases of the modern national defense industry that would eventually provide most materiel at the turn of the century. The most important programs were[12]

- Building small arms locally, centered on the CETME assault rifle and the license-built MG-3 machine gun, as well as the Star submachine guns of the Z-45/70 series and Astra and Llama handguns.
- Acquisition of self-propelled artillery in the United States and the patent to build the Bofors 40/70 AA gun.
- Building locally a medium tank under license, the French AMX-30 being selected.
- Modernizing the tank park of American origin updating the vehicles to their latest versions.
- Design and production of an indigenous Armored Personnel Carrier and a Cavalry Reconnaissance Vehicle, which eventually materialized in the BMR-600 and the VEC, respectively.
- Design and production of an indigenous shipboard Air Defense system, which eventually became the multibarrel Meroka automatic cannon.
- Replacement of U.S. automotive equipment by locally built vehicles, the Land Rover 88 and 109, license built by Santana, and the Pegaso 3045 and 3055.
- Construction of 3,500-ton guided missile frigates of the U.S. *Knox* class under license as the five-ship *Baleares* class.
- Revitalization of national submarine construction with the licensing of the *Daphné* class from France.

- Refurbishment of the latest fighters of the U.S. F-104 and F-4 types and French Mirage F-1 series fighters for Spanish service.
- Design and construction of the C.101EB Aviojet trainer.

Helicopters came into general use in Spain, and in 1967, the World War II light aircraft carrier *Cabot* was loaned to Spain, converted to a sale in 1972. Until 1989, carrier *Dedalo* operated as the new fleet flagship and symbol of the resurgence of the Spanish Navy, equipped with several marks of anti-submarine and troops transport helicopters. The army's helicopter force (FAMET) began as a helicopter company in the armored division in 1965, succeeded by a battalion the next year and became an army branch in 1973.

The navy also benefited from the acquisition of several amphibious ships from the United States—two attack transports in 1964–65, three tank landing ships and a dock landing ship in 1971–72, and two replacement attack transports in 1980. Together with a revitalized minesweeper force, the Spanish Navy now disposed of two escort groups, an amphibious assault group, a mine warfare group, and a submarine group, having built four *Daphné* class submarines in 1973–75.

The end of this period saw a partial modernization of the Spanish Air Force, with thirty-six F-4C transferred from the USAF to Spain in 1971 and four more with four reconnaissance types supplied in 1978. The ever-thirsty F-4s were accompanied by acquisition of the first aerial tankers, the first being surplus KC-97L aircraft. Spain had acquired as well an interceptor squadron of F-104G Starfighters from Holland in 1965, and the extraordinary accomplishment of operating these last without loss through their 1972 retirement established the air force as a first-line professional force.

Restoration at Home and in Europe, 1975–90

The military restoration after the death of General Franco fell upon the shoulders of President Adolfo Suárez and his army chief of staff, Lieutenant General Manuel Gutiérrez Mellado. The reforms posed a striking counterpoint to the previous moribund decade as well as traditional Spanish military influence upon the state. Gone were the three service ministries and a new civilian-led defense ministry erected in substitution, supported by a subordinate armed forces defense chief and general staff. The Constitution of 1978 provided for the forces and the organic laws governing them as bases for their organization, recruitment, and financing.

In alliance politics, the relationship with the United States became more balanced and Spain applied for NATO membership. The latter achieved in 1982, the new Socialist government deferred full operational participation, in the then-current French style, but in the end only for a period of six years. The end of the Cold War and Spain's entry into the European Union rendered this doctrine obsolete, and full integration into NATO began in May 1990. By that time, the perceived military dependency upon the United States had largely dissipated, achieving another goal of the Socialist government.

The forces themselves shrank under the needs of modernization. The army's 1983 modernization plan (META) retained most of the 1960s establishment, but created functional and more effective agencies and commands, arrayed in a hierarchy of command, operating forces, and supporting echelons. Only six administrative military governors remained and 116 units disappeared as the army fell to half its previous strength. Hopes that such reductions would free funds for adequate materiel failed to materialize, however. Long before NATO membership was achieved, the Spanish government had issued a requirement for a new fighter/attack aircraft that would replace its fleet of U.S. F-4 and F-5 and French F-1 aircraft. Initially offered sale of the F-16 by the United States, the navy's F-18 was added later and its twin-engine reliability proved decisive because of the Spanish air force requirements for distant over-water operations. Spain selected the F-18 and placed an initial order for seventy-two aircraft, the largest Spanish foreign purchase order to date.

As if by compensation, the Spanish navy was authorized the purchase of five F-80-type missile frigates, Spanish-built versions of the U.S. *Perry* class, as well as four *Agosto* class submarines, built under French license in Cartagena. The long desired replacement for *Dédalo* came in approval of a new type light carrier, built domestically from U.S. plans originally conceived for its abortive sea control ship. With the delivery of the new flagship *Principe de Asturias*, the navy received its most expensive acquisition in history and Spanish shipbuilding achieved a significant benchmark. A near sister ship was built for Thailand in 1997.

Ironically, Spain in the moment of reconstruction had to bear a brief revival of the old Spanish military revolt, the *Pronunciamiento*. The pending restoration of the monarchy had alienated certain small elements of the forces, which frequently had to discipline an occasional officer or two for expansive behavior or demonstration. The increasing incidence of labor unrest, the appearance of a political opposition, and a new outbreak of terrorism or banditry did not sit well with the officer corps in general. The officers on these margins suffered more, however, as Spain established a new constitutional monarchy, passed liberal laws (including the legalization of the Communist Party), and saw a Socialist government nearing power in 1980. This galvanized officers of the Tejero Faction on February 23, 1981, to take the parliament hostage at pistol point with the aid of over 100 soldiers, whereupon part of the garrisons in Madrid and Valencia began to occupy checkpoints in city streets; although only in Valencia did this activity enter public view. No general rising, this demonstration was foiled because of the continuing loyalty of most regional military commanders and the officer corps in general. Once the king had ensured the support of the military governors, other than Valencia's, his orders and a public radio-television announcement brought the affair to an end.

On December 2, 1982, the Socialists finally took power but the armed forces leadership had no further interest in duplicating the spectacle of the already notorious "23-F" plot.[13] The new professionalization and modernization of the Spanish military establishment thus took a curious benchmark from this abortive plot, followed soon by formal entry into NATO and increasing self-confidence in its missions, organization, and status a world apart from that of the Civil War and colonial policing. This new epoch for the Spanish forces reflected nowhere better than in the renewal of the defense cooperation agreement with the United States. Negotiated in 1988, Spain formally requested that U.S. forces vacate Torrejón Air Base, located on the outskirts of the capital and frequent site of incipient public NATO protests. In return, Spain recognized the end of military assistance (which had not impressed most of its military leaders over the previous two decades as particularly generous) and announced that it was prepared to pay its own way in acquisition, services, training, and support. Although the American negotiating team (unprepared in 1988 for what later became a commonplace event for U.S. forces in foreign countries) likely bungled the opportunity to rebase the forces concerned to the idle standby base at Morón, the rest of the changes to the agreement concerned the status of personnel and turnover of radar, seismic, and logistics sites other than at Zaragoza (which the United States abandoned unilaterally in 1994 under its European force reductions), Morón, and Rota, the latter becoming the single most important U.S. tenant activity in Spain to the present day.

Although relations were strained and the U.S. Air Force highly inconvenienced, the surprisingly quick end to the Cold War and the resulting move toward defense cuts by the United States and other NATO members mollified the worst aspects of the new Spanish position, and the latter's support for the 1990–91 Gulf War exceeded all expectations and renewed a spirit of partnership between the two countries. The continuing orders for materiel and training from Spain also served to compensate the downward turn in the U.S. defense industry. In the end, U.S.–Spanish military cooperation continued almost unmolested by the 1988 renewal accord.[14] Spain's defense industry by now produced warships in the submarine, corvette, missile frigate, and light aircraft carrier categories for the navy; produced transport aircraft for the air force; and continued to produce small arms, artillery, and armored and logistical vehicles of all types for the army.

In Step with Europe, 1990–2006

The final decade of the century saw the culmination of reforms and modernization programs that saw Spanish military forces engaged in almost all activities of its alliances, international peacekeeping and humanitarian relief, and the consolidation of organizational trends and requirements of alliance obligations. The defense industrial base demonstrated an unusually robust capacity for native armaments production, innovation, and cooperation that far exceeded the primitive autarky dreams of the old regime. The army continued the trend of the META plan with a 1990 reform plan (RETO), which brought a further reduction of forces by 25% and the retention of a single heavy division, the former armored division "Brunete," converted to a mechanized infantry division. The most effective units composed brigades of airborne, air landing infantry, light infantry, and light armored cavalry grouped with support battalions under a FAR (Rapid Action Force) for use in national and NATO contingencies. Before it was completed, the successor plan for the New Organization of the Terrestrial Army (NORTE) in 1994 continued the reorientation to modern contingencies post–Cold War by arraying the fifteen brigades of combat troops with a reorganized support establishment into commands ready to provide support to the deployments of expeditionary units up to the size of the entire FAR as well as the deployment of a major Force of Maneuver built around the "Brunete" Division, the cavalry regiment and army aviation of the FAMET.

These contingencies now swelled with the introduction of the first major change in the long dormant WEU (West European Union), the defense arm of the European Community (later European Union). The showcase for this change, calculated to energize European capabilities without recourse to NATO and, in particular, the United States, became the Eurocorps in which the Spanish contribution of the "Brunete" (1994) demonstrated a new Spanish presence in European affairs. Building on the Eurocorps formula, the WEU continued the next year with inceptions of EuroFor and EuroMarFor standing forces earmarked by Spain, France, Italy, and Portugal. A Spanish admiral led the standing naval force in the Mediterranean in the first year of its existence.

In addition, the army refurbished its inactive reserve forces to provide a true mobilization capacity built around three infantry and one armored cavalry brigades, plus regiments of field artillery and engineers. Equipment concerns were partly relieved when the United States disposed of a considerable armor and artillery park in Europe, rendered excess by the Conventional Forces Europe Treaty, distributing it free of charge to NATO and other countries. In late 1994, however, Spain decided to acquire 390 Leopard II main battle tanks from Germany, thus advancing to current fourth generation armor. Some fifty-four Leopard 2A4 tanks were leased in 1995 and another fifty-four in 1996. The Spanish defense industry, led by the experienced Santa Bárbara Blindados firm, began deliveries starting in 2003 of license-built Leopard 2A6E tanks in the most expensive army procurement package to date. This program exemplified the key innovation of government "complimentary actions" or collaboration in its financing. The Industry and Energy Ministry signed its guarantee for 244B *pesetas* on December 29, 1999, with Santa Bárbara Blindados. The funds will be disbursed to SBB during the period 1999–2006, with repayment from proceeds during 2007–16. These intra-ministry loans have enabled the Spanish MOD to pursue simultaneous tank, aircraft, and warship purchases otherwise infeasible under current defense appropriations.

Ironically, the first chance for Spanish military action in this decade came in supporting the United States in Spain as part of the UN prosecution against Iraq during 1990–91. So soon after breaking away from further dependence upon U.S. aid in 1988, the Socialist government of President Felipe González proved surprisingly helpful to U.S. forces in Spain. Permission was given to base twenty-two B-52 bombers at Morón and fly their bombing missions against Iraqi forces. Another forty aerial refuelers operated out of Morón and supported these aircraft, and the hundreds of U.S. tactical aircraft ferried through Spain to the Gulf region. When the bombers at Morón began to run out of ordnance, Spanish air force and army aircraft and heavy lift helicopters carried the bombs from storage sites at Torrejón and Zaragoza to maintain the operational tempo. Over 60% of U.S. airlift to the Gulf transited Spanish bases and local commanders stepped up security at the U.S. facilities; Spanish forces deployed ships to the Gulf in 1990 and took over other allied responsibilities in the Mediterranean to free them for deployments. Finally, Spanish air force and army troops deployed to Turkey in mid-1991 as part of Combined Task Force Provide Comfort, a U.S.-led UN mission into Northern Iraq to furnish local security to Iraqi Kurds in wake of the Iraqi defeat in Operation Desert Storm. A reinforced battalion of the Parachute Brigade (586 troops) operated with the U.S. and British forces on the ground, including the U.S. 24th Marine Expeditionary Unit, which had exercised that spring with the Spanish Legion at Almería.[15]

In addition to its commitment to the WEU, the NATO commitments of Spain produced a Land Component Command headquarters for Allied Forces, South located at Camp Retamar, outside of Madrid. Spain also joined the NATO Early Warning and Control group in 1998 and dispatched forces to NATO interventions in Albania, Kosovo, and Afghanistan.

The CSCE (Conference on Security and Cooperation in Europe) concluded its fall 1994 meeting in Budapest with the announcement of a contact group to study methods of cooperation between CSCE member nations and the Mediterranean periphery: Israel, Egypt, Tunisia, Algeria, and Morocco. The European Community held the long awaited Euro-Mediterranean Conference at the ministerial level in Barcelona on November 27–28. Spain first proposed this conference in 1990, but the Gulf War delayed its inception. The conference included in addition to the EC members twelve Mediterranean states, including the littoral states, the Palestinian Autonomy, Cyprus, and Malta. Only Libya remained ostracized from these meetings.

Spanish defense doctrine created a so-called strategic "Axis" drawn along the line Balearic Islands–Straits–Canary Islands in the 1980s, both to orient its planning and to convince allies of the importance of the southern flank. In particular, Spain sought to advise allies of its archipelago responsibilities in both the Atlantic and the Mediterranean and to stress the vital role of the Straits zone, including the Ceuta and Melilla enclaves.

Spanish defense forces undertook developing a joint warfighting doctrine. Cooperation among the three services traditionally had proven nonexistent. However, the replacement of the former service ministries by a modern MOD structure and the demands for modernization of forces and warfighting techniques for national and European defense needs brought joint operations to the forefront. Approved in 1995, the new policy formally charged the chief of the defense staff (JEMAD) with the operational command of the units assigned by the separate services for a mission. The staff exercised this control for years in exercises and simulations, and first put the doctrine into action in the Perejil Island recovery operation of 2002.

The services were ordered each to form "operational commands" suitable for expeditionary service in 1991. The commanders of the *Mandos Operativos* take the character of service component chiefs, each responsible for deploying and tactically directing their units under the command of the JEMAD or a joint deployment headquarters. The Army initially designated its FAR headquarters, the Air Force created its Aerial Operational Command (MOA), and the Navy entrusted its fleet commander (ALFLOT) with these responsibilities. The defense structure changes and force modernization programs fleshed out these and other organizational aims during 1996–2000.

In terms of the military balance, Maghreb nations pose so little offensive threat to Spain and other nearby countries that Spanish Defense Minister Gustavo Suarez Pertierra could assert (1995) "we have no enemies" as the slogan of Spanish defense policy. Reduced tensions in Central Europe, however, contrasted with increased instability in the Mediterranean littoral. Spanish defense policy continued to evolve from the old Francoist policy of peninsular defense and colonial policing to embrace a modern version of territorial defense (mainly air defense and a ground reserve) coupled with modern forces necessary to maintain Spain's status in NATO, the EC, and the UN.

Even in the event of ruptured relations, the Maghreb nations pose very little military threat to Spanish territory. The Spanish Air Force will replace its older U.S.-supplied radars and command and control systems with a modern SIMCA system (Sistema Integrado de Mando y Control Aereo), featuring three-dimensional radars, NATO and AWACS interoperability, and hardened command bunkers at Morón, Torrejón, and Canary Island sites. The NATO AWACS also serves to fill in radar gaps in the south, especially against low-fliers. Fighter squadrons are well exercised in the defense of Spanish airspace, and, with a few deployments from garrison bases—e.g., to the Balearic and Canary Islands—should be capable of handling a level of intrusion in excess of the threat.

Seaward defenses against raiding patrol craft, mines, and submarines remained the primary effort of the Spanish Navy, assisted by P-3C aircraft of the Air Force and Harpoon-armed EF-18 fighters. The light carrier Task Group Alpha, centered on the carrier *Principe de Asturias,* is fully oriented to classic sea control missions. The Mine Warfare Flotilla was transferred from its idyllic base at Palma de Mallorca to the naval base at Cartagena in 1992 mainly so that it could concentrate better on the vital shipping lanes into Cádiz, where 70% of Spanish sea imports arrive. The eight (recently reduced to five) Spanish submarines are kept in technically upgraded condition and exercise frequently in ASW roles. Amphibious potential continued to grow in Task Group Delta with the replacement of older transport ships with two Spanish-built amphibious assault ships and the naval infantry of the *Tercio de la Armada,* composed of a regimental landing team. The amphibious arm would prove essential in the event of a forced evacuation from Maghreb ports or a reinforcement of the Spanish enclave cities. The excellent Spanish Navy combat divers and the special operations companies of the naval infantry can perform hostage rescue actions.

The Army, in the event of increased tensions with the Maghreb, will bear the weight of the defense of the cities of Ceuta and Melilla, garrisoned in peacetime with mixed brigades stiffened by two regiments of the Spanish Legion. The final deliveries of the Spanish-built Leopard 2A6 tanks in 2008 will go to the 3rd Cavalry Regiment "Montesa" and 10th Cavalry Regiment "Alcántara," which form part of the garrisons of Ceuta and Melilla, respectively. This last measure will introduce the Leopard tank to the African continent for the first time and pose a technological advantage vs. Morocco and the other Maghreb countries.[16]

The Conservative government of 1995 planned a 50% professional force by the end of the century, but instead announced the end of conscription by 2002. The end strength authorized but never realized to date for the all-professional force of 2003 was 265 generals, 48,000 officers, and 120,000 enlisted personnel, including a growing proportion of women, fully active in the forces since 1988. The support given by the government to U.S.-led operations against Iraq in 2003 aroused considerable public opposition, both in the initial deployment of forces to protect NATO ally Turkey and the humanitarian missions focused at the port of Umm Qasr at the time of the U.S. invasion. The army brigade deployed in 2004 to peacekeeping and anti-insurgency duties at Ad Diwaniyah was withdrawn with the change of government.[17]

The return of a Socialist government in 2004 ushered in a significant change in the strategic outlook of the Spanish armed forces, exemplified by the National Defense Directive signed on December 30, 2004. The most significant changes introduced the assignments and missions of the armed forces in support of civilian organizations to an unprecedented level, including the setting up of a dedicated unit, the Military Emergency Unit (UME), dedicated to supporting civilian agencies in disasters, but also on day-to-day operations. The other significant change was a reorientation of military operations abroad, focusing on peace missions, but with the following *preconditions* being necessary before commitment of forces:

- Strict respect of international law, recognizing the UN as the organization responsible for international peace and security, and defining force as a last resource.
- Fighting terrorism globally becomes the main priority of operations abroad, assuming all previous compromises with international organizations, namely the European Union, NATO, and the OSCE.
- Finally, all operations abroad will need the approval of the Parliament.

The end of conscription has forced the army to reinvent itself once again, to adapt to an environment where missions outside the national borders become commonplace but where the financial environment places significant limits on both acquisitions and recruitment. For 2006, the Army had a budget of 2,518 million, 68% of which were personnel expenses. The Army budget amounted to 33.5% of the total Defense budget. The troop strength amounted to some 51,000 soldiers, 5,000 of them enlisting during 2005. The redefinition of the threat from conventional to irregular enemies meant that some of the weapon systems being procured were no longer suitable and the acquisition programs would have to be restructured.

The force of maneuver headquarters (FMA) at Valencia monitors all operational organizations capable of rapid reaction and force projection capabilities. To achieve such a broad and demanding mission, it has the best resources available. The units under its command include the

- 1st Mechanized Division "Brunete"
- 10th Mechanized Brigade: three mechanized and one tank battalion
- 11th Mechanized Brigade: three mechanized and one tank battalion

- 12th Armored Brigade: two tank and one mechanized battalion
- 12th Cavalry Regiment "Farnesio"
- 11th Artillery Regiment: two artillery battalions
- 1st Engineer Regiment
- 1st Logistic Group

The FAR include the

- Legion Light Infantry Brigade: two motorized and one air-assault battalions
- Parachute Brigade: three parachute battalions.
- Light Airmobile Brigade: three light infantry battalions
- 8th Light Cavalry Regiment
- 81st Antiaircraft Artillery Regiment
- 1st Mountain Brigade "Aragón": three mountain battalions
- 2nd Cavalry Brigade "Castillejos": with one armored, two light, and three mechanized cavalry battalions

Each brigade also includes an artillery battalion, a sapper company, and a headquarters battalion and may include specialized companies for antiarmor combat, ski and high mountain warfare, etc., while all cavalry regiments are battalion sized.

- The Telecommunications Brigade
- The Intelligence Regiment
- The NBC Regiment
- Special Operations Command
- Field Artillery Command
- Engineering Command
- Army Airmobile Forces

The FMA is therefore able to provide the headquarters for a corps-level organization capable of being used beyond the national borders on short notice, though not all elements are in a high level of readiness. The Operational Logistic Command is charged with providing logistical support to the other force units.

The Air Force

With 22,000 military and 6,000 civilians, of which 10,000 are officers and 7,000 NCOs, and a 2006 budget line of 1,035 million, the smallest component of the armed forces was a balanced force that aimed at achieving a qualitative edge. Its combat units consist of

- 11th Wing at Morón (near Seville), with three squadrons of new Eurofighters (111th and 112th being the operational units, while the 113th was the conversion unit), which aims to achieve complete operational readiness by 2010.
- 12th Wing at Torrejón, with three squadrons of F-18s (121st and 122nd being the fighter and reconnaissance units and 113th the conversion and trial units for the Mid-Life Update).
- 14th Wing at Albacete has three squadrons of modernized Mirage F.1C/E fighters redesignated F.1M, now on the last quarter of their operational life and slated to be replaced by Eurofighters once the 11th Wing is operational.
- 15th Wing at Zaragoza is also equipped with F-18 but only with two squadrons.
- 21st Wing at Morón outfitted in its 22nd Group with five P-3B patrol aircraft for antisubmarine warfare and maritime surveillance.
- 46th Wing in Gando has one squadron of F-18s bought second hand from the United States.

Finally yet importantly are two ground units: the Combat Parachute Sapper Squadron, charged with offensive missions including Forward Air Control and pathfinding, and the Air Defense Artillery Squadron, detailed to protecting air force units deployed abroad from air and ground attack.

The most important programs underway are the acquisition of fifty-four Eurofighters "Typhoon" (with options for another thirty-four), which eventually will become the most expensive Spanish military acquisition in history, the acquisition of twenty-seven A-400 military transports, nine of which were to be equipped as tankers, due to enter service in 2011, and the midlife update for sixty-seven F-18 Hornet fighter-bombers to enable them to serve until 2020.

The Navy

The Spanish Navy of the twenty-first century also aims at achieving a technological edge over its possible opponents, and musters over 11,000 enlisted personnel and draws 1,056 million of the 2006 budget. The navy takes advantage of an excellent relationship with the United States to purchase advanced systems such as the Aegis combat system, the Tomahawk land attack missile, and the SH-60 helicopter, but also has led the other services in establishing a solid national industrial base now producing and exporting advanced ships such as the F-100 air defense frigate and the S-80 submarine (*Nansen* and *Scorpene* class ships being built for Norway and Chile, respectively).

In 2005, the navy could line up one light aircraft carrier, five submarines (though one is scheduled to be retired in 2006), eleven frigates, six minesweepers, four amphibious ships, twelve patrol ships or corvettes, forty aircraft of all classes, and around fifty auxiliary ships, including an underway replenishment ship. In the same vein as the other services, the operational fleet, based at Rota, includes

Fleet Projection Group with the carrier *Principe de Asturias* and the amphibious ships carrying units of the naval infantry *Tercio de Armada* (TEAR). This *Tercio* forms as a brigade-sized formation that combines light infantry (two battalions), mechanized units (a tank company and a mechanized battalion supported by a self-propelled battery), and a special operations company, making it the most versatile unit in the Spanish armed forces.

- 41st Escort Squadron: six F-80 FFG frigates
- 31st Escort Squadron: three F-100 class frigates and two F-70 frigates
- Submarine Squadron: four *Agosta* class and one *Daphné* class submarines
- Aircraft flotilla: with helicopter and AV-8B Harrier squadrons
- Minesweeper flotilla: with six *Segura* class minesweepers
- Fleet replenishment ship *Patiño*

New programs include the Strategic Projection Ship (a large through-deck amphibious assault ship), an additional replenishment unit, two more F-100 frigates, four S-80 advanced diesel submarines, and four Maritime Action Ships (with a possible ten more to follow), as well as lesser units, like the twelve landing craft. The helicopter force is expected to receive twenty NH-90 helicopters, and it is hoped that JSF will be bought to replace the Harriers.[18]

Conclusion

Not surprisingly, the evolution of Spain's military institutions reflected the transitions of the political, social, and economic realities of the postwar era. Certainly, the severe restrictions imposed on the Spanish state prevented any recovery of the armed forces from the depredations of the Civil War and the armed nonbelligerency stance of World War II. Only with the beginnings of postwar foreign trade and financial assistance and the primitive initial recovery of the Spanish economy could any reforms be undertaken. Handicapped then by the political limitations imposed on the Franco regime, the period of decolonization, and the restricted diplomatic options of *Pax Americana* and European politics, Spain eventually reentered the European Community of nations. In certain respects, the armed forces by the 1970s provided precursors for European and international cooperation for Spain in advance of other state functions, but only with the abandonment of the old regime and

embracing of European and international cooperation could the modernization of the Spanish forces be undertaken across the new operational
and technological spectra of warfare. Today, Spanish forces stand in
the first rank of European military powers, participating in all types
of operations as valued partners in peace and conflict.[19]

Appendices

Spanish Defense Budget, Including Ordinary and Extraordinary Budgets (Not Adjusted for Inflation)

Year	Total Budget	Military Ministries	% Spent on Defense
1940	7,161,222,337.29	1,959,198,237.90	27.36%
1941	8,318,801,213.11	1,839,059,381.65	22.11%
1942	7,880,194,669.28	1,908,569,938.16	24.22%
1943	9,456,475,296.41	2,525,525,830.54	26.71%
1944	13,292,690,130.06	4,067,236,103.32	30.60%
1945	13,235,065,791.53	5,341,440,582.74	40.36%
1946	13,239,379,995.61	4,576,658,315.13	34.57%
1947	14,223,254,787.39	4,841,708,896.30	34.04%
1948	15,196,093,593.05	5,105,084,782.01	33.59%
1949	16,782,924,001.50	5,494,258,030.98	32.74%
1950	18,052,138,062.64	5,703,792,664.76	31.60%
1951	19,502,526,431.17	5,912,543,312.71	30.32%
1952	22,762,147,700.51	7,401,677,892.38	32.52%
1953	24,357,131,447.71	7,373,849,875.87	30.27%
1954	26,339,908,110.88	7,505,228,708.26	28.49%
1955	31,955,956,383.93	8,473,763,548.49	26.52%
1956	35,832,671,087.45	9,537,790,960.29	26.62%
1957	43,080,850,284.33	10,952,612,638.28	25.42%
1958	48,004,958,031.92	10,920,171,723.59	22.75%
1959	50,462,072,076.52	11,367,597,249.06	22.53%
1960	55,757,212,341.00	13,598,795,429.00	24.39%
1961	59,149,897,080.00	13,616,258,286.00	23.02%
1962	75,017,934,938.00	17,449,384,688.00	23.26%
1963	89,073,446,932.00	17,839,083,716.00	20.03%
1964	120,966,310,365.00	19,953,204,183.00	16.49%

Source: Juan Luis Coello Lillo, *Buques de la Armada Española, la ayuda Americana y el Programa de Modernizacion* (Madrid: Aldaba Ediciones, 1992), 187; and Juan Luis Coello Lillo, *Buques de la Armada Española, los Años de la Posguerra* (Madrid: Aldaba Ediciones, 1995), 295.

Spanish Defense Budget (Adjusted for inflation)

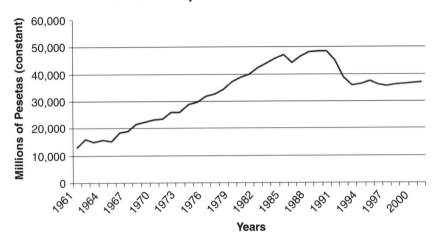

Source: Francisco Pérez Muinelo, *Panorámica Del Presupuesto De Defensa En España, 1946–1995*
(Madrid: Instituto de Cuestiones Internacionales y Política Exterior, Ensayos Incipe n° 15,
1996), 48. Inflation data from INE base: 100=1961.

Missions and Tasks of the Armed Forces

GENERAL MISSIONS	DERIVED MISSIONS	TASKS
TO IMPEDE ANY TYPE OF AGGRESSION AND RESPOND TO IT IF NECESSARY	NATIONAL DEFENCE OPERATIONS	• Surveillance, control and protection of land, sea and air space • Territorial defence • Protection of lines of communication
	OPERATIONS WITHIN THE FRAMEWORK OF THE ATLANTIC ALLIANCE	• Operations within the context of collective defence (Art. 5) • External terrorism
	OPERATIONS WITHIN THE FRAMEWORK OF THE EUROPEAN SECURITY AND DEFENCE POLICY (ESDP)	• Common evaluation of the external terrorist threat (military intelligence) • Protection of deployed forces and civil population from terrorist attacks
	MULTINATIONAL DEFENCE OPERATIONS	• Operations with ad hoc coalitions • Operations under other International Security and Defence Organisations
TO CONTRIBUTE MILITARILY TO INTERNATIONAL PEACE AND STABILITY	PEACE AND HUMANITARIAN AID OPERATIONS	• Preventive diplomacy • Peace making • Peace keeping • Peace enforcement and re-establishment • Peace consolidation • Humanitarian assistance in a bilateral or multilateral framework • Support for governmental and non-governmental organisations • Combat external terrorism

	CONFIDENCE- AND SECURITY- BUILDING MEASURES, ARMS CONTROL, AND THE NON- PROLIFERATION OF WEAPONS OF MASS DESTRUCTION	• Arms control and disarmament • Inspection of units or physical spaces in other countries • Verification
	DEFENCE DIPLOMACY	• Bilateral relations • Multilateral cooperation • Presence abroad
TO CONTRIBUTE WITH OTHER STATE INSTITUTIONS AND PUBLIC ADMINISTRATIONS TO MAINTAINING CITIZEN SECURITY AND WELL-BEING	ASSISTANCE IN CRITICAL EMERGENCY AND CATASTROPHE SITUATIONS	• Fire fighting • Civil emergency plans • Civil Protection (NBCR) • Action against natural or environmental disasters
	EVACUATING CITIZENS	• Evacuating non-combatants
	SUPPORTING KEY AREAS OF THE NATIONAL ECONOMY	• Support for fishing, farming, sanitation and transport
	SUPPORTING SCIENTIFIC AND TECHNOLOGICAL PROGRESS	• Cartography, oceanography, aerospace and hydrodynamic industries, and dual-use technologies • Support for the Spanish defence industry
	SUPPORTING THE STATE SECURITY FORCES AND CORPS	• Combating external terrorism • Extraordinary and uncontrolled migratory movements • Combating organised crime and drug trafficking

TRANSPORT SUPPORT FOR STATE ACTIVITIES	• Supporting other Ministries • Official and state travel
SEARCH AND RESCUE	• Air Rescue Service (S.A.R) • Maritime rescue • Land rescue

Source: Spain MOD, *Strategic Defense Review* (Madrid, 2000), II: 175–77.

CHAPTER **9**

War on Terrorism:
The Spanish Experience, 1939–2006

José A. Olmeda

The theoretical model used in this chapter is that of a non-state terrorist group competing for absolute power with a government against which its efforts are targeted. I would contend that—strictly for the purposes of this analysis—it is possible to describe terrorism as the deliberate creation of a sense of fear, usually by the use or threat of use of symbolic acts of physical violence, to influence the political behavior of a given target group. This definition highlights three facets of the phenomenon: The violent quality of most terrorist acts; the nature of the violence itself; and the symbolic character of the violent act, the terrorist act can only be understood by appreciating its symbolic content or "message." Unlike conventional warfare, however, the aim of a strategy of terrorism is not to kill or destroy but to break the spirit and create a sensation of fear within a target group, which will cause it to initiate political change. In this regard, terrorism bears many similarities to forms of guerrilla warfare. Terrorism, therefore, is a particular form of psychological warfare; a battle of wills played out in people's minds. Terrorism should more appropriately be viewed as a military strategy. It is a method that has been employed by actors who believe, rightly or wrongly, that through such means they can advance their agenda. It belongs to the different methods of military coercion, those efforts to change the behavior of a state by manipulating costs and benefits, affecting political and military outcomes through indirect military measures. Coercion seeks to change the behavior of the victim without decisive military victory, with actions directed at targets mainly behind the battlefield. The aim is to have a significant impact on the victim's willingness to continue the fight.[1]

Spain has been one of the countries with stronger nationalist and revolutionary terrorism during last century. Martha Crenshaw rightly identifies the existence of grievances and the lack of opportunity for political participation as the two most important "direct causes" of terrorism, and this may explain well the appearance of communist and anarchist irregular forces after the end of the Civil War and of *Euskadi Ta Askatasuna* [ETA (Basque Homeland and Freedom)] in 1959, and minor groups of different ideological persuasions later in Spain during Francoist dictatorship (1939–75). However, terrorism is about effecting radical political change, and it seems implausible that "access to the electoral arena" alone would persuade a terrorist group to abandon its military campaign though that was the case with an ETA faction in 1982. At the empirical level, the available evidence seems to suggest that democracy actually encourages terrorism. As the various studies have shown, democracies are more than three times as likely to become the target of terrorist groups than nondemocracies, because only democracies offer both the "oxygen" and the audience that are necessary for terrorism to communicate their message and gain legitimacy. Based on this evidence, one could argue that, since political fronts enable the terrorists to gain direct access to the mass media and facilitate all forms of political communication at the grassroots level, they actually contribute to making terrorism more effective.[2] In fact, this is what has happened with the terrorist upsurge with the transition to democracy in Spain (1976–82). In what follows, we are trying to analyze the interplay of two factors: the strategic choices of the terrorist organizations (in our case mainly ETA) and the different government responses to terrorism.[3]

Low-Intensity Conflict Under Francoism, 1939–75: From Minor Guerrilla Warfare to Terrorism

The authoritarian regime produced by the Spanish Civil War (1936–39) was going to cope with two different kinds of armed opposition: the remnants of communist and anarchist units just after the war and the terrorist Basque nationalism branch since 1968. Beyond its direct effects, research has shown that political repression also contributes indirectly to a number of forms of political violence. After the defeat of the Republicans, some refused to give up the war and fled north mainly to the mountains on Spain's border with France. Then in 1947, the Socialists voted to leave the movement, leading others to give up the armed conflict. Yet there were still guerrillas in the northern mountains as late as 1952.

The Basque nationalist movement is hardly unique with respect to its internal fragmentation, its historical process of splits and mergers. The movement's organizational field represents an increasingly heterogeneous mix of organizations and aims. Its branches compete with each other for resources, legitimacy, and the right to speak on behalf of the Basque society. In 1959, a group of militant activists within the relatively moderate Basque Nationalist Party (PNV) formed a breakaway faction seeking more extremist policy goals and committed to outspoken, direct action against the Spanish government. At its inception, ETA appeared generally unified behind a shared vision of a future independent, socialist Basque Country, to be achieved through "armed struggle." It mixed nationalist secession with imitation of Third World national liberation from colonialism struggles.

While ETA indicated a formal commitment to guerrilla war from its beginnings, it did not carry out its first killings until 1968. In the meantime, it passed through an ideological ferment, moving rapidly from Catholic social radicalism through a spectrum of anticolonialist positions, ultimately defining itself as a Marxist-Leninist movement committed to Basque independence and socialism. More crucial than its theoretical debates, however, was its commitment to armed action, which remains dominant up till today. The organization began pursuing the model "spiral of action-repression-action," which operated along the following lines: (1) ETA carried out a provocative violent action against the political system; (2) the system responded with repression against "the masses"; and (3) the masses responded with a mixture of panic and rebellion, whereupon ETA embarked on a further action that brought the masses a step further along the road to revolution. This grim motor shifted into gear when ETA carried out its first attacks, and the Francoist dictatorship obliged with brutal and often indiscriminate repression against the general Basque population. Its momentum has proved very difficult to halt ever since. However, the popular guerrilla war the terrorist envisaged never took off. ETA's most spectacular action under Francoism was the assassination, in Madrid in 1973, of the dictator's prime minister, Luis Carrero Blanco. Many militants of the Leftist opposition privately applauded the attack. Nevertheless, only a few opposition forces verbally condemned ETA's use of violence as morally unacceptable and politically counterproductive.[4]

In Search of Strategy: Terrorism and Counterterrorism Policy Under Democracy, 1976–2006

The nature of the armed threat to Spain's transition to democracy (1976–82) was going to be more than noteworthy: ETA (1959) with its mixture of nationalist and revolutionary terrorism; GRAPO [*Grupo de Resistencia Antifascista Primero de Octubre* (First of October Antifascist Resistance Group); 1976], a deadly revolutionary terrorist organization; minor nationalist terrorist organizations; and a disperse network of extreme right terrorist cells (1976–81).[5]

The Basque Country was not the only region on Spain's geographical periphery where extreme nationalists sought to make an impact on political developments by turning to terrorism[6]. For example, in 1976 the MPAIAC [*Movimiento para la Autodeterminación y la Independencia del*

Archipiélago Canario (Movement for the Self-Determination and Independence of the Canary Archipelago)] set up its so-called military wing, which was supposed to serve as the embryo of the future Armed Forces of the independent Canary Islands. But the cult of personality around which it coalesced and the indifference of the society it had set out to liberate meant that its turn to violence only hastened its eventual breakup. Not even the backing it eventually received from the Algerian authorities could make up for the near-total lack of support at the local level. A police crackdown, coupled with timely diplomatic maneuvers to ensure that the group received no support from African countries, and the number of militants who abandoned the minuscule group as soon as it showed its violent character, resulted in the MPAIAC's definitive liquidation in 1978. In 1979, the Catalonian nationalist movement gave rise to *Terra Lliure* (Free Land) (1980–95), a group claiming to be the vanguard of a grassroots independence movement. That this organization never really got off the ground was due largely to the overwhelming rejection of violence that prevails among the long-established and relatively moderate Catalonian nationalist movement, despite the calculated ambivalence which some of its leaders have occasionally manifested in that respect. *Terra Lliure*'s attempts at mobilizing support were a dismal failure. The state's selective response, added to their lack of popular backing, meant that *Terra Lliure* ended in a political blind alley from which the group has emerged by renouncing violence, but not until after a handful of people were killed. Radical extremists in the mainly agrarian northwestern region of Galicia also set up for a while the exaggeratedly so-called EGPGC [*Exército Guerrilheiro do Povo Galego Ceive* (Free Galician People's Guerrilla Army)], a tiny secret group which committed its first murder in 1987 and was dissolved in 1994. Once again, some efficacious police work and the total lack of support from the Galician society on whose behalf it was supposed to be fighting forestalled any hopes it may have entertained of achieving notoriety through sustained terrorist activity. The fact is that only a few of all terrorist organizations made the momentous step of killing people. They knew that killing meant a higher level of confrontation with the system and therefore harsher repression by the State if possible. In the end, they had a low impact measured as a function of its killings and its persistence.[7]

Leaving aside from the nationalist-rooted conflicts mentioned above, the most dramatic example of revolutionary terrorism during the democratic transition years was the one practiced by the GRAPO, which carried out their first attack in mid-1976. Once again, we are dealing with a tiny group isolated from the political change process which sought to acquire the influence it felt it was entitled to by resorting to violence. Of course, the perpetrators claimed to be the revolutionary vanguard capable of evolving into a people's army that would avert all possibility of Francoist rule being perpetuated and lead to a millennial insurrection. The result, however, was no more than a wave of terrorist killings by three dozen or so militants who received no external support whatsoever except perhaps some indirect aid provided by the then totalitarian Albanian authorities. GRAPO's bloodiest year was 1979, and since that time the number of killings and its activities in general have fallen off sharply, despite several attempts at reorganization. Measured by its impact, GRAPO is the bloodiest revolutionary terrorist organization in the developed world.[8]

Finally, the extreme right-wing groups at one time were infiltrated by members of the security services who were hostile to the democratization process and used the killings to destabilize the reform of the political system, based on a narrow idea of patriotism, and justified their action on grounds of self-defense. As the new regime took on a more pronounced democratic character, these extreme right-wing groups took on an increasingly insurgent cast. These groups were most active in 1980, although it must be noted that more crimes were claimed by individuals identified with the extreme right than by terrorist organizations who espoused this ideology. A considerable number of overlapping right-wing acronyms, barely distinguishable among themselves as far as their objectives, targeted individuals or organizations whom they supposed to be linked with leftist or Basque nationalist parties in a first example of the dirty war against terrorism.

Fighting Terrorism in a New Political Environment, 1976–81: The Legacy of the Past

The experience of Spain during its transition to democracy offers another case in point of increasing terrorism with democratization. Under the new Constitution approved in 1978, the Basque Country was granted a historically unprecedented degree of self-rule under a power-sharing arrangement which was endorsed in a 1979 referendum by the vast majority of its inhabitants. However, the rising nationalists were perceived by the military as a threat to the unity of the fatherland. So the military looked with suspicion toward the self-government of the regions granted by the new Constitution and exerted through the Autonomy Statutes. Many Spaniards thought that democracy's territorial distribution of power would end terrorist Basque nationalism and ETA, but this belief has proved mere wishful thinking. The pattern of terrorist activity during transition increased by the number of deadly attacks perpetrated. The terrorist Basque nationalism became more and more virulent as democratic change gained momentum. A bloody escalation got underway in 1978 and culminated in 1980. It remained at levels not quite as high, but no less alarming, until 1986, at which point it began to decline even more sharply.

The number and length of kidnappings by ETA follow a similar pattern, with a peak of kidnappings occurring in 1979 and 1980.[9]

On July 21, 1978, ETA killed General Juan Manuel Sánchez Ramos-Izquierdo and Lieutenant Colonel Juan Antonio Pérez Rodríguez while the project of a democratic Constitution was being debated in the Congress.[10] That implied a change of target selection. The military was now a target for the terrorists who were against the newborn democracy. Equally, a main target was the Civil Guard (*Guardia Civil*), a security force of military nature, which took the burden of fighting ETA and took heavy casualties. In fact, the Armed Forces and the Security Forces (Civil Guard and National Police) would carry the heaviest casualties of the total in the transition (1976–82). Given the large number of military casualties, it is hardly surprising the military perception of the threat posed by escalating terrorist Basque nationalism. However, ETA apparently did not want to provoke the February 23, 1981, coup. Rather, it appears that ETA used the assassination of military personnel to force the government into accepting the terrorists' demands, to be acknowledged as a belligerent, and open political negotiations.[11] It did not realize the effects of its own actions, and that says much about the organization's isolation from reality.

The effects of the authoritarian regime's treatment of terrorist Basque nationalism would be a heavy legacy on the shoulders of the democratic regime. There was a blind repressive reaction which was implemented without police professionalism, precision, and efficiency. An inept response to the terrorist threat can equally be related to a lack of adequate command and control by the executive over the activities of its security agencies. Cases of abuse reported from Spain's Basque provinces, especially during the crucial years of the democratic transition, appear to fall within this category. These were mostly attributed to agents and officials who had been trained and steeled in a system that was authoritarian and purely repressive in its approach to the maintenance of law and order.[12] The upsurge in violence registered during Spain's transition to democracy, especially during the 1978–80 period, was to some extent a consequence of the transfers of command, personnel shuffles, and organizational restructuring involved in the orderly and peaceful changeover from an authoritarian to a democratic regime.

As the country moved toward democracy, the more terrorist violence increased. This was because a favorable political opportunity structure existed for this to happen. First, the changeover from a repressive regime to another, more tolerant one is bound to lead to a relaxation of social control mechanisms that, in turn, tends to reinforce the likelihood of success for any type of collective action attempting to achieve a direct influence on the distribution of power. Apart from that factor, however, police counterterrorist efforts were not being very efficiently coordinated, and a coherent political consensus as to how to address the problem had not yet emerged. These circumstances meant that all legislative measures attempting to deal with the phenomenon of terrorism ended up quite limited in their effectiveness and, in a number of cases, were merely counterproductive. As to external factors, one may refer to the role of other countries or foreign-based groups in providing logistical support or cover to the domestic terrorists especially in France.

Until the latter months of 1980, counterterrorist policies implemented by successive governments of the *Unión de Centro Democrático* [UCD (Democratic Center Union)] had been particularly erratic. The guardians of public order at that time proved to be incapable of establishing a coherent and effective series of measures to replace the predominantly military-inspired repertory of responses that the Franco regime applied to all internal security matters. The policing apparatus which the defunct dictatorship had left in place was thus only partially susceptible to pressures from the parliamentary opposition and the informal political arrangements that greased the wheels of the democratic transition. Some veteran specialists were reclassified or given new duties, the hierarchy was shuffled here and there, but it was not until 1979 that the security forces were given the thoroughgoing shake-up they needed. The whys and wherefores of this delay may be quite simply put: the politicians were afraid of provoking a rebellion by the militarized security forces, as evidenced by the eloquent testimony of Rodolfo Martín Villa, first Minister of Interior, 1976–79.[13] As a result, the information-gathering mechanisms which are of critical importance in the fight against terrorism were not only inadequate but frequently fairly crude, and operated with little if any type of governmental controls. A total lack of coordination between the intelligence arms answerable to the various state security services was self-evident, indeed, notorious. At the end of 1975, as many as ten different information police, military, and intelligence services were operating in competition with one another, instead of pooling and coordinating their efforts. Under such circumstances, it is scarcely to be wondered that most successful results in counterterrorist operations were obtained at the local or provincial level, though these, of course, were necessarily limited in their impact. Given such an outlook, the Spanish government had no choice but to turn to neighboring countries for intelligence and direct help in dealing with its terrorist problem.[14]

In February 1977, Spain's *Audiencia Nacional* (National Court) held its first sessions in Madrid. At present it shares with the *Juzgados Centrales de Instrucción* (Central Prosecution Tribunals) exclusive competence for preparing and trying cases involving terrorist activities carried out anywhere on Spanish territory by individuals who are members of armed organizations or otherwise acting in collusion with them. Though controversial at the time of its creation, this tribunal set an important precedent in helping to remove jurisdiction over terrorist crimes from the military courts, barely two years after Franco's death, at a time when the transition to democracy was by no means complete or even on a solid footing.[15] One of the legal measures most likely to give rise to civil rights abuses by the state security apparatus is that of allowing suspects to be held without charge and without access to legal counsel for prolonged periods. Regardless of whether this type of policy is tolerated for long or short periods of time, it is indeed one of the most widespread measures adopted by democratic governments as a means of reinforcing their counterterrorist policies. It is disconcerting to see how the vast majority of those detained in the mass roundups authorized by any of several special measures passed in the Basque provinces were subsequently set free with no charges filed against them.[16]

The National Police was the agency preferred by the UCD politicians who were responsible for internal security issues in those days. At the same time, Martín Villa, the then Minister of Interior, went abroad looking for advice on how to counter terrorism properly. In July and November of 1978, for instance, he traveled to the Federal Republic of Germany and the United Kingdom, respectively, to find out about specialized antiterrorist units and appropriate information-gathering systems. The executive wanted to increase the number of agents, to articulate adequate intelligence services, and to modernize technical resources within the police in order to improve the efficiency in the fight against terrorism, a threat that by then was undoubtedly perceived as a major danger. However, as terrorism continued to escalate, the then civilian Minister of Interior was replaced in April 1979 by an army general. During this period, a delegation of the central government for security matters was opened in the Basque autonomous community and also in the autonomous community of Navarre, headed by another general linked to the National Police.[17]

The point at which counterterrorist policy began to attain the operational agility it hitherto had so conspicuously lacked and, thus, to achieve the results it had so desperately failed to achieve coincided with the naming of Juan José Rosón as Interior Minister (1980–82). That was the point when terrorism was at its bloodiest and most feverish peak, and the government was still unable to get a grip on the police forces. The new minister lost no time putting his department in order and did not hesitate to use his authority to bring into line and coordinate the efforts of the various policing bodies, including those that had been conspicuous for their reluctance to pursue right-wing groups that were all but flaunting their impunity. Following the abortive attempt at a right-wing military coup in February 1981, Rosón made a long-overdue effort to create a professional intelligence-gathering apparatus, created a Single Command for the Fight against Terrorism, and finally special operations groups and antiterrorist units from both the National Police [the *Grupos Especiales de Operaciones* (Special Groups of Operations)] and the Civil Guard [the

Unidades Antiterroristas Rurales (Rural Counter-terrorist Units)] were deployed in the Basque Country. All this paled, however, alongside the audacity he showed in pushing for the creation of legal and administrative measures that would lower the costs of exit from terrorist organizations and allow convicted terrorists who laid down their arms to regain a place in society. The most visible result of all this was the unprecedented self-dissolution of ETA "political-military" (p-m) late in September 1982.[18]

ETA had split into two factions in 1974 which made different assessments of political change in Spain according to its opposite organizational strategies. The majority (the so-called "political-military") sector of the terrorist organization ETA decided to participate in the first democratic general election through its political arm in 1977. The minority sector, ETA "military," rejected the new democratic realities self-designing itself as the vanguard of the Basque nationalist movement, and its political arm, *Herri Batasuna*, was not formed until 1979. The evolution of the two branches illustrates how both of these contrasting strategies work: in the first case, increasing civilian control and political considerations set the strategy; in the second, military autonomy and rigid extreme nationalist considerations established the terrorist direction. In response to changes in the power structure, the leaders of what was originally the majority faction, ETA (p-m), decided to restrict and ultimately renounce the use of violence, ruling out its offensive use and subordinating it to political initiatives. The strategy now was to carry on through legal, institutionalized channels the mobilization of forces in the cause of what may be described as the left-wing variant of Basque nationalism. While still operating clandestinely, the organization began to transform itself into an aboveboard political party. The party which emerged from this initiative, *Euskadiko Ezkerra* (Left of Basque Country), took part in the first post-Franco democratic elections of 1977 in which it obtained relatively satisfactory results. It continued to do well in subsequent ballots at the local and national level until, in the wake of numerous internal divisions, it merged with the Basque offshoot of the then ruling *Partido Socialista Obrero Español* [PSOE (Spanish Socialist Worker's Party)] in 1993. As democracy continued to evolve and the new juridical order conceded ample possibilities of self-government to Spain's regions, the contradictions between the political exchange which one sector of the party was carrying on within legitimated institutions and the violence of the underground militants became more and more pronounced. As a result, in 1982 ETA (p-m) announced that it was dissolving in the wake of an internal debate stimulated by its political wing. The decision to lay down their arms was spurred by deals securing them pardons and reprieves that were agreed on a one-by-one basis between Left-leaning Basque nationalist politicians and the then center-right Spanish government.[19]

As a result, it was ETA (m) that was left to dominate the center stage, claiming responsibility for well over 90% of the terrorist attacks that have been carried out since 1981. But even as they did so, a number of factors helped buttress the counterterrorist policies which the government developed to counter the organization.

The Socialist Counterterrorism Policy: Cover Action, Negotiations, and Penitentiary Dispersion, 1982-95

The impact which the new democratic rules of the game as a favorable political opportunity structure had on the terrorist escalation during the democratic transition would appear to be confirmed by the fact that, when democracy began to be consolidated, the factors that once had favored terrorist violence began to have negative repercussions on it. The average number of deaths per year from terrorism dropped by 70% between 1981 and 1985 compared to the figures for the 1978–80 period, and after 1986, they slumped even further. GRAPO was dismantled, despite a few later attempts at reorganization. Extreme right-wing groups found their operational capacity reduced to nil once its political sector vanished and officials sympathetic to their aims were rooted out of the security services. ETA (m) thus remained the main focal point of terrorist activity.

Following the victory of the Spanish Socialist Party (PSOE) in the October 1982 general elections, efforts were made to continue and develop existing counterterrorist policies. The primary guidelines around which the strategy has evolved may be summarized as follows. First of all, an emphasis was put on more effective police work and on channeling greater human and logistic resources to this end. Special security plans were drawn up for most contingencies, and considerable progress was made in developing infrastructure for a coordinating authority in the intelligence sector, despite some remaining confrontations eventually observed between the National Police and the Civil Guard. As a result, security forces obtained a better idea of how the terrorist organizations are internally articulated and of the identity and likely whereabouts at any given moment of its militants. Next, as Spain adopted an increasingly high profile on the international scene, the government finessed a number of diplomatic initiatives aimed at producing specific accords on intergovernment cooperation on terrorist questions. Then, over a period of time, it became possible though not always easy to bring legislation gradually into line so as to allow for a more effective policing action. Nevertheless, measures allowing terrorist suspects to be held incommunicado for a certain time remained in force, so the allegations of mistreatment persisted. The last factor of significance is the standing offer that allowed terrorists to regain their place in society providing they renounce violence and agree to respect the basic laws of democracy. Up to 1996, over 370 members of different Basque terrorist organizations have accepted the terms of this offer.[20]

A buildup of momentum toward deeper European integration (Spain became a member state of the European Community in 1986) similarly brought little comfort to ETA terrorists. They were also affected somewhat by the criminal attacks of the so-called *Grupos Antiterroristas de Liberación* [GAL (Anti-Terrorist Liberation Groups)]. This shadowy organization emerged in 1983 in an attempt to complement the government's counterterrorism initiatives with an illegal "dirty war" campaign against suspected members of ETA. Using the same terrorist methods employed by their adversaries, the GAL killed twenty-five persons between 1983 and 1987, though surprisingly many of their victims had no links whatsoever to ETA due to its very poor intelligence. Most of these killings took place in southern France, and the GAL vanished from the scene as soon as the French government began lending its active cooperation to turning the screws on ETA members residing in its territory. The GAL was instigated by some incumbent politicians and high-ranking members of the security forces. It was composed of deviant police functionaries and mercenary delinquents, with the passive acquiescence, if not the active complicity, of some high-ranking socialist politicians. Actually, two relevant policemen were eventually given long jail terms for their role in recruiting the common criminals and foreigners with links to transnational organized crime who had carried out the assassinations. Former high-ranking officers in command of counterterrorism units and a Basque politician affiliated in the past to the PSOE have confessed their involvement in GAL actions, after they were prosecuted and imprisoned. Due to their links with GAL, the Spanish Supreme Court sentenced the then Minister of Interior and some of the highest authorities of the Interior Ministry when the GAL's killings took place to prison. Certainly, the terrorist actions perpetrated by GAL activists had the short-term impact of partially disorganizing the collectivity of ETA members living with impunity in southern France and gaining the French counterterrorist cooperation after years of passive Basque terrorism support, but the long-term consequences of such state-sponsored terrorism have been very pernicious.

On this occasion, we could observe how the illicit use of public resources is meant to enhance and complement existing legal measures through methods that can scarcely be distinguished from those employed by the terrorists themselves. Some police officers or individuals holding political office considered these to be extremely effective in the short term, despite their obvious illegality. In point of fact, not only are these morally reprehensible but also exceedingly counterproductive in that they tend to feed the social unrest from which the terrorists draw their ideological sustenance. Among other effects, the political consensus needed to implement counterterrorism policies was endangered and supporters of insurgent violence found new arguments, precisely at a time when ETA (m) was weaker than ever and increasingly isolated.[21] The credibility of the state security apparatus suffered great damage while at the same time providing ETA with new pretexts for justifying its own terrorism just when support for the organization had sunk to an all-time low.

In 1987, an ETA car bomb exploded in the supermarket *Hipercor* in Barcelona, killing twenty-one people and injuring many more. This attack, ETA's bloodiest and most indiscriminate action caused such great consternation within the left-nationalist movement that the organization did not even try to justify it. Instead, ETA apologized for this action and framed it as a "mistake"; the excuse given was that ETA had warned the police in advance, but that the police, intentionally, had waited too long in clearing the people out of the building, so as to provoke a great number of casualties which would discredit the organization. According to some observers, the action may have been a test case: if the left-nationalist following had accepted its consequences, such indiscriminate actions might have become a normal part of ETA's strategy. However, it had become clear that the members and sympathizers of the movement were "not yet ready" for such actions.[22] As this indiscriminate target selection was meant as a strategic escalation, a new offensive, its failure marked a tipping point in ETA's organizational decline because of the acute loss of legitimacy among its supporters.

Police counterterrorist operations became much more discriminate and selective after 1988. No single episode of illegal violence in the state response to ETA has been reported since that time. ETA since its inception has sought for years to reach a clear and determined aim that it has not abandoned up to date: to get the independence of a reunified Basque Country to the detriment of Spain and France and to establish a revolutionary Socialist regime in this territory under its rule. For ETA to attain its maximalist goal, ETA must force the Spanish State to seek the negotiation. This is what ETA did two years after the Socialists came to power and in the framework of a bloody terrorist campaign in 1984. The campaign grew harsher later, in 1988–89, a period including a cease-fire from September 1988. The cease-fire ended the following year in April when the negotiations between the government and ETA in Algiers failed. In the late 1990s, ETA had been pursuing the "Irish model" after the Holy Friday Agreements in April 1998, including a distorted vision of the situation in Ulster.[23]

Prospects for the survival of terrorist groups depend greatly on maintaining the internal cohesion and unconditional submission of jailed members; these members constitute the main asset for marshalling support and sympathy from the society whose destiny they claim the right to determine. This is not so much a matter of exploiting a political consensus as a preexisting network of friendship and family structures which is uncommonly cohesive with an intense sense of collective identity. Therefore, when the authorities arrange for the dispersal of terrorist prisoners as part of a concerted counterterrorist policy, the reaction by the group's leadership tends to be extreme.[24] In 1989, Spanish authorities had considerable initial success in disrupting the terrorist organization's internal cohesion by both offering generous terms to allow ETA militants to reenter society and dispersing inmates to penitentiaries scattered throughout Spain. In this way, they succeeded in creating fissures and fractures in the iron discipline maintained by ETA over militants serving long prison sentences. After years of successful underground activity, ETA's leadership was arrested in the south of France in 1992 in a joint operation by the *Guardia Civil* and the French police, with the technical support of the CIA. This was the beginning of a new operational decline in the terrorist organization.

During the 1980s, support or tolerance for political violence gradually lost ground in the Basque Country, where despite ever-persistent ambivalence, at the end of the decade fewer people than ever before acknowledged that they identified themselves with ETA. The relative stability of the political power-sharing arrangements that were worked out in the Basque Autonomous Government, giving rise to a coalition between the moderate Basque Nationalist Party and the Basque offshoot of the ruling Spanish Socialist Party, helped bring about a broad-based antiterrorism accord. During the 1990s, a grassroots-level reaction against terrorist violence had begun in Basque society. Groups of citizens have organized protests against ETA activities breaking the spiral of silence developed by Basque nationalism tacit support. All these factors contributed to allowing the built-up tensions and resentments of decades to seep out of the Basque political scene and to delegitimize in political terms ETA (m)'s demands. Most decisive was the unprecedented cooperation Spanish authorities were now receiving from abroad in their fight against terrorism. Especially noteworthy was the change in attitude by France since 1986, which no longer granted political refugee status to ETA militants and logistical sanctuary to the organization and, instead, facilitated the arrest, expulsion, or deportation of many of its ringleaders.[25]

The Success of Popular Party Counterterrorism Policy Against Basque Terrorist Nationalism, 1996–2004

The short-lived cease-fire announced by ETA in June 1996 was designed and timed to serve as a pretext for seizing the political initiative and fracturing the consensus reached by the Basque nationalist and nonnationalist parties opposed to violence, a factor that had clearly diminished the terrorists' ability to mobilize support.

In July 1997, a terrorist cell kidnapped a young Basque councilor in a small town, Miguel Ángel Blanco, who belonged to the *Partido Popular* (PP), then in power with a minority government. ETA threatened to kill him in forty-eight hours if ETA's imprisoned members were not brought back to prisons in the Basque provinces. After his murder, massive demonstrations and expressions of outrage spread throughout Basque territory. This process of mobilization triggered two main reactions in the Basque nationalist movement: its disloyal political branch, PNV, radicalized its posture in order to help the terrorist branch and favored the creation of a pan-nationalist front under its political hegemony and its terrorist branch suffered internal dissent when important activists of older generations demanded the end of the "armed struggle" because of ETA's faltering support and its ineffectiveness. Rogelio Alonso has rightly underscored the underlying rationale of these actions: Basque nationalists' fears that ETA's military defeat would have very negative consequences for the Basque people, rendering its main nationalist party (PNV) insignificant.[26]

On July 15, 1998, Judge Baltasar Garzón closed the daily newspaper *Egin* and the radio station *Egin Irratia*, having proved that ETA appointed its directors and defined its editorial line. In September 1998, this strategic and political climate led to the declaration by ETA of an indefinite cease-fire that broke down in late 1999. ETA's cease-fire was the trade-off for a radicalization of the PNV, which then retreated from every agreement with Spanish democratic political forces (PP and PSOE) and in January 2000 endorsed the terrorist aim of self-determination. This secret pact opened the way to the Estella (*Lizarra* in the Basque language) Declaration, an agreement signed by the main Basque nationalist parties and trade unions, with the addition of the Basque section of the postcommunist coalition *Izquierda Unida* (United Left), then in the Basque regional government.[27]

Before this scenario, the popular government pursued its strategy of no political concessions to the PNV; enforcement of the rule of law against terrorists; elimination of any of its political, financial, and symbolic resources through legal measures; and their encouragement of international cooperation. On December 8, 2000, an agreement between the PP and the PSOE was signed designing several counterterrorism measures. The new comprehensive approach to combat terrorism started with the premise that ETA is not constituted only of its cells but also of a big network with political parties, social organizations, companies, and propagandistic means. That entire network is directly controlled and directed by ETA and provides the political support, welfare services, and logistic and economic assistance rendered to terrorist activity. The PP government approach was, therefore, to fight against that network so as to hinder, on the one hand, the regenerative capacity the armed organization had enjoyed throughout its history and, on the other, the impunity most of the organization had had making use of democratic means in order to destroy democracy.[28]

Another pillar of this strategy was international cooperation with an important Trans-Atlantic dimension after too many years of French reluctance. International cooperation has two basic dimensions: bilateral and multilateral. In the first dimension, the priority was cooperation with France. ETA has historically kept its leadership, its logistic bases, and its training camps in French territory. Throughout the 1990s, police cooperation with France had significantly improved, as shown by the seventy-eight terrorists arrested in French territory in that decade and the thirty-two terrorists extradited. Regarding the multilateral dimension, September 11 has had a catalyzing effect, especially at the core of the European Union. Thus, after the attacks against the United States, the EU triggered new mechanisms such as the compilation of a common list of terrorist organizations, a boost to the fight against their funding, implementation of the European arrest warrant and surrender procedures, the setting up of joint investigation teams, or reinforcing of Europol. Lastly, the growing Trans-Atlantic police cooperation, both in the bilateral field and in the creation of a permanent mechanism of liaison between the FBI and the Europol, is worth mentioning.[29]

The new strategy has produced several important legislation changes and judicial decisions. The amendment of the Criminal Law or the Criminal Responsibility of Under-aged Persons in January 2000 put an end to this impunity, toughening the sentences for this kind of terrorist attacks (*kale borroka*). This was decisive for undercutting the recruitment of young activist to the terrorist group. The sentences for terrorist crimes became more severe after Law 7/2003 was passed by Parliament as of June 30, 2003. The new rule extends the punishments for terrorist crimes from thirty to forty years, and in the most serious cases, those convicted will have to serve their sentences fully. Before the law was passed, it was a common occurrence for terrorists to remain in prison for a maximum of twenty years.[30]

The Supreme Court sentence of March 17, 2003, that dissolved the *Batasuna* political party in accordance with the Political Parties Law passed one year earlier, with the votes of the PP, the PSOE, and regionalist and nationalist groups. This sentence prevented ETA from counting on a powerful propagandistic tool, which used to benefit from public money. The illegalization brought about the inability for *Batasuna* to participate in the May 25 local elections, consequently losing power over the forty-nine little towns of the Autonomous Regions of Navarre and the Basque Country, with a budget of more than 90 million. On February 20, 2003, Judge Del Olmo ordered the preventive closing of the daily newspaper *Euskaldunon Egunkaria* on the grounds that the direction of the paper was under the control of ETA. On April 29, 2003, the police neutralized the direction of the *Udalbiltza Kursaal* Assembly as part of an operation coordinated by the *Audiencia Nacional* Judge Baltasar Garzón. The *Udalbitza Kursaal* Assembly was created in February 2001 by local representatives of *Batasuna* and served as a political platform to support ETA.

The success of this strategy cannot be denied. Different data can sustain this assertion. For example, in 2003, ETA launched eighteen attacks, causing three fatalities. This is one of the lowest figures in thirty years. Equally noteworthy was the decline of the so-called low-intensity terrorism, i.e., launching Molotov cocktails or stones, that the media usually refers to as *kale borroka*—a Basque idiom for street violence—and the Ministry of Interior as urban terrorism. In 2003, there were 150 attacks of this kind, fewer than in any of the recent years, including 1999, as this sort of terrorism was not discontinued during ETA's cease-fire. This point is extremely important, as such acts of terror contribute to magnify the alarm caused by more brutal attacks among the Basque population. More importantly, many of the terrorists that joined ETA in the last years were initiated into violence through this type of action.

In recent years, these efforts have brought about the capture of large numbers of ETA terrorists, including some of its leaders. In contrast to the 100 arrested in the year 2000, as ETA resumed its terrorist activities following the cease-fire, 187 ETA members were arrested in the year 2003. And last but not least, social support for the terrorist group has also significantly decreased. The support for ETA, which in the 1980s was around 10%, is nowadays around 2%. In contrast, total rejection has increased from 40% around the middle of the 1980s to the current 64%. The remaining 30% takes a position of rejection but with some qualifications, for instance, to support the group's aims but not the violent means used to achieve them and to justify the existence of ETA during the dictatorship but not in democracy. These results produced a polarization of Basque nationalist forces, leading to serious confrontation with the national PP government due to the threat of secession invoked by the Basque regional government.

However, I want to stress the consequences of this success for the Spanish population's perception of the terrorist threat. According to data from the CIS [*Centro de Investigaciones Sociológicas* (Center for Sociological Research)], the answer "terrorism, ETA" as a Spanish problem has almost disappeared (the wording of the question was: "Which are, in your opinion, the three main problems in Spain? Multiple answer) beginning in 2002." However, one year after 9/11, the CIS asked "Do you think that there can be terrorist attacks of the same magnitude as 9/11/2001 in the next weeks or months in the United States or in another developed country?" 62.6% of those asked said "yes."[31]

The reappearance of Islamist terrorism at the end of the PP's tenure in office could not be more dramatic. Nevertheless, before that on April 12, 1985, after a visit by President Ronald Reagan and in the peak of the campaign against Spanish membership to NATO, a bomb exploded in a restaurant frequented by American military personnel, killing eighteen persons and wounding nearly one hundred. *Hezbollah* issued a statement of responsibility, through its international affiliate *Islamic Jihad* from Beirut. Years later, in the penultimate day of the general elections campaign to be held on March 14, 2004, terrorist attacks were perpetrated in Madrid; 192 persons were killed and 1,430 wounded. Though the formal connection to Al-Qaeda has not been proved, the attack had at least an Islamist component.[32]

The Beginning of the End?

After all these years, ETA is one of the longest-lived terrorist organizations in the Western world, with more than forty years of existence, more than thirty years of personal attacks, about a thousand assassinations, and an important destabilizing problem for Spanish democracy. Traditionally, ETA has assessed the results of its fight in political terms, considering the fight is bound to solve a political conflict. Initially, ETA envisaged the possibility of defeating Spain in military terms. Later, it sought to create the conditions leading up to the negotiations with the Spanish government. It did not think, however, how to negotiate with the French State the independence of the Basque territories in France. ETA has engaged in a Vietnamese strategy obliging the enemy to be the one to ask for the negotiations. Following that strategy, it has launched more or less hard blows by committing terrorist acts or activating street rioting to gain social control through destabilization. From top down, ETA has activated its fronts: the military front using armed struggle; the mass front using street rioting; and the political front using its political wing that has kept changing names to adapt to the new circumstances.

The average yearly number of fatalities caused by ETA was eighty-one between 1978 and 1980, thirty-four between 1981 and 1990, and sixteen between 1991 and 2000. ETA's murderous campaign has progressively declined since then. In 2001 the group killed thirteen people. The following year ETA caused five fatalities followed by three killings in 2003. It should be noted that this terrorist organization perpetrated an average of seven assassinations per year between 1968 and 1977, which was under the dictatorship and before the first free elections were held in Spain. Paradoxically, though, this operational decline, caused by changing political conditions and governmental responses, has modified both internal structures and victimization patterns of the terrorist organization. For instance, the range of targets has been successively expanded, from mainly military and police personnel at the beginning to civilians (often highly indiscriminately killed outside the Basque Country) and, finally, Basque-elected politicians from the local to the national levels of government, university lecturers, journalists, businessmen and judges, among other categories of people explicitly known for not endorsing nationalist propositions. In addition, the terrorist organization established new expressions of daily violence (practiced by a number of supporters in their late teens and early twenties) intended to harass and prosecute nonnationalist sectors of Basque society, which account for half the population in the autonomous community. According to ETA's strategy, the maintenance of street rioting has served to remind the importance of violence in the ordinary life of the Basque people and to prevent them from adopting pliable attitudes.[33]

On March 24, 2006, ETA declared a permanent cease-fire but has never mentioned the possibility of giving up arms and has pursued street level terrorism, economic extortion, and logistical activities in France. The current Socialist government declared its intention to negotiate with the terrorist organization. Only time will tell if this was the beginning of the end or another make-believe tactical move. However, from a strategic point of view, the terrorists would win if they provoke a government into defeating itself by setting a process of rolling concessions.

Are there some lessons learned from the Spanish fight against terrorism? I could make several points. There is not a local vs. a transnational type of terrorism: terrorism is only one, a military strategy pursued by very different groups. It is a method that has been employed by actors who believe, rightly or wrongly, that through such means they can advance their agenda. Spain's longer-than-forty-year experience in the fight against ETA shows us how important the international factor is in any kind of terrorism and how necessary it is to curb its support bases or its recognition abroad. Terrorism is the main actual enemy of democratic regimes. In the case of ETA, its terrorist activities were activated during Spain's democratic transition. Such regimes should be consistent with their principles, typify clearly what a democracy considers a crime, and be strict with the compliance with democratic rules and the fight against crime. The counterterrorist struggle is a long-term fight and is perceived as such by terrorists of any kind. Western nations and especially its public opinions should be aware of this, avoiding rush and discouragement.

Notes

Chapter 1

1. Works covering the political history of the nineteenth-century Spanish Army include Stanley G. Payne, *Politics and the Military in Modern Spain* (Stanford: Stanford University Press, 1967); Manuel Ballbé, *Orden público y militarismo en la España constitucional (1812–1983)* (Madrid: Alianza, 1983); E. Christiansen, *The Origins of Military Power in Spain 1800–1854* (Oxford: Oxford University Press, 1967); Daniel R. Headrick, *Ejército y política en España (1866–1898)* (Madrid: Tecnos, 1981); and Carlos Seco Serrano, *Militarismo y civilismo en la España contemporánea* (Madrid: Instituto de Estudios Politicos, 1984).

2. Headrick, *Ejército y política*, 38–39.

3. Charles J. Esdaile, *The Spanish Army in the Peninsular War* (Manchester, UK, New York: Manchester University Press, 1988), 106–7. For an overview of Prussia's response to the French military threat in the wake of the Revolution, see Robert Michael Citino, *The German Way of War: From the Thirty Years' War to the Third Reich* (Lawrence, KS: University Press of Kansas, 2005), 104–41.

4. Esdaile, *Spanish Army*, 14.

5. Rory Muir, *Tactics and the Experience of Battle in the Age of Napoleon* (New Haven: Yale University Press, 1998), 71–72; and Esdaile, *Spanish Army*, 50.

6. Muir, *Tactics*, 51–67; and Citino, *German Way of War*, 106–7.

7. Esdaile, *Spanish Army*, 45–46.

8. Ibid., 85–90.

9. Ibid., 81.

10. Carlos Martínez de Campos y Serrano, *España belica: el siglo XIX* (Madrid: Aguilar, 1961), 79–81; Esdaile, *Spanish Army*, 89.

11. Esdaile, *Spanish Army*, 90–95.

12. Martínez de Campos y Serrano, *España belica*, 40–44; John Lawrence Tone, *The Fatal Knot: The Guerrilla War in Navarre and the Defeat of Napoleon in Spain* (Chapel Hill: University of North Carolina Press, 1994), 57–58; and Esdaile, *Spanish Army*, 98–101.

13. Esdaile, *Spanish Army*, 121–23.

14. Ibid., 136–38.

15. Ibid., 137.

16. Ibid., 143, 168–70, 175; Martínez de Campos y Serrano, *España belica*, 44.

17. Tone, *Fatal Knot*, 4.

18. Ibid.

19. John F. Coverdale, *The Basque Phase of Spain's First Carlist War* (Princeton, NJ: Princeton University Press, 1984), 3.

20. *Tratado sobre la guerra de Montaña* (Madrid: 1834), cited in Alfonso Bullón de Mendoza y Gómez de Valugera, *La primera guerra carlista* (Madrid: Actas, 1992), 113–14.

21. Bullón de Mendoza y Gómez de Valugera, *Primera guerra carlista,* 114–15.

22. Ibid., 118.

23. These estimates in troop numbers are based on the figures in Bullón de Mendoza y Gómez de Valugera, *Primera guerra carlista,* 181, 199–200, 208–9, 219.

24. Except where otherwise noted, the following account of the war comes from Bullón de Mendoza y Gómez de Valugera, *Primera guerra carlista,* 247–73 and Coverdale, *Basque Phase,* 120–225, 284–94.

25. See José Álvarez Junco, "El nacionalismo español como mito movilizador. Cuatro guerras," in *Cultura y movilización en la España contemporánea,* ed. Rafael Cruz and Manuel Pérez (Madrid: Alianza, 1997), 35–67.

26. María Rosa de Madariaga, *España y el Rif: Crónica de una historia casi olvidada,* 2nd ed. (Ciudad Autónoma de Melilla: UNED-Centro Asociado de Melilla, 1999), 78–79.

27. Karl Marx and Frederick Engels, *Revolution in Spain* (1939; repr., Westport, CT: Greenwood, 1975) (originally appeared as an article by Engels in the *New York Daily Tribune,* January 19, 1860); Madariaga, *España y el Rif,* 75–76.

28. Thilo Wittenberg, *Mut Und Ehre: Die Professionelle, Ideologische Und Politische Entwicklung Des Spanischen Offizierskorps Im 19. Jahrhundert (1808–1908)* (Freiburg, Germany: Albert-Ludwigs-Universität, 1995), 29.

29. Marx and Engels, *Revolution,* 208 (originally appeared in an article by Engels in the *New York Daily Tribune,* March 17, 1860).

30. Federico Villalobos Goyarrola, *El sueño colonial: las guerras de España en Marruecos* (Barcelona: Ariel, 2004), 21–22.

31. Madariaga, *España y el Rif,* 77–79.

32. José M. Rodríguez Gómez, *La tercera guerra carlista, 1869–1876* (Madrid: Almena, 2004), 38, 46.

33. Headrick, *Ejército y política,* 190–96; and Rodríguez Gómez, *Tercera guerra carlista,* 65.

34. Rodríguez Gómez, *Tercera guerra carlista,* 66.

35. Ibid., 66–67, 75–76.

36. Headrick, *Ejército y política,* 186–89.

37. Rodríguez Gómez, *Tercera guerra carlista,* 78–79; and Citino, *German Way of War,* 81, 176.

38. Headrick, *Ejército y política,* 190–92.

39. Ibid., 192–94.

40. Rodríguez Gómez, *Tercera guerra carlista,* 99–100; and Headrick, *Ejército y política,* 194–95.

41. Rodríguez Gómez, *Tercera guerra carlista,* 139–41.

42. Headrick, *Ejército y política,* 214–15.

43. John Lawrence Tone, "The Machete and the Liberation of Cuba," *Journal of Military History* 62 (January 1998): 11–16.

44. Quoted in John Lawrence Tone, *War and Genocide in Cuba, 1895–1898* (Chapel Hill: University of North Carolina Press, 2006), 120. On Martínez Campos attitude and approach to the war in general, see Tone, *War and Genocide,* 113–21.

45. Tone makes this argument very convincingly in *War and Genocide.*

46. On reconcentration in Cuba, see Tone, *War and Genocide,* especially 193–224.

47. Tone, *War and Genocide,* 150, 196.

48. Valeriano Weyler, *Memorias de un general. De caballero cadete a general en jefe,* ed. María Teresa Weyler (Barcelona: Ediciones Destino, 2004), 63–64; Gabriel Cardona and Juan Carlos Losada Málvarez, *Weyler, nuestro hombre en la habana* (Barcelona: Planeta, 1997), 50.

49. Weyler, *Memorias,* 65; Cardona and Losada Málvarez, *Weyler,* 50–51, 187–89.

50. See, for example, Cardona and Losada Málvarez, *Weyler.*

51. John Grenier, "Continental and British *Petite Guerre,* circa 1750," in *The First Way of War: American War Making on the Frontier* (New York: Cambridge University Press, 2005), chap. 3.

52. Weyler, *Memorias,* 63–64, 69–72.

53. Tone, *War and Genocide,* 225–38.

54. Robert M. Cassidy, *Counterinsurgency and the Global War on Terror: Military Culture and Irregular War* (Westport, CT: Praeger Security International, 2006), 99–114. The Spanish Army's dominant institutional culture began to reflect the importance of counterinsurgency only in the 1920s, as reflected in its publications and the reestablishment of its all-arms academy for future officers. Geoffrey Jensen, "The Politics and Practice of Spanish Counterinsurgency, 1895–1936," in *Nation and Conflict in Modern Spain,* ed. Sasha D. Pack (Madison: Parallel Press, forthcoming).

55. Weyler, *Memorias,* 54.

Chapter 2

1. John Keegan, *World Armies* (London: The MacMillan Press, 1979), 644. For more on the problems, as well as the powerful influence of the Spanish Army on the government, see Gabriel Cardona, *El poder militar en la España contemporánea hasta la Guerra Civil* (Madrid: Siglo XXI de España editores, 1983); Julio Busquets, *El militar de carrera en España* (Barcelona: Editorial Ariel, 1984); and Miguel Alonso Baquer, *El Ejército en la sociedad española* (Madrid: Ediciones del Movimiento, 1971).

2. Walter B. Harris, *France, Spain and the Riff* (London: Edward Arnold & Co., 1927), 50. Without an adequate fleet, Spain wisely sold the Palau, Caroline, and Mariana Islands to Germany in 1899. José Alvarez Junco and Adrian Shubert, eds., *Spanish History since 1808* (London: Arnold, 2000), 118.

3. Raymond Carr, *España: De La Restauración A La Democracia, 1875–1980* (Barcelona: Editorial Ariel, S.A., 1983), 120–21. For more on the animosity between the Army (officers) and Catalan nationalism, see Charles J. Esdaile, *Spain in the Liberal Age* (Oxford, UK/Malden, MA: Blackwell Publishers, 2000), 208–9.

4. Payne, *Politics and the Military in Modern Spain,* 86–89; Seco Serrano, *Militarismo y civilismo,* 233; Carr, *España: De La Restauración,* 120; Busquets, *El militar de carrera en España,* 25; Esdaile, *Spain in the Liberal Age,* 207; and Mark Williams, *The Story of Spain* (Málaga, Spain: Santana Books, 2000), 189, noted that a panel of generals recommend increasing the number of men in the Army, instead of reducing the number of officers to correct the imbalance.

5. Esdaile, *Spain in the Liberal Age,* 207–8; and Carr, *España: De La Restauración,* 121. Seco Serrano, *Militarismo y civilismo,* 237, also covers the subsequent passage

of the "Law of Jurisdictions" (*Ley de Jurisdicciones*) on March 20, 1906. Payne, *Politics and the Military in Modern Spain*, 94–97.

6. Esdaile, *Spain in the Liberal Age*, 208; and Carr, *España: De La Restauración*, 120.

7. For information on Spanish and German iron ore mining interests in the Rif, see Pessah Shinar, "Abd al Qadir and Abd al Krim: Religious Influences on Their Thought and Action," *Asian and African Studies*, I, Annual of the Israeli Oriental Society (Jerusalem, 1975), 161; and J.D. Fage and Roland Oliver, eds., "Morocco," in *The Cambridge History of Africa* (London and New York: Cambridge University Press, 1975), 7, 300.

8. George Hills, *Spain* (New York: Praeger Publishers, 1970), 114; Robert Rezette, *The Spanish Enclaves in Morocco*, trans. Mary Ewalt (Paris: Nouvelles Editions Latines, 1976), 53–54; Joaquín Arraras, ed., *Historia de la Cruzada Española* (Madrid: Ediciones Españolas, 1939), 38–42. For more on the 1909 campaign around Melilla and the "Tragic Week" draft riots, see Payne, *Politics and the Military in Modern Spain*, 105–12; and Joan Connelly Ullman, *The Tragic Week: A Study of Anti-Clericalism in Spain, 1875–1912* (Cambridge, MA: Harvard University Press, 1968). See also, Alal al-Fasi, *The Independence Movements in Arab North Africa*, trans. Hazem Zaki Nuseibeh (New York: Octagon Press, 1970), 92; Robert B. Asprey, *War in the Shadows: The Guerrilla in History* (New York: Doubleday & Co., 1975), 402; and Tomás García Figueras, *Marruecos: La Acción de España en el Norte de Africa* (Barcelona: Ediciones Fe, 1939), chap. 10.

9. Sebastian Balfour, *The End of the Spanish Empire 1898–1923* (Oxford: Clarendon Press, 1997), 200–1. Following the Melillan campaign of 1909, the Spanish occupied the coastal cities of Arcila, Larache, and Alcazarquivir on the Atlantic, and advanced toward the Kert River in the Rif. Seco Serrano, *Militarismo y civilismo*, 252.

10. Carlos Blanco Escolá, *La Academia General Militar de Zaragoza (1928–1931)* (Barcelona: Labor Universitaria, 1989), 82–83. Seco Serrano, *Militarismo y civilismo*, 253, noted that about the time of the 1909 Melillan campaign, the system of promotion known as "*méritos de guerra*" (war merits) was put into effect. They were discontinued after the Spanish-Cuban-American War (replaced by promotion based on seniority) in order to reduce rank inflation among the officers. It caused great animosity between the *peninsulares* and the *Africanistas*.

11. Shannon E. Fleming, "Disaster of Annual: Spanish Colonial Failure in Northern Morocco, 1902–1921" (Master's thesis, University of Minnesota, 1969), 17–18.

12. J. Ramón Alonso, *Historia Politica del Ejercito Español* (Madrid: Editora Nacional, 1974), 455; and Balfour, *The End of the Spanish Empire*, 187. Alvarez Junco and Shubert, *Spanish History since 1808*, wrote on 119 that the Army's casualties in the 1909 Melillan campaign had been 2,517, with more than 700 of that number having been killed, while independent sources put the numbers as high as 4,131. For more on the *Regulares*, see María Rosa de Madariaga, *Los Moros Que Trajo Franco...La Intervención de Tropas Coloniales en la Guerra Civil Española* (Barcelona: Ediciones Martínez Roca, S.A., 2002), 75–86.

13. Ron Vaughan, "The Forgotten Army: The Spanish in Morocco," *Savage & Soldier* XVI, no. 2 (April–June 1984): 2; and Hills, *Spain*, 118. See Fage and Oliver, "Morocco," 288–89. Rosita Forbes, *El Raisuni, the Sultan of the Mountains. His Life as Told to Rosita Forbes* (London: Thornton Butterworth, 1924). For more on the

establishment of the Protectorate, see García Figueras, *Marruecos,* chap. 11. Payne, *Politics and the Military in Modern Spain,* 115–19.

14. Alvarez Junco and Shubert, *Spanish History since 1808,* 119–20; and Payne, *Politics and the Military in Modern Spain,* 120.

15. Payne, *Politics and the Military in Modern Spain,* 123–51, 183; Esdaile, *Spain in the Liberal Age,* 234–39; Carr, *España: De La Restauración,* 121–26; and Seco Serrano, *Militarismo y civilismo,* 261–65.

16. Fleming, "Disaster of Annual," 49, 78–80; David S. Woolman, *Rebels in the Rif: Abd el Krim and the Rif Rebellion* (Stanford, CA: Stanford University Press, 1968), 100; Arturo Barea, *The Forging of a Rebel,* trans. Ilsa Barea (New York: Reynal & Hitchcock, 1946), 67–69; Payne, *Politics and the Military in Modern Spain,* 155; Esdaile, *Spain in the Liberal Age,* 250–51; and Seco Serrano, *Militarismo y civilismo,* 293. See Sebastian Balfour, *Deadly Embrace: Morocco and the Road to the Spanish Civil War* (New York: Oxford University Press, 2002), chap. 3.

17. Woolman, *Rebels in the Rif,* 67; and Payne, *Politics and the Military in Modern Spain,* 156.

18. *Archivo General Militar,* Legajo (File) #246, SECCIÓN (Section) #2, DIVISIÓN (Division) #10. Carlos De Silva, *General Millán Astray (El Legionario)* (Barcelona: Editorial AHR, 1956), 110. Subinspección de La Legión, ed., *La Legión Española (Cincuenta años de historia) 1920–1936* (Madrid: Leganes, 1975), 18. See De Silva, *General Millán Astray,* 111; and page 1 of *Resumen Historico De La Legión, Diario de Operaciones de la Legión* (Serrallo de la Legión, Plana Mayor del Tercio, Archivo General, Ceuta). *Servicio Historico Militar,* DO #22 (29-I-1920), Tomo (Volume) I, Año de 1920, Primer Trimestre (Madrid: Talleres del Deposito de la Guerra, 1920), 293, L 128. *Servicio Historico Militar,* Colección Legislative del Ejército— 1920—Ministerio de la Guerra #49 (Legislative Collection of the Army) #35 (28-I-1920) (Madrid: Talleres del Deposito de la Guerra, 1920), 60. John H. Galey, "Bridegrooms of Death: A Profile Study of the Spanish Foreign Legion," *Journal of Contemporary History* 4, no. 2 (April 1969): 49–51. Although the Legion was officially created on September 4, 1920, Legionaries celebrate the anniversary of the founding of the Legion on September 20, the date on which the first Legionary joined its ranks. For more on the creation of the Legion, see José E. Álvarez, *The Betrothed of Death: The Spanish Foreign Legion During the Rif Rebellion, 1920–1927* (Westport, CT: Greenwood Press, 2001), chap. 2; José Luis Rodríguez Jiménez, *¡A MÍ LA LEGIÓN!: De Millán Astray a las misiones de paz,* 2nd ed. (Barcelona: Editorial Planeta, S.A., 2005), chap. 2; and de Madariaga, *Los Moros Que Trajo Franco,* 86–104.

19. Carolyn Boyd, *Praetorian Politics in Liberal Spain* (Chapel Hill, NC: University of North Carolina, 1979), 172. According to Julio Busquets, *El militar de carrera en España,* 99–100, Gabriel Cardona looked at the impact of *"méritos de Guerra"* on promotions in the Infantry branch for the class of 1910. Because of the Moroccan War (1909–1927), twenty years after they left the Academy of Toledo, *Africanistas* like Franco (jumped 2,438 places) and Yagüe (jumped 1,595 places) enjoyed meteoric promotions, while classmates who remained in Spain languished in the lower ranks.

20. Brian Crozier, *Franco: A Biographical History* (London: Eyre & Spottiswoode, 1967), 51–52; J.W.D. Trythall, *Franco: A Biography* (London: Rupert Hart-Davis, 1970), 34; and George Hills, *Franco: The Man and His Nation* (New York: The Mac-Millan Company, 1967), 106. Luis De Galinsoga, *Centinela De Occidente,* with the

collaboration of Lieutenant General Franco Salgado (Barcelona: Editorial AHR, 1956), 37. Ricardo De La Cierva, *Franco* (Barcelona: Editorial Planeta, 1986), 57.

21. Álvarez, *Betrothed of Death,* 16–23; Rodríguez Jiménez, *¡A MÍ LA LEGIÓN!* 101, 106–19; and Carr, *España: De La Restauración,* 133.

22. Woolman, *Rebels in the Rif,* 69–71.

23. Seco Serrano, *Militarismo y civilismo,* 294–95; Esdaile, *Spain in the Liberal Age,* 251–52; and Carr, *España: De La Restauración,* 133–34.

24. Ricardo Fernández De La Ruguera and Susana March, *El Desastre De Annual* (Barcelona: Editorial Planeta, 1968), 37.

25. Fleming, "Disaster of Annual" and *Primo de Rivera and Abd-el-Krim: The Struggle in Spanish Morocco, 1923–1927* (New York and London: Garland Publishing, 1991); Rupert Furneaux, *Abdel Krim—Emir of the Rif* (London: Secker & Warburg, 1967); Vincent Sheean, *An American Among the Riffi* (New York: The Century Co., 1926) and *Personal History* (Garden City: Country Life Press, 1934–35); C. Richard Pennell, *A Country with a Government and a Flag: The Rif War in Morocco, 1921–1926* (Wisbech, Cambridgeshire, England: Middle East and North African Studies Press, 1986); Ramón Salas Larrazábal, *El Protectorado De España En Marruecos* (Madrid: Editorial MAPFRE, S.A., 1992); García Figueras, *Marruecos;* Asprey, *War in the Shadows,* vol. 1; Emilio Ayensa, *Del Desastre De Annual A La Presidencia Del Consejo* (Madrid: Rafael Caro Raggio, 1930); and Basil Davidson, *The People's Cause—A History of Guerrillas in Africa* (London: Longman Studies in African History, 1981). Antonio Carrasco García, *Las Imágenes del Desastre: Annual 1921* (Madrid: Almena Ediciones, 1999). In addition, the Riffians were now very well armed having captured thousands of rifles, as well as numerous machine guns and artillery pieces.

26. *DOL,* Negociado de Campaña, July 1921, 7; and *AGM,* Legajo #M-3204, SECCIÓN #1, DIVISIÓN #1, July 1921, 8. See Dámaso Berenguer Fusté, *Campañas en el Rif y Yebala 1921–1922: Notas y documentos de mi diario de operaciones* (Madrid: Sucesores De R. Velasco, 1923), 242. Estado Mayor Central del Ejército, Servicio Histórico Militar, *Historia de las Campañas de Marruecos,* vols. 3 and 4 (Madrid: Imprenta Ideal, 1981), 195.

27. Antonio Azpeitua, *Marruecos, la mala semilla; ensayo de analisis objetivo de como fue sembrada la guerra en África* (Madrid, 1921), 83.

28. Carlos de Arce, *Historia de la Legión Española* (Barcelona: Editorial Mitre, 1984), 96; José Millán Astray, *La Legión* (Madrid: V.H. Sanz Calleja, 1923), 182–85. *AGM,* Legajo #M-3204, SECCIÓN #1, DIVISIÓN #1, 8–9; Joaquín Arraras, ed., *Historia de la Cruzada Española* (Madrid: Ediciones Españolas, 1921), 115; Subinspección de La Legión, *La Legión Española,* 111; De La Cierva, *Franco,* 66, 182; and García Figueras, *Marruecos,* 181.

29. Payne, *Politics and the Military in Modern Spain,* 169–72; Fleming, *Primo de Rivera,* 70–73; Boyd, *Praetorian Politics in Liberal Spain,* 183–208; Woolman, *Rebels in the Rif,* 97; and Victor Morales Lezcano, *España y el Norte de África—El Protectorado en Marruecos (1912–1956)* (Madrid: U.N.E.D., 1986), 233. Rafael Bañon Martínez and Thomas M. Barker, eds., *Armed Forces and Society in Spain Past and Present* (New York: Columbia University Press, 1988), 233, wrote that the Annual disaster ended the Defense Juntas. They had discredited themselves and were abolished by Sánchez Guerra's government in November 1922. For more on the demise of the *Juntas de Defensa,* see Arraras, *Historia de la Cruzada Española,* 121; and Seco

Serrano, *Militarismo y civilismo*, 296–98. Though officially disbanded in 1922, the *Junteros* remained a powerful entity within the Army.

30. García Figueras, *Marruecos*, 182–83.

31. Subinspección de La Legión, *La Legión Española*, 117.

32. Delfín Salas, *Tropas Regulares Indígenas*, vol. 2 (Madrid: Aldaba Militaria, 1989), 7–8 (and Álvarez, *Betrothed of Death*, 51–52), describes the gruesome sights discovered at Nador. Barea, *The Forging of a Rebel*, 103–4.

33. The conscripts included many middle class *soldados de cuota*. For more on the *soldados de cuota*, see Boyd, *Praetorian Politics in Liberal Spain*, 200–1.

34. Payne, *Politics and the Military in Modern Spain*, 177.

35. The *Conferencia de Pizarra* had many ramifications which caused differences between the attendants. One major point of contention, which rightly had major consideration between the government and the military, was the POW question. Should they be ransomed for the amount asked for by Abd-el-Krim, or as the Army wanted, should they be liberated by their brothers-in-arms? The government wanted what was politically expedient, particularly since Spanish lives were at stake. On the other hand, the Army felt that it needed to vindicate itself after the drubbing it received at Annual, and they were certain that the ransom money paid would be used to buy weapons and mercenaries which would extend the course of the war and lead to more Spanish losses (which it did). Needless to say, what was agreed upon at the Conference of Pizarra came to naught as the Maura government was replaced on March 7 by one headed up by Sánchez Guerra. Subsequently, the staid Sánchez Guerra moved quickly to cancel all arrangements for a landing at Alhucemas Bay. For more on the various aspects of the *Conferencia de Pizarra*, see Arraras, *Historia de la Cruzada Española*, 118–19; García Figueras, *Marruecos*, 183–84; Berenguer Fusté, *Campañas en el Rif y Yebala*, 175–77 and 252–53; Estado Mayor Central del Ejército, *Historia de las Campañas de Marruecos*, 533–34; De La Cierva, *Franco*, 191; Fleming, *Primo de Rivera*, 73–75; and Morales Lezcano, *España y el Norte de África*, 234. Of the 570 Spaniards (soldiers and civilians) captured after Annual in 1921, 330 survivors were finally ransomed on January 27, 1923, for just over 4 million *pesetas*. Álvarez, *Betrothed of Death*, 85.

36. Juan Picasso González, *Expediente Picasso: Documentos relacionados con la información instruida por el señor general de división D. Juan Picasso sobre las responsabilidades de la actuación española en Marruecos durante julio de mil novecientos veintiuno*, with a Prologue by Diego Abad de Santillan (Mexico, D.F.: Frente de Afirmación Hispanista, A.C., 1976), 294–96.

37. Boyd, *Praetorian Politics in Liberal Spain*, 221–22. See also, Fleming, *Primo de Rivera*, 75–77; Payne, *Politics and the Military in Modern Spain*, 179–81; Woolman, *Rebels in the Rif*, 106–7; Fernando Cano Velasco, ed., "Las Fuerzas Regulares Indigenas" & "La Legión," in *Historia de las fuerzas armadas*, vol. 4 (Zaragoza: Ediciones Palafox, 1984), 152; and Estado Mayor Central del Ejército, *Historia de las Campañas de Marruecos*, 270. Berenguer, *Campañas en el Rif y Yebala*, 211–24. De La Cierva, *Franco*, 192. Arraras, *Historia de la Cruzada Española*, 120. de Arce, *Historia de la Legión Española*, 159.

38. Boyd, *Praetorian Politics in Liberal Spain*, 236–61; Payne, *Politics and the Military in Modern Spain*, 187–89; Woolman, *Rebels in the Rif*, 120–21; Fleming, *Primo de Rivera*, 85–87; Paul Preston, *Franco: A Biography* (New York: Basic Books,

1994), 40; García Figueras, *Marruecos*, 191–95; Arraras, *Historia de la Cruzada Española*, 128–32; and De La Cierva, *Franco*, 208–12.

39. Alonso Baquer, *El Ejército en la sociedad española*, 278, wrote that on two occasions, once in Cádiz in 1917 and the other in Madrid in 1922, Primo de Rivera had recommended that Morocco be abandoned. Esdaile, *Spain in the Liberal Age*, 260.

40. Fleming, *Primo de Rivera*, 87–108; and Boyd, *Praetorian Politics in Liberal Spain*, 262–73. García Figueras, *Marruecos*, 198.

41. García Figueras, *Marruecos*, 198; Payne, *Politics and the Military in Modern Spain*, 208; Fleming, *Primo de Rivera*, 108–11; Woolman, *Rebels in the Rif*, 124; Subinspección de La Legión, *La Legión Española*, 199; De La Cierva, *Franco*, 213; and Cano Velasco, Las Fuerzas Regulares Indigenas, 154.

42. See Álvarez, *Betrothed of Death*, 120–22, and Payne, *Politics and the Military in Modern Spain*, 211–12, for the "Ben Tieb incident." Susana Sueiro Seoane, "Spanish Colonialism During Primo de Rivera's Dictatorship," trans. Jessica Brown, *Mediterranean Historical Review* 13 (June–December 1998): 48–64.

43. Payne, *Politics and the Military in Modern Spain*, 209; García Figueras, *Marruecos*, 200; Woolman, *Rebels in the Rif*, 125; and Fleming, *Primo de Rivera*, 119–20.

44. Álvarez, *Betrothed of Death*, 113–41; Woolman, *Rebels in the Rif*, 128–45; and Payne, *Politics and the Military in Modern Spain*, 212–16.

45. Fleming, *Primo de Rivera*, 215–17.

46. Cano Velasco, Las Fuerzas Regulares Indigenas, 157, noted that the French defeat was similar to the Spaniard's defeat at Annual, but that the facts and figures were well concealed, and that Fez was in the same position as Melilla in July 1921. Payne, *Politics and the Military in Modern Spain*, 219. Woolman, *Rebels in the Rif*, 177 and 183–85. De La Cierva, *Franco*, 251, gave the number of soldiers sent by France to Morocco in order to counterattack Abd-el-Krim's forces as 100 battalions of infantry plus their support services.

47. Francisco Gómez-Jordana y Souza, *La Tramoya De Nuestra Actuación En Marruecos* (Madrid: Editora Nacional, 1976), 75–98. Fleming, *Primo de Rivera*, 247–55. de Arce, *Historia de la Legión Española*, 182, wrote that the Spanish and French agreed on France contributing 160,000 men, the majority being colonial troops and attacking from the south, while the Spanish would contribute 75,000 men, mostly Europeans, who would land at Alhucemas Bay and drive inland. Estado Mayor Central del Ejército, *Historia de las Campañas de Marruecos*, 20–21. De La Cierva, *Franco*, 247–50. García Figueras, *Marruecos*, 205–6. Woolman, *Rebels in the Rif*, 179–82.

48. Estado Mayor Central del Ejército, *Historia de las Campañas de Marruecos*, 59, 64–67. Pennell, *A Country with a Government and a Flag*, 199, noted that 5,000 Riffians opposed the Spaniards at Alhucemas. Fleming, *Primo de Rivera*, 285–99; De La Cierva, *Franco: Un Siglo*, 255–65; Preston, *Franco: A Biography*, 47–48; Payne, *Politics and the Military in Modern Spain*, 220; and Woolman, *Rebels in the Rif*, 190–91. Álvarez, *Betrothed of Death*, 168–72.

49. Álvarez, *Betrothed of Death*, 172–89, 191–204; Payne, *Politics and the Military in Modern Spain*, 221–23; and Woolman, *Rebels in the Rif*, 197–214. Alvarez Junco and Shubert, *Spanish History since 1808*, 211.

50. Alvarez Junco and Shubert, *Spanish History since 1808*, 210, 215. Esdaile, *Spain in the Liberal Age*, 274–76. Payne, *Politics and the Military in Modern Spain*, 242.

51. Alvarez Junco and Shubert, *Spanish History since 1808,* 215, noted that Primo de Rivera reduced the officer corps by 10%, and the troops by a third, while at the same time paring down the number of cadets from 1,200 in 1922 to 200 in 1929. Payne, *Politics and the Military in Modern Spain,* 241–42.

52. Payne, *Politics and the Military in Modern Spain,* 224–25.

53. Ibid., 256–57.

54. Williams, *The Story of Spain,* 195–96; and Payne, *Politics and the Military in Modern Spain,* 260–65.

Chapter 3

1. See Gabriel Cardona, *El problema militar en España* (Madrid: Historia 16, 1990), 121–27.

2. Fernando de Bordejé y Morencos, *Vicisitudes de una política naval* (Madrid: Editorial San Martín, 1978), chap. 2.

3. Steven E. Miller, ed., *Military Strategy and the Origins of the First World War* (Princeton, New Jersey: Princeton University Press, 1985); D.G. Herrmann, *The Arming of Europe and the Making of the First World War* (New Jersey: Princeton University Press, 1996).

4. Enrique Rosas Ledezma, "Las Declaraciones de Cartagena (1907): significación en la política exterior de España y repercusiones internacionales," *Cuadernos de Historia Moderna y Contemporánea* 2 (1981): 213–29; and Rosario de la Torre del Río, "Los acuerdos anglo-hispano-franceses de 1907: una larga negociación en la estela del 98," *Cuadernos de la Escuela Diplomática* 1 (June 1988): 81–104.

5. For information on Spain's attitude concerning the impending war, the French chargé d'affaires in Madrid commented in a letter to Paris that the Spanish were indifferent on this matter; confidential, Mathieu de Vienne, French chargé d'affaires in Madrid, a Bienvenu-Martin, acting Minister for Foreign Affairs, July 27, 1914, *Documents Diplomatiques Français* (Paris: Imprimerie Nationale, 1929–1959), 3rd series, XI, n. 174. Gerie B. Bledsoe, "Spanish Foreign Policy, 1898–1936," in *Spain in the Twentieth-Century World. Essays on Spanish Diplomacy, 1898–1978,* ed. James W. Cortada (London: Aldwych Press, 1980), 11–14. José María Jover Zamora, "Caracteres de la política exterior de España en el siglo XIX," in *Política, diplomacia y humanismo popular* (Madrid: Turner, 1976), 137–38.

6. Víctor Morales Lezcano, *León y Castillo, Embajador (1887–1918). Un estudio sobre la política exterior de España* (Las Palmas de Gran Canaria: Cabildo Insular de Gran Canaria, 1975), 140n10.

7. Pierre Renouvin, *Historia de las relaciones internacionales,* 2nd. ed. (Madrid: Akal, 1990), 530–31; and Rosario de la Torre del Río, "Entre 1898 y 1914: la orientación de la política exterior española," in *Política española y política naval tras el desastre (1900–1914). VII Jornadas de Historia Marítima,* vol. 15 of *Cuadernos Monográficos del Instituto de Historia y Cultura Naval* (Madrid: Instituto de Historia y Cultura Naval, 1991), 19–21.

8. See Julián Cortés Cavanillas, *Alfonso XIII y la guerra del 14* (Madrid: Alce, 1976).

9. Hipólito de la Torre Gómez, "El destino de la *regeneración* internacional de España (1898–1918)," *Proserpina* 1 (1984): 9–22.

10. Juan Carlos Pereira Castañares, *Introducción al estudio de la política exterior de España (siglos XIX y XX)* (Madrid: Akal, 1983), 155. A study of the country's internal situation can be found in two classic works: Melchor Fernández Almagro, *Historia del reinado de D. Alfonso XIII* (Barcelona: Montaner y Simón, 1933); and Carlos Seco Serrano, *Alfonso XIII y la crisis de la Restauración* (Barcelona: Ariel, 1969). To understand fully the public opinion toward the war, see Fernando Díaz-Plaja, *Francófilos y germanófilos* (Madrid: Alianza, 1981). See also Gerald H. Meaker, "A Civil War of Words: The Ideological Impact of the First World War on Spain, 1914–18," in *Neutral Europe Between War and Revolution, 1917–23* (Cherlottesville: University Press of Virginia, 1988), 1–65.

11. Gloria Solé Romeo, "La Conferencia de Algeciras de 1906: Una solución europea al conflicto marroquí y a la crisis internacional de 1905," *Revista de la Universidad Complutense, Estudios de Hª Moderna y Contemporánea, Homenaje a D. Jesús Pabón III* XXVIII, no. 116 (1979): 261–79.

12. *Diario de Sesiones* (hereafter *DS*), *Senado,* session of 1918, V, January 22, 1919, n. 108, 1811–1813.

13. Undated draft for a speech delivered on his return in 1916 to the Paris embassy, Archivo Histórico Provincial de Las Palmas (hereafter AHPLP), *Fernando León y Castillo,* file 21.

14. Morales Lezcano, *León y Castillo,* 141–74.

15. Jean-Marc Delaunay, "España trabajó por la victoria," *Historia 16* 63 (1981): 38–44.

16. For a study of relations between Spain and Germany, within the framework of neutrality in the Spanish government during the war, see Lilian Gelos de Vaz Ferreira, *Die Neutralitätspolitik Spaniens während des Ersten Weltkrieges. Unter besonderer Berücksichtigung der deutsch-spanischen Beziehungen* (Hamburg: Institut für Auswärtige Politik, 1966).

17. Ron M. Carden, *German Policy Toward Neutral Spain, 1914–1918* (New York and London: Garland Publishing, Inc., 1987), 37–38.

18. Morales Lezcano, *León y Castillo,* 140n11.

19. Polo de Bernabé, Spanish Ambassador in Berlin, to Marquis of Lema, Minister of State, March 18, 1915, Archivo del Ministerio de Asuntos Exteriores, Madrid (hereafter AMAE), *Guerra Europea,* H 2988.

20. Carden, *German Policy Toward Neutral Spain,* 46.

21. Alfonso XIII to Wilhelm II, January 19, 1918, Politisches Archiv des Auswärtigen Amts, Berlin (hereafter PAAA), *Spanien 61,* R 12005.

22. The work by Carden, *German Policy Toward Neutral Spain,* mainly considers the able German diplomacy which, along with the pragmatism of Madrid, led to Spanish neutrality; however, no Spanish sources are included.

23. Telegram from Ratibor, Imperial Ambassador in Madrid, to *Auswärtiges Amt,* December 30, 1915, PAAA, *Spanien 55 Nr. 2,* R 11950.

24. Strictly confidential note from the Austro-Hungarian Embassy in Berlin, April 4, 1916, PAAA, *Spanien 61,* R 11999.

25. Morales Lezcano, *León y Castillo,* 147–48.

26. See Hipólito de la Torre Gómez, *Antagonismo y fractura peninsular. España-Portugal, 1910–1919* (Madrid: Espasa-Calpe, 1983).

27. Telegram from Ratibor, Imperial Ambassador in Madrid, to *Auswärtiges Amt,* October 6, 1914, PAAA, *Spanien 61,* R 11998.

28. PAAA, *Spanien 61*, cited in Carden, *German Policy Toward Neutral Spain*, 96–97.

29. Telegram from Bethmann Hollweg to Lancken, August 29, 1915, PAAA, *Der Weltkrieg Nr. 11 q Geheim*, R 21239.

30. PAAA, *Der Weltkrieg Nr. 11 q Geheim*, cited in Carden, *German Policy Toward Neutral Spain*, 98–99.

31. Private correspondence, Marquis of Lema, Minister of State, to Polo de Bernabé, Spanish Ambassador in Berlin, November 2, 1915, AMAE, *Guerra Europea*, H 3055.

32. Albert Mousset, *La política exterior de España, 1873–1918* (Madrid: Bib. Nueva, 1918), refers to Spanish neutrality as static in the first part of the war and dynamic in the final stages of the conflict.

33. See Gabriel Cardona, "La reforma militar que nunca existió," *Historia 16* 63 (1981): 31–38.

34. Bordejé y Morencos, *Vicisitudes de una política naval*, chaps. 1–3.

35. Undated draft for a speech delivered on his return in 1916 to the Paris embassy, AHPLP, *Fernando León y Castillo*, file 21.

36. *DS, Senado*, session of 1918, V, January 22, 1919, n. 108, 1812.

37. Royal Order April 11, 1911, applying Royal Decree dated March 17, 1891, which established military zone on coasts and borders, extended to the Balearic and Canary Islands and possessions in Africa through Royal Orders September 30 of the same year and September 27, 1902, AMAE, *Guerra Europea*, H 3163.

38. *DS, Senado*, session of 1914, VIII, February 8, 1915, n. 138, 2203–7.

39. *DS, Congreso de los Diputados*, session of 1918, V, 13 and 14 June 1918, n. 56 and 57, 1655–70 and 1688–90.

40. F. Javier Ponce Marrero, *Canarias en la Gran Guerra, 1914–1918: estrategia y diplomacia. Un estudio sobre la política exterior de España* (Las Palmas de Gran Canaria: Ediciones del Cabildo, 2006), 108.

41. For an analysis of the agreement, see Isidro Fabela, *Neutralité* (Paris: Pedone, 1949), 69–77.

42. For a study of Spanish policy in the international conference, see María Victoria López-Cordón Cortezo, "España en las Conferencias de La Haya de 1899 y 1907," *Revista de Estudios Internacionales* 3 (July–September 1982): 703–56.

43. Memorandum, November 1914, AMAE, *Guerra Europea*, H 3097.

44. Telegrams from the Minister of the Navy to the Naval Commanders in Tenerife and Las Palmas, September 5, 1914, AMAE, *Guerra Europea*, H 2984.

45. Royal Decree November 23, 1914, concerning the XIIIth Agreement of The Hague regarding rights and responsibilities of the neutral powers in the event of war at sea, AMAE, *Guerra Europea*, H 3097.

46. Central Staff of the Ministry of the Navy to Minister of State, November 7, 1914, Ibid.

47. Archivo de la Capitanía General, Tenerife (hereafter ACGT), section 2, division 4, file 4.

48. Royal Order May 29, 1915, Ibid.

49. Royal Order June 2, 1915, Ibid.

50. Royal Order June 30, 1915, ACGT, section 2, division 3, file 82.

51. Ministry of the War to General Captaincy of the Canary Islands, October 1, 1915, ACGT, section 2, division 4, file 4.

52. Ponce Marrero, *Canarias en la Gran Guerra*, 117–18.

53. The British Embassy believed that some German ships were armed and stocked to flee; private correspondence, Hardinge, British Ambassador in Madrid, to Villanueva, Minister of State, February 20, 1916, The National Archives, Kew (hereafter NA), FO 372/885.

54. According to the list of German and Austrian ships sheltered in Spanish ports in May 1918 by the naval attaché at the British Embassy in Madrid, NA, FO 372/1169.

55. Ponce Marrero, *Canarias en la Gran Guerra*, 118–20.

Chapter 4

1. The best overview of civil–military relations during the Restoration era can be found in Boyd, *Praetorian Politics in Liberal Spain*. See also, Seco Serrano, *Militarismo y civilismo*.

2. Led by battle-hardened officers like José Millán Astray and Francisco Franco, the latter quickly gained notoriety for its discipline, ruthlessness, and efficient fighting abilities.

3. Frank E. Manuel, *The Politics of Modern Spain* (New York: McGraw-Hill, 1938), chap. 7, 129–50.

4. By early 1936, there were an estimated 30,000 members throughout Spain as a whole. Carlist efforts to overthrow the government also received financial support from Mussolini's government. Martin Blinkhorn, *Carlism and Crisis in Spain, 1931–1939* (New York and London: Cambridge University Press, 1975), 136–37.

5. Though the clandestine *Unión Militar Española* (UME)—composed of around one-fourth of the active officer corps (3,436)—played a role in the early planning of the uprising, the organization itself lacked the kind of cohesive organization and forceful leadership which would have made it, in the words of Stanley Payne, "an effective instrument of conspiracy." See his, *Spain's First Democracy* (Madison: The University of Wisconsin Press, 1993), 290.

6. In addition, to ensure that there would not be any organized effort to resist the rebellion, Mola's directive called for the violent suppression of all groups and individuals who were deemed enemies of the insurrectionary movement.

7. Hagiographical treatments of several of the leading conspirators can be found in the following: General Jorge Vigón, *General Mola* (Barcelona: Editorial AHR, 1957); General Emilio Esteban-Infantes, *General Sanjurjo* (Barcelona: Editorial AHR, 1957; General Francisco Javier Mariñas, *General Varela* (Barcelona: Editorial AHR, 1957).

8. On Franco's role at this time and during the Civil War period: Paul Preston, *Franco* (New York: Basic Books, 1994).

9. Sebastian Balfour, *Deadly Embrace*, 271.

10. Gerald Howson, *Aircraft of the Spanish Civil War* (Smithsonian, 1990; Putnam Aeronautical, 2003), 12.

11. Both Italy and Germany deepened their commitment to Franco over time. The first organized Italian troops arrived in Spain in early 1937, while Germany formalized its military support to the Nationalists by organizing the Condor Legion in October 1936.

12. Raymond Carr, *The Spanish Tragedy: The Civil War in Perspective* (London: Phoenix, 2000), 66.

13. According to Stanley Payne, Nationalist mobilizing efforts were highly successful. See, *Politics and the Military in Modern Spain,* 389.

14. Anthony Beevor, *The Battle for Spain* (London: Weidenfeld & Nicolson, 2006), 199.

15. *British Documents on Foreign Affairs,* Part II, Series F, vol. 27, 169.

16. *Documents on German Foreign Policy,* Series "D," vol. III, no. 96, 106.

17. Beevor, *The Battle for Spain,* chap. 18, 189–207.

18. *Documents on German Foreign Policy,* Series "D," vol. III, 554.

19. As we have seen, Franco had successfully decapitated the leadership of the civilian movements that could rival his authority. The head of the Falange, Manuel Hedilla, was placed under arrest and the independent-minded Carlist leader, Manuel Fal Conde, had been sent into exile in Portugal.

Chapter 5

1. See, for example, *ABC (Madrid), passim.*

2. Enrique Líster, *Nuestra Guerra* (Paris: Librairie du Globe, 1966), 74.

3. R. Radosh, Mary Habeck, and G. Sevastianov, *Spain Betrayed* (New Haven and London: Yale UP, 2001), 18.

4. For a close study of Soviet aid to the Republic, see D. Kowalsky, *La Unión Soviética y la guerra civil española: una revisión crítica* (Barcelona: Crítica, 2004), 191–240.

5. M. Aroca Mohedano, *General Juan Hernández Saravia* (Madrid: Oberón, 2006), 159–81.

6. Carlos Engel, *Historia de las Brigadas Mixtas del Ejército Popular de la República* (Madrid: Almena, 1999), lists all the commanders.

7. Radosh, Habeck, and Sevastianov, *Spain Betrayed,* 127.

8. For a list and comparison of Republican and Nationalist commanders, see Michael Alpert, *El ejército republicano en la guerra civil española* (Madrid: Siglo XXI, 1989), 343–58.

9. Ibid. on militia, 130–75.

10. *Gaceta de Madrid,* August 3, 1936.

11. See Alpert, *El ejército republicano en la guerra civil española,* 320–24 for a list of militia units.

12. Ibid., 48–54.

13. Líster, *Nuestra Guerra,* 61–73; and Juan Modesto, *Soy del Quinto Regimiento* (Paris: Librairie du Globe, 1969), 44.

14. Cipriano Mera, *Guerra, exilio y cárcel de un anarcosindicalista* (Paris: Ruedo Ibérico, 1976), especially 111.

15. Alpert, *El ejército republicano en la guerra civil española,* 70–71.

16. J.I. Martínez Paricio, ed., *Los papeles del general Rojo* (Madrid: Espasa-Calpe, 1989), 182–84.

17. On the Mixed Brigade, see Alpert, *El ejército republicano en la guerra civil española,* 76–80; Ramón Salas, *Historia de Ejército Popular de la República* (Madrid: Editora Nacional, 1973), 504–7.

18. Alpert, *El ejército republicano en la guerra civil española*, 80–86.

19. Ibid., 305–10.

20. Remi Skoutelsky, *Novedad en el frente: las brigadas internacionales en la guerra civil española* (Madrid: Ediciones Temas de Hoy, 2005), is an up-to-date study supported by recent research in Russian archives.

21. Antonio Elorza and Marta Bizcarrondo, *Queridos camaradas: el Comintern en España 1919–1939* (Barcelona: Planeta, 1999), 324.

22. Salas, *Historia de Ejército Popular de la República*, 1294.

23. Skoutelsky, *Novedad en el frente*, 282.

24. Notably by Kowalsky, *La Unión Soviética y la guerra civil española*, 211–31, and Gerald Howson, *Arms for Spain: The Untold Story of the Spanish Civil War* (London: John Murray, 1998), 136–45.

25. Michael Alpert, *A New International History of the Spanish Civil War*, 2nd ed. (1994; repr., Basingstoke: Palgrave, 2004), chap. 16.

26. Howson, *Arms for Spain*, 218–29.

27. Kowalsky, *La Unión Soviética y la guerra civil española*, 216–320, discusses Russian personnel in Spain in detail.

28. Michael Alpert, "The Clash of Spanish Armies: Contrasting Ways of War in Spain 1936–1939," *War in History* 6, no. 3 (1999): 331–51.

29. Kowalsky, *La Unión Soviética y la guerra civil española*, 312.

30. Radosh, Habeck, and Sevastianov, *Spain Betrayed*, 158.

31. Alpert, *El ejército republicano en la guerra civil española*, 268–74.

32. On the Casado coup, see Angel Bahamonde and Javier Cervera, *Así terminó la guerra de España* (Madrid: Marcial Pons, 2000).

33. Alpert, *El ejército republicano en la guerra civil española*, 293–304.

34. Alpert, *Clash of Spanish Armies*, 338.

Chapter 6

1. Wayne H. Bowen, *Spain During World War II* (Columbia: University of Missouri Press, 2006), 1.

2. *Arriba*, April 2, 1939.

3. Gustau Nerín and Alfred Bosch, *El imperio que nunca existió* (Barcelona: Plaza y Janés, 2001), 30, 215. US Army Military History Institute, Carlisle Barracks, Box 62A, Letter and attached Memoranda, "Basic data pertaining to Spanish military, naval and air forces," October 26, 1944, U.S. Ambassador and Military Attachés, Madrid, to Secretary of State.

4. José Luis Casas Sánchez, ed., *La postguerra española y la Segunda Guerra Mundial* (Córdoba: Diputación Provincial de Córdoba, 1990), 43. Elena Hernández-Sandoica and Enrique Moradiellos, "Spain and the Second World War," in *European Neutrals and Non-Belligerents during the Second World War*, ed. Neville Wylie (Cambridge: Cambridge University Press, 2002), 248–49. *Arriba*, September 6–7, November 24, 1940, June 24, 1941, March 22, 1944.

5. Gabriel Cardona, *Franco y sus generales* (Madrid: Temas de Hoy, 2001), 46.

6. *Arriba*, July 6 and 25, 1939. *YA*, July 5 and 25, 1939. Stanley G. Payne, *The Franco Regime* (London: Phoenix Press, 2000), 242–43. Frances Lannon and Paul Preston, eds., *Elites and Power in Twentieth-Century Spain* (Oxford: Oxford University Press, 1990), 206.

7. José Antonio Olmeda Gómez, *Las Fuerzas Armadas en el Estado Franquista* (Madrid: Ediciones El Arquero, 1988), 110–12, 135. Miguel Alonso Baquer, *Franco y sus generales* (Madrid: Taurus, 2005), 102.

8. *Ejército, Indice de los trabajos publicados desde Febrero de 1940 (N. 1) a fin de Diciembre de 1945 (N. 71)*, Madrid, Army Ministry, 1946.

9. *Revista General de Marina*, Madrid, Naval Ministry, 1941–1945.

10. Cardona, *Franco y sus generales*, 39–40.

11. Geoffrey Jensen, *Franco: Soldier, Commander, Dictator* (Dulles, VA: Potomac Books, 2005), 101–2.

12. Cardona, *Franco y sus generales*, 96.

13. Paul Preston, "Decay, Division, and the Defence of Dictatorship: The Military and Politics, 1939–1975," in *Elites and Power in Twentieth-Century Spain*, ed. Frances Lannon and Paul Preston (Oxford: Oxford University Press, 1990), 205.

14. *Arriba*, June 15, 1941.

15. Cardona, *Franco y sus generales*, 49–50. *YA*, July 29, 1939. *Arriba*, July 22, 1939.

16. Payne, *The Franco Regime*, 244–45; Cardona, *Franco y sus generales*, 78, 90–91; and *Arriba*, November 18, 1942.

17. Olmeda Gómez, *Las Fuerzas Armadas*, 131–32, 160.

18. Payne, *The Franco Regime, 1936–1975*, 245–46; Cardona, *Franco y sus generales*, 42; and Raymond Carr, *Spain: 1808–1975*, 2nd ed. (Oxford: Oxford University Press, 1990), 698.

19. Preston, "Decay, Division, and the Defence of Dictatorship," 209–10; and Olmeda Gómez, *Las Fuerzas Armadas*, 206, 218.

20. Cardona, *Franco y sus generales*, 121.

21. Preston, "Decay, Division, and the Defence of Dictatorship," 206–7.

22. Cardona, *Franco y sus generales*, 56.

23. Ibid., 108–9.

24. José María Gil-Robles, *La monarquía por la que yo luché* (Madrid: Taurus, 1976), 61; and Cardona, *Franco y sus generales*, 48.

25. Preston, "Decay, Division, and the Defence of Dictatorship," 206–7.

26. Cardona, *Franco y sus generales*, 57; Preston, "Decay, Division, and the Defence of Dictatorship," 208; and Carr, *The Spanish Tragedy*, 260.

27. Cardona, *Franco y sus generales*, 120–21; and *YA*, August 25, 1942.

28. Cardona, *Franco y sus generales*, 112–14.

29. Preston, "Decay, Division, and the Defence of Dictatorship," 205.

30. Baquer, *Franco y sus generales*, 66.

31. Alfredo Kindelán, *La verdad de mis relaciones con Franco* (Barcelona: Planeta, 1981), 129.

32. Payne, *The Franco Regime*, 235; and Preston, *Franco*, 339–40.

33. Gil-Robles, *La monarquía por la que yo luché*, 62.

34. Rafael Abella, *La vida cotidiana en España bajo el regimen de Franco* (Barcelona: Argos Vergara, 1985), 64–65.

35. Payne, *The Franco Regime*, 266–67.

36. Antonio Marquina Barrio, *La diplomacia vaticana y la España de Franco* (Madrid: CSIC, 1983), 269–70; Payne, *The Franco Regime*, 260–61; and Preston, *Franco*, 365.

37. Marquina Barrio, *La diplomacia vaticana y la España de Franco*, 270.

38. Abella, *La vida cotidiana en España bajo el regimen de Franco*, 70.

39. Cardona, *Franco y sus generales*, 72.
40. *YA*, June 27 and 29, 1941. *Arriba*, June 25–29, July 1–3, 1941.
41. *Arriba*, July 3, 8, 11, 13, 15, and 20, 1941.
42. *YA*, October 29, 1941, March 3, 1942. *Arriba*, July 25 and 29, August 12 and 17, September 7, 1941, January 2, February 24, March 25, June 12 and 14, July 15 and 24, August 25, November 3, 10, and 29, December 3–4, 1942, June 16, July 23, 1943.
43. *Arriba*, January 2, 1942.
44. *Arriba*, December 16, 18, and 19, 1942, January 3, 6, 9, and 13, 1943. Payne, *The Franco Regime*, 347 and *Fascism in Spain, 1923–1977*, 385.
45. Payne, *The Franco Regime*, 306–9. Preston, *Franco*, 466–68. Carr, *Spain, 1808–1975*, 720. Payne, *Fascism in Spain, 1923–1977*, 378–79. *Arriba*, August 19 and 25, September 4, December 9, 1942.
46. *Arriba*, September 4, 1942.
47. Preston, *Franco*, 470.
48. Gil-Robles, *La monarquía por la que yo luché*, 19.
49. Cardona, *Franco y sus generales*, 86–87.

Chapter 7

1. See, for instance, the Moroccan situation just prior to and during the European penetration of that empire in the late nineteenth and early twentieth centuries in C.R. Pennell, *Morocco since 1830* (New York: New York University Press, 2000), 68–153. On the state of the Spanish Army in terms of colonial involvement see Javier Ramiro de la Mata, *Origen y dinámica del colonialismo español en Marruecos* (Ceuta: Ciudad Autónoma de Ceuta, 2001), 53–63.
2. See José Luis Villanova, *Los interventores: la piedra angular del Protectorado español en Marruecos* (Barcelona: Edicions Bellaterra, 2006). On the Second Republican policies in Spanish Morocco, see S.E. Fleming, "Spanish Morocco and the Second Republic: Consistency of Colonial Policy?" in *Spain and the Mediterranean since 1898*, ed. Raanan Rein (London: Frank Cass, 1999), 80–98.
3. José Luis Villanova, *El Protectorado de España en Marruecos: organización política y territorial* (Barcelona: Edicions Bellaterra, 2004), 190–96.
4. This information is taken from entries dated April 26, 1940 (148) and June 19, 1940 (195) in the "Journal des marches et operations du Quartier Général du Commandement en Chef du Théâtre d'Opérations de l'Afrique du Nord (2 septembre 1939–31 juillet 1940)" in the Nogues Papers, Paris. The author would like to thank Professor William A. Hoisington for this information. Morales Lezcano, *España y el Norte de África*, 136. The Ministerio del Ejército in the *Organización del Ejército, Plantillas 1940* (Madrid: Ministerio del Ejército, 1941), 194, puts this figure at 86,232. The author would like to thank Lucas Molina Franco for providing this information.
5. For Francoist imperial aspiration, see among others, Lluís Riudor, "Sueños imperiales y africanismo durante el franquismo (1939–1956)," in *España en Marruecos (1912–1956): discursos geográficos e intervención territorial*, ed. Joan Nogué and José Luis Villanova (Lleida: Editorial Milenio, 1999), 251–76. For the full text of President Roosevelt's November 8, 1942, message to General Franco, see http://www.ibiblio.org/pha/policy/1942/421108e.html.

6. This figure was provided to the author in correspondence dated August 29, 2006, with the Subdirección de Estudios Históricos del Instituto de Historia y Cultura Militar (Ministerio de Defensa). The author would like to thank Comandante Antonio de Pablo Cantero for this information.

7. Juan B. Vilar, "España y la descolonización de Marruecos," in *Relaciones entre España y Marruecos en el Siglo XX*, ed. José U. Martínez Carreras (Madrid: Asociación Española de Africanistas, 2000), 68. Salas Larrazábal, *El Protectorado de España en Marruecos*, 245–68.

8. These figures are provided in Tables 16 and 17 in Salas Larrazábal, *El Protectorado de España en Marruecos*, 325.

9. Víctor Morales Lezcano, *El final del Protectorado Hispano-Francés en Marruecos: el desafío del nacionalismo magrebí (1945–1962)* (Madrid: Instituto Egipico de Estudios Islámicos, 1998), 137–43.

10. M.D. Algora Weber, *Las relaciones hispano-árabes durante el régimen de Franco: la rupture del aislamiento internacional (1946–50)* (Madrid: Ministerio de Asuntos Exteriores, 1995). See also M.D. Algora Weber, "La política árabe del régimen franquista: planteamientos generales y fases," *Estudios Africanos*, 5 (1990): 93–100.

11. María Concepción Ybarra Enríquez de la Orden, *España y la descolonización del magreb: rivalidad hispano-francesa en Marruecos (1951–1961)* (Madrid: U.N.E.D., 1998), 75; Salas Larrazábal, *El Protectorado de España en Marruecos*, 337. See also Mohammed Ibn Azzuz Hakim's interesting reassessment of Spanish contributions to Northern Morocco during the Protectorate years in "Una visión realista del Protectorado ejercido por España en Marruecos," in Martínez Carreras, *Relaciones entre España y Marruecos*, 53–64.

12. Ybarra, *España y la descolonización del magreb*, 139.

13. Ibid., 243, ft. 11 for figures dealing with terrorist incidents in French Morocco; 101 for Spanish Army staffing; and 117–235 for the events of 1953–55. For the state of Spanish forces in Spanish Morocco, see Paul Preston, *Franco: A Biography* (New York: Basic Books, 1994), 643.

14. Francisco Franco Salgado-Araujo, *Mis conversaciones privadas con Franco* (Barcelona: Planeta, 1976), 158. Preston, *Franco: A Biography*, 643–44. Preston repeats the famous Franco quote on 652: "Without Africa, I can scarcely explain myself to myself." Ybarra, *España y la descolonización del magreb*, 239–52.

15. Franco Salgado-Araujo, *Mis conversaciones privadas con Franco*, 170; and Salas Larrazábal, *El Protectorado de España en Marruecos*, 280–87, 324.

16. Salas Larrazábal, *El Protectorado de España en Marruecos*, 280–87, 324.

17. Franco Salgado-Araujo, *Mis conversaciones privadas con Franco*, 172.

18. Ybarra, *España y la descolonización del magreb*, 252–59.

19. Franco Salgado-Araujo, *Mis conversaciones privadas con Franco*, 168.

20. Ministerio del Ejército, *Memoria del Repliegue a Soberanía de las Fuerzas Españolas en Marruecos, 1956–1961* (Madrid: Impresa del Servicio Geográfico del Ejercito, 1962), 121. The author would like to thank Lucas Molina Franco for providing this resource.

21. *Memoria del Repliegue a Soberanía*, 39–101. Ybarra, *España y la descolonización del magreb*, 292. On the Liberation Army see, among others, Pennell, *Morocco since 1830*, 289–92 and Douglas E. Ashford, *Political Change in Morocco* (Princeton, NJ: Princeton University Press, 1961), 176–77.

22. Gastón Segura Valero, *Ifni: la guerra que silenció Franco* (Madrid: Ediciones Martínez Roca, 2006), 242–43. José Ramón Diego Aguirre, *La última guerra colonial de España: Ifni-Sáhara (1957–1958)* (Málaga: Editorial Algazara, 1993), 128–30.

23. Ramón Diego Aguirre, *La última guerra colonial de España*, 71–124. Segura Valero, *Ifni*, 118–51.

24. Ramón Diego Aguirre, *La última guerra colonial de España*, 167–228. Ybarra, *España y la descolonización del magreb*, 341.

25. Ybarra, *España y la descolonización del magreb*, 337. Franco Salgado-Araujo, *Mis conversaciones privadas con Franco*, 221. Elena del Pozo Manzano, "La campaña de Ifni en la última guerra de Africa: 1957–1958," *Estudios Africanos* 5 (1990): 123.

26. Segura Valero, *Ifni*, 297 for the French commitment; for the Spanish figure see page 301. Segura Valero also provides a discussion of the shortcomings of Spanish equipment and logistics on 248–51. See also Jesús F. Salafranca Ortega, *El sistema colonial español en África* (Málaga: Editorial Algazara, 2001), 315–18 concerning command issues. See also Alfredo Bosque Coma, *Guerra de Ifni, las banderas paracaidistas 1957–1958* (Madrid: Almena, 1998).

27. Guadalupe Pérez García, "La falacia histórica sobre la colonia de Ifni," *Historia y Comunicación Social* 8 (2003): 207–22. José Ramón Diego Aguirre, *Historia del Sahara Español* (Madrid: Kaydeda, 1988), 405–29.

28. A detailed study of Equatorial Guinea's decolonization is furnished by Alicia Campos Serrano, *De colonia a estado: Guinea Ecuatorial, 1955–1968* (Madrid: Centro de Estudios Políticos y Constitucionales, 2002). For the police figures, see ft. 4, 169.

29. Javier Tusell Gómez, *Carrero. La eminencia gris del régimen de Franco* (Madrid: Temas de Hoy, 1993), 308–9.

30. Salafranca Ortega, *El sistema colonial español en África*, 330–34.

31. José Ramón Diego Aguirre, *Guerra en el Sáhara* (Madrid: Ediciones Istmo, 1991), 78–90.

32. For a new look at this crisis and the United States role in it, see Jacob Mundy, "Neutrality or Complicity? The United States and the 1975 Moroccan Takeover of the Spanish Sahara," *Journal of North African Studies* 11 (September 2006): 275–306.

33. The most complete discussion of the Sahara crisis of 1974–75 from a Spanish military perspective is contained in Diego Aguirre, *Historia*, 632–725. For Spanish military staffing in the Sahara in 1975, see 734–46.

34. Diego Aguirre, *Historia*, 726–33. See also, Jerome B. Weiner, "The Green March in Historical Perspective," *Middle Eastern Journal* 33 (Winter 1979): 20–33.

35. One of the most complete narratives of these events is provided by Tony Hodges, *Western Sahara: The Roots of a Desert War* (Westport, CT: L. Hill, 1983).

36. Segura Valero, *Ifni*, 359.

Chapter 8

1. Stanley G. Payne, *The Franco Regime* (London: Phoenix Press, 2000), 357–61.

2. Juán Vasques García, "Spanish Coastal Defenses of the Rias Baixas," *Coast Defense Journal* 18, no. 18 (February 2004): 42–54; Juán Vasques García, "Modern Coastal Defenses of the Spanish Naval Base of Ferrol," *Coast Defense Journal* 14, no. 2 (May 2000): 29–39.

3. Jean-Louis Blanchon, "Linea P—ligne de fortification de la chaîne des Pyrénées," *Fortifications & Patrimoine*, no. 2 (April 1997): 4.

4. Payne, *The Franco Regime*, 344–45, 375–76, 381; see also Louis Stein, *Beyond Death and Exile: The Spanish Republicans in France, 1939–1955* (Cambridge: Harvard University Press, 1979).

5. References for construction of 1945 order of battle data include: http://orbat.com/site/ww2/drleo/080_spain/44_army/_army.html. Francisco Fernandez Mateos, *Medio siglo de caballeria española Defensa Extra 17* (Madrid: Edefa, 1991), 56. Rafael Reig de la Vega (ed.), *Los 75 Años de La Legión Española, Defensa, Extra 41* (Madrid: Edefa, 1995). Francisco Javier Álvarez Laita, inter alia (ed.), *Artilleria de Costa en la España del siglo XIX Defensa Extra 76–77* (Madrid: Edefa, 2006). "La Brunete, 60 años de historia" *Defensa* n.231/232 (July–August, 1977), 21. Spain. Circular November 16, 1939, organizing the troops of the Air Force. BOE Database (http://www.boe.es). José Luis Gonzalez Serrano, *Unidades y Material del Ejercito del Aire en la Segunda Guerra Mundial* (Valladolid: Quiron Ediciones, 2006). Payne, *The Franco Regime*, 425–26, refers to a 1953 reduction of 24 to 18 divisions, and asserts that only U.S. military assistance of the 1950s permitted the formation of Spain's first armored division. Actually the Republican army first formed such divisions, based upon paper strength.

6. Fernando Puell de la Villa, "Política De Defensa Y Política Militar En El Siglo XX," *Claves de la España del siglo XX. Estudios* (Valencia: Sociedad Estatal España Nuevo Milenio, 2001), also available at http://www.iugm.es/estudioshistoricos/estudioshis.htm, 10.

7. David Garoz, "Divisiónes de Infantería Experimentales, las 'pentómicas,'" *Trubia* (2005): 27–29.

8. Friedrich Wiener, *Die Armeen der neutralen und blockfreien Staaten Europas; Organisation, Kriegsbild, Waffen und Gerät* (München: J.F. Lehmann, 1969), 151–55.

9. *La Legión Española: Cincuenta Años de Historia*, 2 vols. (Leganés: La Legión, 1970, 1974), II, 480.

10. During the period September 20, 1920–August 31, 1930, the Legion recruited 24,521 men to its ranks, of whom 4,304 were foreigners from 48 nations. Nations contributing over a hundred volunteers were Portugal (1,086), Germany (912), Cuba (546), France (365), Italy (194), and Argentina (140). Foreign recruitment officially terminated with Royal Decree 611/1986 of March 21, 1986. Data compiled by author Estes from G-1 files, Legion Inspectorate, 1994.

11. Wiener, *Die Armeen der neutralen und blockfreien Staaten Europas*, 151–55.

12. Jose Luis Manuel Hidalgo, "Las Fuerzas de Intervención Inmediata" and "Las Fuerzas de Defensa Operacional del Territorio," unpublished manuscripts, 2004.

13. Puell de la Villa, "Política De Defensa," 17–19.

14. Author Estes worked with members of the negotiating team of the 1988 renewal team in the aftermath of the negotiations and oversaw local arrangements for the withdrawal of U.S. forces from Torrejón in 1991.

15. Author Estes served as bilateral exercise coordinator and later Chief of International Affairs Section in the U.S. military mission (ODC), Madrid, 1989-91.

16. Kenneth W. Estes, "Spain's View of Maghreb as NATO's Southern Flank," *International Defense Review* (January 1996): 20–22.

17. Puell de la Villa, "Política De Defensa," 20. Spanish recruitment to date has not produced an enlisted force exceeding 76,000 men and women (including 17.6% women and 4.27% foreigners, mostly from Latin America, in 2006).

18. Octavio Diéz Cámara, "España el Rumbo de la Defensa," *Soldier-Raids* 127 (April 2006): 8–11.

19. Ian Kemp and Craig Hoyle, "Coming of Age," *Jane's Defense Weekly* 48, no. 23 (2003): 25–29

Chapter 9

I want to thank F. Reinares for his generous information sharing on this topic along the years.

1. Robert A. Pape, "Coercive Air Power in the Vietnam War," *International Security* 15, no. 2 (1990): 103–46, for the coercive dimension, and Peter R. Neumann and M.L.R. Smith, "Strategic Terrorism: The Framework and its Fallacies," *Journal of Strategic Studies* 28, no. 4 (2005): 571–95, 574, for the definition. Compare with another definition "the sustained use, or threat of use, of violence by a small group for political purposes such as inspiring fear, drawing widespread attention to a political grievance and/or provoking a draconian or unsustainable response," in James D. Kiras, "Terrorism and Irregular Warfare," in *Strategy in the Contemporary World. An Introduction to Strategic Studies,* ed. John Baylis, James Wirtz, Eliot Cohen, and Colin S. Gray (Oxford: Oxford University Press, 2002), 208–32, definition in 211. Schmid and others devoted 38 pages to their investigation of the constituent parts of terrorism in Alex P. Schmid and others, *Political Terrorism. A New Guide to Actors, Authors, Data Bases, Theories, and Literature* (New Brunswick: Transaction, 1988). Professor Schmid is preparing a new handbook of terrorism research.

2. See Martha Crenshaw, "The Causes of Terrorism," *Comparative Politics* 13, no. 4 (1981): 383–84; William Lee Eubank and Leonard Weinberg, "Does Democracy Encourage Terrorism?" *Terrorism and Political Violence* 6, no. 4 (1994): 417–43; also Leonard Weinberg and William Eubank, "Terrorism and Democracy: What Recent Events Disclose," *Terrorism and Political Violence* 10, no. 1 (1998): 108–18; and Peter R. Neumann, "The Bullet and the Ballot Box: The Case of the IRA," *Journal of Strategic Studies* 28, no. 6 (2005): 941–75.

3. Martha Crenshaw, "The Concept of Revolutionary Terrorism," *Journal of Conflict Resolution* 16, no. 3 (1972): 383–96; Martha Crenshaw, "How Terrorism Declines," *Terrorism and Political Violence* 3, no. 1 (1991): 69–87; and Ignacio Sánchez-Cuenca, "Revolutionary Terrorism: A Political Selection Model," Instituto Juan March, Madrid, November 2005.

4. Paddy Woodworth, "Why Do They Kill? The Basque Conflict in Spain," *World Policy Journal* 18, no. 1 (2001).

5. Inserted between parenthesis the date of founding of the organization or of the period of its criminal activities.

6. In this and the next paragraph I follow closely Fernando Reinares, "The Political Conditioning of Collective Violence: Regime Change and Insurgent Terrorism in Spain," *Research on Democracy and Society* 3 (1996): 310–11.

7. According to the comparative statistical analysis performed by Sánchez-Cuenca, it is reasonable to suggest that the strength of an organization is a function

of the number of killings, but also of the number of years that the organization is active. For the sake of simplicity, he considers that a terrorist organization is active during the period that goes from the first killing to the last one. Let $i = \{1, \ldots, I\}$ represent the set of active organizations in a country. The impact of nationalist, revolutionary, and extreme right terrorism in Spain can be measured according to this index: $\mathrm{Ln}(\sum_{i=1}^{I} \mathrm{deaths}_i \times \mathrm{years}_i)$. See Sánchez-Cuenca, *Revolutionary Terrorism*, 16.

8. Sánchez-Cuenca, *Revolutionary Terrorism*, 17.

9. Key references about ETA are Florencio Domínguez Iribarren, *ETA: estrategia organizativa y actuaciones, 1978–1992* (Bilbao: Universidad del País Vasco, 1998); Florencio Domínguez Iribarren, *De la negociación a la tregua ¿el final de ETA?* (Madrid: Taurus, 1998); Fernando Reinares, *Patriotas de la muerte. Quiénes han militado en ETA y por qué* (Madrid: Taurus, 2001); Ignacio Sánchez-Cuenca, *ETA contra el Estado. Las estrategias del terrorismo* (Barcelona: Tusquets, 2001); Goldie Shabad and Francisco José Llera Ramo, "Political Violence in a Democratic State: Basque Terrorism in Spain," in *Terrorism in Context*, ed. Martha Crenshaw (University Park: Pennsylvania State University Press, 1995), 410–69.

10. General Sánchez was the first general of the Armed Forces killed since Civil War. The first military killed by ETA was major Imaz Martínez on November 26, 1977.

11. Domínguez Iribarren, *ETA: estrategia organizativa*, 225–31.

12. Fernando Reinares, "Democratic Regimes, Internal Security Policy and the Threat of Terrorism," *Australian Journal of Politics and History* 44, no. 3 (1998): 369.

13. Rodolfo Martín Villa, *Al servicio del Estado* (Barcelona: Planeta, 1984), 150–58.

14. Fernando Reinares, "Political Conditioning," 313.

15. Domínguez Iribarren, *De la negociación a la tregua*, 215–16; Fernando Reinares, "Democratic Regimes," 361.

16. Fernando Reinares, "Democratic Regimes," 363.

17. Fernando Reinares, "Political Conditioning," 318–19.

18. Ibid., 313.

19. Robert P. Clark, *Negotiating with ETA. Obstacles to Peace in the Basque Country, 1975–1988* (Reno: University of Nevada Press, 1990), 93–115.

20. Domínguez Iribarren, *De la negociación a la tregua*, 227.

21. Paddy Woodworth, *Guerra sucia, manos limpias. ETA, el GAL y la democracia española* (Barcelona: Crítica, 2002); and Rogelio Alonso and Fernando Reinares, "Terrorism, Human Rights and Law Enforcement in Spain," *Terrorism and Political Violence* 17 (2005): 265–78.

22. Hans Peter van der Broek, "*Borroka*. The Legitimation of Street Violence in the Political Discourse of Radical Basque Nationalists," *Terrorism and Political Violence* 16, no. 4 (2004): 733.

23. Clark, *Negotiating with ETA*, 165–221; Ignacio Sánchez-Cuenca, *ETA contra el Estado. Las estrategias del terrorismo* (Barcelona: Tusquets, 2001), 109–42, with sound criticism for Algiers and later negotiations; Rogelio Alonso, "Pathways Out of Terrorism in Northern Ireland and the Basque Country: The Misrepresentation of the Irish Model," *Terrorism and Political Violence* 16, no. 4 (2004): 695–713.

24. Reinares, "Democratic Regimes," 359.

25. Domínguez Iribarren, *De la negociación a la tregua*, 282–83; María J. Funes, "Social Responses to Political Violence in the Basque Country. Peace Movements and Their Audience," *Journal of Conflict Resolution* 42, no. 4 (1998): 493–510.

26. Alonso "Pathways Out of Terrorism," 705.

27. Ibid., 696–97.

28. Ignacio Cosidó, "Spanish Policy Against Terrorism: The Guardia Civil and ETA," *Análisis* 28 (octubre 2002), Grupo de Estudios Estratégicos (www.gees.org).

29. Ibid.

30. Juan Avilés, "Assessment of Terrorism in Spain. Year 2003," *Análisis* 64 (mayo 2004), Grupo de Estudios Estratégicos (www.gees.org); L. Luis Romero, *Las políticas de prevención y seguridad desarrolladas durante la VII Legislatura, 2000–2004* [Madrid: Instituto Universitario de Investigación sobre Seguridad Interior (UNED), 2004].

31. Centro de Investigaciones Sociológicas [CIS (Center for Sociological Research)]: Estudio n° 2.466. *Barómetro de septiembre*, 2002.

32. José A. Olmeda, "Fear or Falsehood? Framing the 3/11 Terrorist Attacks in Madrid and Electoral Accountability," *WP 24/2005* (5/5/2005), Real Instituto Elcano, Madrid, http://www.realinstitutoelcano.org/documentos/195.asp.

33. Alonso and Reinares, "Terrorism, Human Rights," 265–78.

Bibliography

Abella, Rafael. *La vida cotidiana en España bajo el regimen de Franco.* Barcelona: Argos Vergara, 1985.

Aguirre, José Ramón Diego. *Guerra en el Sáhara.* Madrid: Ediciones Istmo, 1991.

———. *Historia del Sahara Español.* Madrid: Kaydeda, 1988.

———. *La última guerra colonial de España: Ifni-Sáhara (1957–1958).* Málaga: Editorial Algazara, 1993.

al-Fasi, Alal. *The Independence Movements in Arab North Africa.* Translated by Hazem Zaki Nuseibeh. New York: Octagon Press, 1970.

Algora Weber, María Dolores. *Las relaciones hispano-árabes durante el régimen de Franco: la rupture del aislamiento internacional (1946–50).* Madrid: Ministerio de Asuntos Exteriores, 1995.

———. "La política árabe del régimen franquista: planteamientos generales y fases." *Estudios Africanos* 5 (1990).

Alonso, J. Ramón. *Historia Política del Ejercito Español.* Madrid: Editora Nacional, 1974.

Alonso, Rogelio. "Pathways Out of Terrorism in Northern Ireland and the Basque Country: The Misrepresentation of the Irish Model." *Terrorism and Political Violence* 16, no. 4 (2004): 695–713.

Alonso, Rogelio, and Fernando Reinares. "Terrorism, Human Rights and Law Enforcement in Spain." *Terrorism and Political Violence* 17 (2005): 265–78.

Alpert, Michael. *El ejército republicano en la guerra civil.* Paris-Barcelona: Ruedo Ibérico, 1977; Madrid: Siglo XXI, 1989. 3rd edition pending, Barcelona: Crítica.

———. "The Clash of Spanish Armies: Contrasting Ways of War in Spain 1936–1939." *War in History* 6, no. 3 (1999): 351–51.

Álvarez, José E. *The Betrothed of Death: The Spanish Foreign Legion During the Rif Rebellion, 1920–1927.* Westport, CT: Greenwood Press, 2001.

Álvarez Junco, José. "El nacionalismo español como mito movilizador. Cuatro guerras." In *Cultura y movilización en la España contemporánea.* Edited by Rafael Cruz and Manuel Pérez, 35–67. Madrid: Alianza, 1997.

Alvarez Junco, José, and Adrian Shubert, eds. *Spanish History since 1808.* London: Arnold, 2000.

Aguilar Olivencia, Mariano. *El Ejército durante el Franquismo.* Madrid: Ediciones Akal, 1999.

Arce, Carlos de. *Historia de la Legión Española.* Barcelona: Editorial Mitre, 1984.

Aroca Mohedano, Manuela. *General Juan Hernández Saravia: el ayudante militar de Azaña.* Madrid: Oberón, 2006.

Arraras, Joaquín, ed. *Historia de la Cruzada Española.* Madrid: Ediciones Españolas, 1939.

Asprey, Robert B. *War in the Shadows: The Guerrilla in History.* New York: Doubleday & Co., Inc., 1975.

Ashford, Douglas E. *Political Change in Morocco.* Princeton, NJ: Princeton University Press, 1961.

Aubert, Paul. "La propagande étrangère en Espagne pendant la Première Guerre
Mondiale." In *Españoles y franceses en la primera mitad del siglo XX,* 357–411.
Madrid: CSIC, 1986.

Avilés, Juan. "Assessment of Terrorism in Spain. Year 2003." *Análisis* 64 (May
2004), Grupo de Estudios Estratégicos (www.gees.org).

Ayensa, Emilio. *Del Desastre De Annual A La Presidencia Del Consejo.* Madrid: Rafael
Caro Raggio, 1930.

Azpeitua, Antonio. *Marruecos, la mala semilla; ensayo de analisis objetivo de como fue
sembrada la guerra en África.* Madrid, 1921.

Azzuz Hakim, Mohammed Ibn. "Una visión realista del Protectorado ejercido por
España en Marruecos." In *Relaciones entre España y Marruecos en el Siglo XX.*
Edited by José U. Martínez Carreras. Madrid: Asociación Española de Africa-
nistas, 2000.

Bahamonde, Angel, and Javier Cervera. *Así terminó la guerra de España.* Madrid:
Marcial Pons, 2000.

Balfour, Sebastian. *Deadly Embrace: Morocco and the Road to the Spanish Civil War.*
Oxford and New York: Oxford University Press, 2002.

———. *The End of the Spanish Empire 1898–1923.* Oxford: Clarendon Press,
1997.

Ballbé, Manuel. *Orden público y militarismo en la España constitucional (1812–1983).*
Madrid: Alianza, 1983.

Bañon Martínez, Rafael, and Thomas M. Barker, eds. *Armed Forces and Society in
Spain Past and Present.* New York: Columbia University Press, 1988.

Baquer, Miguel Alonso. *Franco y sus generales.* Madrid: Taurus, 2005.

———. *El Ejército en la sociedad española.* Madrid: Ediciones del Movimiento,
1971.

Barea, Arturo. *The Forging of a Rebel.* Translated by Ilsa Barea. New York: Reynal &
Hitchcock, 1946.

Beevor, Anthony. *The Battle for Spain.* London: Weidenfeld & Nicolson, 2006.

Berenguer Fusté, Dámaso. *Campañas en el Rif y Yebala 1921–1922: Notas y
documentos de mi diario de operaciones.* Madrid: Sucesores De R. Velasco,
1923.

Blanco Escolá, Carlos. *La Academia General Militar de Zaragoza (1928–1931).*
Barcelona: Labor Universitaria, 1989.

Blinkhorn, Martin. *Carlism and Crisis in Spain.* Cambridge: Cambridge University
Press, 1975.

Bordejé y Morencos, Fernando de. *Vicisitudes de una política naval.* Madrid: Editorial San Martín, 1978.

Bosque Coma, Alfredo. *Guerra de Ifni, las banderas paracaidistas 1957–1958.* Madrid:
Almena, 1998.

Bowen, Wayne H. *Spain During World War II.* Columbia: University of Missouri
Press, 2006.

———. *Spaniards and Nazi Germany: Collaboration in the New Order.* Columbia:
University of Missouri Press, 2000.

Boyd, Carolyn P. *Praetorian Politics in Liberal Spain*. Chapel Hill: University of North Carolina Press, 1979.

Bullón de Mendoza y Gómez de Valugera, Alfonso. *La primera guerra carlista*. Madrid: Actas, 1992.

Busquets, Julio. *El militar de carrera en España*. Barcelona: Editorial Ariel, 1984.

Cabanellas, Guillermo. *La Lucha por el Poder. Cuatro Generales 2*. Barcelona: Planeta, 1977.

Cámara, Octavio Díez. *Brigada Legionaria Alfonso XIII*. Madrid: Fundación Rodrigo, 1999.

Campos Serrano, Alicia. *De colonia a estado: Guinea Ecuatorial, 1955–1968*. Madrid: Centro de Estudios Políticos y Constitucionales, 2002.

Carden, Ron M. *German Policy Toward Neutral Spain, 1914–1918*. New York and London: Garland Publishing, Inc., 1987.

Cardona, Gabriel. *El poder militar en la España contemporánea hasta la guerra civil*. Madrid: Siglo XXI de España Editores, 1983.

———. *El problema militar en España*. Madrid: Historia 16, 1990.

———. *Franco y sus generales*. Madrid: Temas de Hoy, 2001.

Cardona, Gabriel, and Juan Carlos Losada Málvarez. *Weyler, nuestro hombre en la Habana*. 1st ed. Barcelona: Planeta, 1997.

Carr, Raymond. *España: De La Restauración A La Democracia, 1875–1980*. Barcelona: Editorial Ariel, S.A., 1983.

———. *The Spanish Tragedy: The Civil War in Perspective*. London: Phoenix, 2000.

Carrasco García, Antonio. *Las Imágenes del Desastre: Annual 1921*. Madrid: Almena Ediciones, 1999.

Casas Sánchez, José Luis, ed. *La postguerra española y la Segunda Guerra Mundial*. Córdoba: Diputación Provincial de Córdoba, 1990.

Cassidy, Robert M. *Counterinsurgency and the Global War on Terror: Military Culture and Irregular War*. Westport, CT: Praeger Security International, 2006.

Centro de Investigaciones Sociológicas [CIS (Center for Sociological Research)]: Estudio n° 2.466. *Barómetro de septiembre*, 2002.

Cerezo Martínez, Ricardo. *Armada española siglo XX*. Madrid: Poniente, 1983.

Christiansen, E. *The Origins of Military Power in Spain 1800–1854*. Oxford: Oxford University Press, 1967.

Citino, Robert Michael. *The German Way of War: From the Thirty Years' War to the Third Reich*. Lawrence, KS: University Press of Kansas, 2005.

Clark, Robert P. *Negotiating with ETA. Obstacles to Peace in the Basque Country, 1975–1988*. Reno: University of Nevada Press, 1990.

Connelly Ullman, Joan. *The Tragic Week: A Study of Anti-Clericalism in Spain, 1875–1912*. Cambridge, MA: Harvard University Press, 1968.

Cortés Cavanillas, Julián. *Alfonso XIII y la guerra del 14*. Madrid: Alce, 1976.

Cosidó, Ignacio. "Spanish Policy Against Terrorism: The Guardia Civil and ETA." *Análisis* 28 (October 2002), Grupo de Estudios Estratégicos (www.gees.org).

Coverdale, John F. *The Basque Phase of Spain's First Carlist War*. Princeton, NJ: Princeton University Press, 1984.

———. *Italian Intervention in the Spanish Civil War*. Princeton, NJ: Princeton University Press, 1975.

Crenshaw, Martha.. "The Causes of Terrorism." *Comparative Politics* 13, no. 4 (1981): 383–84.

———. "The Concept of Revolutionary Terrorism." *Journal of Conflict Resolution* 16, no. 3 (1972): 383–96.

———. "How Terrorism Declines." *Terrorism and Political Violence* 3, no. 1 (1991): 69–87.

Crozier, Brian. *Franco: A Biographical History.* London: Eyre & Spottiswoode, 1967.

Davidson, Basil. *The People's Cause—A History of Guerrillas in Africa.* London: Longman, 1981.

De la Cierva, Ricardo. *Franco.* Barcelona: Editorial Planeta, 1986.

de Madariaga, María Rosa. *Los Moros Que Trajo Franco...La Intervención de Tropas Coloniales en la Guerra Civil Española.* Barcelona: Ediciones Martínez Roca, S.A., 2002.

Díaz-Plaja, Fernando. *Francófilos y germanófilos.* Madrid: Alianza, 1981.

———. *ETA: estrategia organizativa y actuaciones, 1978–1992.* Bilbao: Universidad del País Vasco, 1998.

Domínguez Iribarren, Florencio. *De la negociación a la tregua ¿el final de ETA?* Madrid: Taurus, 1998.

Fernando Reinares. *Patriotas de la muerte. Quiénes han militado en ETA y por qué.* Madrid: Taurus, 2001.

Elorza, Antonio, and Marta Bizcarrondo. *Queridos Camaradas, la Internacional Comunista y Espana 1919–1939.* Barcelona: Planeta, 1999.

Engel, Carlos. *Historia de las brigadas mixtas del Ejército Popular de la República.* Madrid: Almena, 1999.

Esdaile, Charles J. *Spain in the Liberal Age.* Oxford, UK/Malden, MA: Blackwell Publishers, 2000.

———. *The Spanish Army in the Peninsular War.* Manchester, UK, New York: Manchester University Press, 1988.

Espadas Burgos, Manuel. "Las Fuerzas Armadas durante la Gran Guerra." In *Las Fuerzas Armadas Españolas. Historia institucional y social,* V, 197–227. Madrid: Alhambra-Asuri, 1985.

Estes, Kenneth W. "New Brigade Structure Cements Future of Spanish Legion." *International Defense Review,* May 1995, 67–69.

Estado Mayor Central del Ejército, Servicio Histórico Militar. *Historia de las Campañas de Marruecos.* Vols. 3 and 4. Madrid: Imprenta Ideal, 1981.

Eubank, William Lee, and Leonard Weinberg. "Does Democracy Encourage Terrorism?" *Terrorism and Political Violence* 6, no. 4 (1994): 417–43.

———. "Terrorism and Democracy: What Recent Events Disclose." *Terrorism and Political Violence* 10, no. 1 (1998): 108–18.

Fage, J.D., and Roland Oliver, eds. "Morocco." In *The Cambridge History of Africa.* London and New York: Cambridge University Press, 1975.

Fernández De La Ruguera, Ricardo, and Susana March. *El Desastre De Annual.* Barcelona: Editorial Planeta, 1968.

Fleming, Shannon E. "Disaster of Annual: Spanish Colonial Failure in Northern Morocco, 1902–1921." M.A. thesis, University of Minnesota, 1969.

———. *Primo de Rivera and Abd-el-Krim: The Struggle in Spanish Morocco, 1923–1927.* New York and London: Garland Publishing, 1991.

————. "Spanish Morocco and the Second Republic: Consistency of Colonial Policy?" In *Spain and the Mediterranean since 1898*. Edited by Raanan Rein. London: Frank Cass, 1999.

Forbes, Rosita. *El Raisuni, the Sultan of the Mountains. His Life as Told to Rosita Forbes*. London: Thornton Butterworth, 1924.

Franco Salgado-Araujo, Francisco. *Mis conversaciones privadas con Franco*. Barcelona: Planeta, 1976.

Funes, María J. "Social Responses to Political Violence in the Basque Country. Peace Movements and Their Audience." *Journal of Conflict Resolution* 42, no. 4 (1998).

Furneaux, Rupert. *Abdel Krim—Emir of the Rif*. London: Secker & Warburg, 1967.

Galey, John H. "Bridegrooms of Death: A Profile Study of the Spanish Foreign Legion." *Journal of Contemporary History* 4, no. 2 (1969).

Galinsoga, Luis De. *Centinela De Occidente*, with the collaboration of Lieutenant General Franco Salgado. Barcelona: Editorial AHR, 1956.

Gárate Córdoba, José María. "Los militares españoles ante la Gran Guerra." *Hispania* 161 (1985): 579–614.

García Figueras, Tomás. *Marruecos: La Acción de España en el Norte de Africa*. Barcelona: Ediciones Fe, 1939.

Gil-Robles, José María. *La monarquía por la que yo luché*. Madrid: Taurus, 1976.

Gómez-Jordana y Souza, Francisco. *La Tramoya De Nuestra Actuación En Marruecos*. Madrid: Editora Nacional, 1976.

Harris, Walter B. *France, Spain and the Riff*. London: Edward Arnold & Co., 1927.

Headrick, Daniel R. *Ejército y política en España (1866–1898)*. Madrid: Tecnos, 1981.

Hernández-Sandoica, Elena, and Enrique Moradiellos. "Spain and the Second World War." In *European Neutrals and Non-Belligerents During the Second World War*. Edited by Neville Wylie. Cambridge: Cambridge University Press, 2002.

Hills, George. *Franco: The Man and His Nation*. New York: MacMillan, 1967.

————. *Spain*. New York: Praeger Publishers, 1970.

Hodges, Tony. *Western Sahara: The Roots of a Desert War*. Westport, CT: L. Hill, 1983.

Howson, Gerald. *Aircraft of the Spanish Civil War, 1936–1939*. Washington DC: Smithsonian Institution Press, 1991.

————. *Arms for Spain: The Untold Story of the Spanish Civil War*. London: John Murray, 1998.

Jensen, Geoffrey. *Franco: Soldier, Commander, Dictator*. Washington, DC: Potomac Books, 2005.

————. "The Politics and Practice of Spanish Counterinsurgency, 1895–1936." In *Nation and Conflict in Modern Spain*. Edited by Sasha D. Pack. Madison: Parallel Press, forthcoming.

Jover Zamora, José María. "La percepción española de los conflictos europeos: notas históricas para su entendimiento." *Revista de Occidente* 57 (1986): 5–42.

Keegan, John. *World Armies*. London: The MacMillan Press, 1979.

Keene, Judith. *Fighting for Franco: International Volunteers in Nationalist Spain During the Spanish Civil War*. London and New York: Leicester University Press, 2001.

Kindelán, Alfredo. *La verdad de mis relaciones con Franco*. Barcelona: Planeta, 1981.

Kiras, James D. "Terrorism and Irregular Warfare." In *Strategy in the Contemporary World. An Introduction to Strategic Studies.* Edited by John Baylis, James Wirtz, Eliot Cohen, and Colin S. Gray, 208–32. Oxford: Oxford University Press, 2002.

Kowalsky, Daniel. *La Unión Soviética y la guerra civil española: una revisión crítica* Barcelona: Crítica, 2004.

Lacomba Avellán, Juan Antonio. *La crisis española de 1917.* Madrid: Ciencia Nueva, 1970.

Líster, Enrique. *Nuestra Guerra.* Paris: Libraire du Globe, 1966.

Locksley, Christopher C. "Condor over Spain: The Civil War, Combat Experience and the Development of Luftwaffe Airpower Doctrine." *Civil Wars,* Frank Cass, London, 2, no. 1 (1999): 69–99.

Madariaga, María Rosa de. *España y el Rif: crónica de una historia casi olvidada.* 2nd ed. Ciudad Autónoma de Melilla: UNED-Centro Asociado de Melilla, 2000.

———. *Los Moros Que Trajo Franco. . .La Intervención de Tropas Coloniales en la Guerra Civil Española.* Barcelona: Ediciones Martínez Roca, 2002.

Marín, Francisco. *Martínez se va a la Guerra.* Barcelona: Edìciones Inèdita, 2005.

Marquina Barrio, Antonio. *La diplomacia vaticana y la España de Franco.* Madrid: CSIC, 1983.

Martín Villa, Rodolfo. *Al servicio del Estado.* Barcelona: Planeta, 1984.

Martínez Bande, José Manuel. *La batalla del Ebro.* Madrid: San Martín, 1978.

———. *La batalla de Teruel.* Madrid: Servicio Histórico Militar, 1974.

———. *La campaña de Andalucía.* Madrid: Servicio Histórico Militar, 1969.

———. *La campaña de Cataluña.* Madrid: San Martín, 1979.

———. *El final de la guerra civil.* Madrid: San Martín, 1985.

———. *La gran ofensiva sobre Zaragoza.* Madrid: Servicio Histórico Militar, 1973.

———. *La guerra en el norte.* Madrid: Servicio Histórico Militar, 1969.

———. *La invasión de Aragón y el desembarco en Mallorca.* Madrid: Servicio Histórico Militar, 1970.

———. *La llegada al mar.* Madrid: San Martín, 1975.

———. *La marcha sobre Madrid.* Madrid: Servicio Histórico Militar, 1982.

———. *La ofensiva sobre Segovia y la batalla de Brunete.* Madrid: San Martín, 1972.

———. *La ofensiva sobre Valencia.* Madrid: San Martín, 1977.

———. *Vizcaya.* Madrid: San Martín, 1971.

Martínez de Campos y Serrano, Carlos. *España belica: el siglo XIX.* Madrid: Aguilar, 1961.

Martínez Paricio, Jesús, I, ed. *Los papeles del general Rojo.* Madrid: Espasa-Calpe, 1989.

Meaker, Gerald H. "A Civil War of Words: The Ideological Impact of the First World War on Spain, 1914–18." In *Neutral Europe Between War and Revolution, 1917–23,* 1–65. Charlottesville: University Press of Virginia, 1988.

Memoria del Repliegue a Soberanía de las Fuerzas Españolas en Marruecos, 1956–1961. Madrid: Impresa del Servicio Geográfico del Ejercito, 1962.

Mera, Cipriano. *Guerra, exilio y cárcel de un anarcosindicalista.* Pis: Ruedo Ibérico, 1976.

Ministerio del Ejército. *Organización del Ejército, Plantillas 1940.* Madrid: Ministerio del Ejército, 1941.

Modesto, Juan. *Soy del Quinto Regimiento.* Paris: Librairie du Globe, 1969.

Morales Lezcano, Víctor. *El final del Protectorado Hispano-Francés en Marruecos: el desafío del nacionalismo magrebí (1945–1962).* Madrid: Instituto Egipico de Estudios Islámicos, 1998.

———. *España y el Norte de África—El Protectorado en Marruecos (1912–1956).* Madrid: U.N.E.D., 1986.

Mundy, Jacob. "Neutrality or Complicity? The United States and the 1975 Moroccan Takeover of the Spanish Sahara." *Journal of North African Studies* 11 (September 2006).

Nerín, Gustau, and Alfred Bosch. *El imperio que nunca existió.* Barcelona: Plaza y Janés, 2001.

Neumann, Peter R. "The Bullet and the Ballot Box: The Case of the IRA." *Journal of Strategic Studies* 28, no. 6 (December 2005).

Neumann, Peter R., and M.L.R. Smith, "Strategic Terrorism: The Framework and its Fallacies." *Journal of Strategic Studies* 28, no. 4 (2005): 571–95.

Nicot, Jean, and Pierre Waksmann. "Les relations franco-espagnoles et la politique extérieure d'Alfonso XIII en 1917." In *94° Congrès National des Sociétés Savantes, Pau, 1969, Section d'histoire moderne et contemporaine,* I, 463–84. Paris: Bibliotheque Nationale, 1971.

Olmeda Gómez, José Antonio. "Fear or Falsehood? Framing the 3/11 Terrorist Attacks in Madrid and Electoral Accountability." *WP 24/2005* (5/5/2005), Real Instituto Elcano, Madrid. http://www.realinstitutoelcano.org/documentos/195.asp.

———. Olmeda Gómez, José Antonio. *Las Fuerzas Armadas en el Estado Franquista.* Madrid: Ediciones El Arquero, 1988.

Pape, Robert A. "Coercive Air Power in the Vietnam War." *International Security* 15, no. 2 (1990): 103–46.

Payne, Stanley G. *The Collapse of the Spanish Republic, 1933–1936: Origins of the Civil War.* New Haven: Yale University Press, 2006.

———. *Ejército y sociedad en la España liberal, 1808–1936.* Madrid: Akal, 1976.

———. *Fascism in Spain, 1923–1977.* Madison: University of Wisconsin Press, 1999.

———. *The Franco Regime, 1936–1975.* Madison: University of Wisconsin Press, 1987.

———. *Politics and the Military in Modern Spain.* Stanford: Stanford University Press, 1967.

———. *Spain's First Democracy: The Second Republic, 1931–1936.* Madison: University of Wisconsin Press, 1994.

Pennell, C. Richard. *Morocco since 1830.* New York, New York University Press, 2000.

———. *A Country with a Government and a Flag: The Rif War in Morocco, 1921–1926.* Wisbech, Cambridgeshire, UK: Middle East and North African Studies Press, 1986.

Pérez García, Guadalupe. "La falacia histórica sobre la colonia de Ifni." *Historia y Comunicación Social* 8 (2003).

Picasso González, Juan. *Expediente Picasso: Documentos relacionados con la información instruida por el señor general de división D. Juan Picasso sobre las responsabilidades de la actuación española en Marruecos durante julio de mil novecientos veintiuno*. Mexico, D.F.: Frente de Afirmación Hispanista, A.C., 1976.

Ponce Marrero, F. Javier. *Canarias en la Gran Guerra, 1914–1918: estrategia y diplomacia. Un estudio sobre la política exterior de España*. Las Palmas de Gran Canaria: Ediciones del Cabildo de Gran Canaria, 2006.

Pozo Manzano, Elena del. "La campaña de Ifni en la última guerra de Africa: 1957–1958." *Estudios Africanos* 5 (1990).

Preston, Paul. "Decay, Division, and the Defence of Dictatorship: The Military and Politics, 1939–1975." *Elites and Power in Twentieth Century Spain*. Edited by Frances Lannon and Paul Preston. Oxford: Oxford University Press, 1990.

———. *Franco: A Biography*. New York: Basic Books, 1994.

———. *Franco: A Biography*. New York: HarperCollins, 1994.

———. *The Politics of Revenge: Fascism and the Military in 20th Century Spain*. London: Unwin Hyman, 1990.

Proctor, Raymond L. *Hitler's Luftwaffe in the Spanish Civil War*. Westport, CT: Greenwood Press, 1983.

Puell de la Villa, Fernando. *Historia del ejército en España*. Madrid: Alianza Editorial, 2000, 2003.

———. "Política De Defensa Y Política Militar En El Siglo XX." In *Claves de la España del siglo XX. Estudios*. Valencia: Sociedad Estatal España Nuevo Milenio, 2001. http://www.iugm.es/estudioshistoricos/estudioshis.htm.

Radosh, S., Mary Habeck, and G. Sevastianov, eds. *Spain Betrayed: The Soviet Union in the Spanish Civil War*. New Haven and London: Yale UP, 2001.

Ramiro de la Mata, Javier. *Origen y dinámica del colonialismo español en Marruecos*. Ceuta: Ciudad Autónoma de Ceuta, 2001.

Redondo Díaz, Fernando. "Los observadores militares españoles en la Primera Guerra Mundial." *Revista de Historia Militar* 59 (1985): 197–208.

Reig de la Vega, Rafael, ed. *Los 75 Años de La Legión Española*. Madrid: Revista Defensa, Extra No. 41, 1995.

Reinares, Fernando. "The Political Conditioning of Collective Violence: Regime Change and Insurgent Terrorism in Spain." *Research on Democracy and Society* 3 (1996).

Rezette, Robert. *The Spanish Enclaves in Morocco*. Translated by Mary Ewalt. Paris: Nouvelles Editions Latines, 1976.

Riudor, Lluís. "Sueños imperiales y africanismo durante el franquismo (1939–1956)." In *España en Marruecos (1912–1956): discursos geográficos e intervención territorial*. Edited by Joan Nogué and José Luis Villanova. Lleida: Editorial Milenio, 1999.

Rodríguez Jiménez, José Luis. *¡A MÍ LA LEGIÓN!: De Millán Astray a las misiones de paz*. 2nd ed. Barcelona: Editorial Planeta, S.A., 2005.

Rodríguez Gómez, José M. *La Tercera guerra carlista, 1869–1876*. 1st ed. Madrid: Almena, 2004.

Romero de Lara, Luis. *Las políticas de prevención y seguridad desarrolladas durante la VII Legislatura, 2000–2004*. Madrid: Instituto Universitario de Investigación sobre Seguridad Interior (UNED), November 2004.

Rosa de Madariaga, Maria. "The Intervention of Moroccan Troops in the Spanish Civil War: A Reconsideration." *European History Quarterly* 22 (1992): 67–97.

Sánchez-Cuenca, Ignacio. *ETA contra el Estado. Las estrategias del terrorismo.* Barcelona: Tusquets, 2001.

Salafranca Ortega, Jesús F. *El sistema colonial español en África.* Málaga: Editorial Algazara, 2001.

Salas, Delfín. *Tropas Regulares Indígenas.* Vol. 2. Madrid: Aldaba Militaria, 1989.

Salas Larrazábal, Jesus. *Air War over Spain.* London: Ian Allen Ltd., 1969.

Salas Larrazábal, Ramón. *El Protectorado De España En Marruecos.* Madrid: Editorial MAPFRE, 1992.

———. *Historia del Ejército Popular de la República.* 4 vols. Madrid: Editora Nacional, 1973.

Sánchez-Cuenca, Ignacio. *ETA contra el Estado. Las estrategias del terrorismo.* Barcelona: Tusquets, 2001.

———. "Revolutionary Terrorism: A Political Selection Model." Instituto Juan March, Madrid, November 2005.

Schmid, Alex P., and Albert J. Jongman. *Political Terrorism. A New Guide to Actors, Authors, Data Bases, Theories, and Literature.* New Brunswick: Transaction, 1988.

Seco Serrano, Carlos. *Militarismo y civilismo en la España contemporánea.* Madrid: Instituto de Estudios Ecónomicos, 1984.

Segura Valero, Gastón. *Ifni: la guerra que silenció Franco.* Madrid: Ediciones Martínez Roca, 2006.

Sheehan, Vincent. *An American Among the Riffi.* New York: The Century Co., 1926.

———. *Personal History.* Garden City: Country Life Press, 1934–35.

Shabad, Goldie, and Francisco José Llera Ramo. "Political Violence in a Democratic State: Basque Terrorism in Spain." In *Terrorism in Context.* Edited by Martha Crenshaw, 410–69. University Park: Pennsylvania State University Press, 1995.

Shinar, Pessah. "Abd al Qadir and Abd al Krim: Religious Influences on Their Thought and Action." *Asian and African Studies,* Vol. I, Annual of the Israeli Oriental Society, Jerusalem, 1975.

Silva, Carlos De. *General Millán Astray (El Legionario).* Barcelona: Editorial AHR, 1956.

Sueiro Seoane, Susana. "Spanish Colonialism During Primo de Rivera's Dictatorship." *Mediterranean Historical Review* 13 (June–December 1998).

Sullivan, Brian R. "Fascist Italy's Military Involvement in the Spanish Civil War." *Journal of Military History* (Chicago) 59 (October 1995): 697–727.

Skoutelsky, Remi. *Novedad en el frente: Las Brigadas Internacionales en la guerra civil española.* Madrid: Temas de hoy, 2006.

Togores Sánchez, Luis E. "La campaña de Levante, 23 de abril-25 de julio de 1938, el penúltimo capítulo de la Guerra Civil." *Aportes,* Madrid, año XXI—1/2006, no. 60, 100–29.

Tone, John Lawrence. *The Fatal Knot: The Guerrilla War in Navarre and the Defeat of Napoleon in Spain.* Chapel Hill: University of North Carolina Press, 1994.

———. "The Machete and the Liberation of Cuba." *Journal of Military History* 62 (January 1998): 11–16.

———. *War and Genocide in Cuba, 1895–1898*. Chapel Hill: University of North Carolina Press, 2006.

Torre Gómez, Hipólito de la. "El destino de la 'regeneración' internacional de España (1898–1918)." *Proserpina* 1 (1984): 9–22.

Trythall, J.W.D. *Franco: A Biography*. London: Rupert Hart-Davis, 1970.

Tusell Gómez, Javier. *Carrero. La eminencia gris del régimen de Franco*. Madrid: Temas de Hoy, 1993.

Van der Broek, Hans Peter. "*Borroka*. The Legitimation of Street Violence in the Political Discourse of Radical Basque Nationalists." *Terrorism and Political Violence* 16, no. 4 (2004): 733.

Vaughan, Ron. "The Forgotten Army: The Spanish in Morocco." *Savage & Soldier* 16, no. 2 (April–June 1984).

Vidal, César. *La Guerra de Franco: Historia Militar de La Guerra Civil Española*. Barcelona: Planeta, 1996.

Villalobos Goyarrola, Federico. *El sueño colonial: las guerras de España en Marruecos*. 1st ed. Barcelona: Ariel, 2004.

Villanova, José Luis. *El Protectorado de España en Marruecos: organización política y territorial*. Barcelona: Edicions Bellaterra, 2004.

———. *Los interventores: la piedra angular del Protectorado español en Marruecos*. Barcelona: Edicions Bellaterra, 2006.

Vilar, Juan B. "España y la descolonización de Marruecos." In *Relaciones entre España y Marruecos en el Siglo XX*. Edited by José U. Martínez Carreras. Madrid: Asociación Española de Africanistas, 2000.

Weiner, Jerome B. "The Green March in Historical Perspective." *Middle Eastern Journal* 33 (Winter 1979).

Weyler, Valeriano. *Memorias de un general. De caballero cadete a general en jefe*. Edited by María Teresa Weyler. Barcelona: Ediciones Destino, 2004.

Whealey, Robert. *Hitler and Spain: The Nazi Role in the Spanish Civil War*. Lexington: University of Kentucky Press, 1989.

Wiener, Friedrich. *Die Armeen der neutralen und blockfreien Staaten Europas; Organisation, Kriegsbild, Waffen und Gerät*. München: J.F. Lehmann, 1969, 1978, 1983, 1986.

———. *La Legion Española: Cincuenta Años de Historia*. 2 vols. Leganés: La Legión, 1970, 1974.

Williams, Mark. *The Story of Spain*. Málaga, Spain: Santana Books, 2000.

Wittenberg, Thilo. "Mut und Ehre: Die professionelle, ideologische und politische Entwicklung des spanischen offizierskorps im 19. Jahrhundert (1808–1908)." Ph.D. dissertation. Freiburg i. Br.: Albert-Ludwigs-Universität, 1995.

Woodworth, Paddy. *Guerra sucia, manos limpias. ETA, el GAL y la democracia española*. Barcelona: Crítica, 2002.

———. "Why Do They Kill? The Basque Conflict in Spain." *World Policy Journal* 18 (Spring 2001).

Woolman, David S. *Rebels in the Rif: Abd el Krim and the Rif Rebellion*. Stanford: Stanford University Press, 1968.

Ybarra Enríquez de la Orden, María Concepción. *España y la descolonización del magreb: rivalidad hispano-francesa en Marruecos (1951–1961)*. Madrid: U.N.E.D., 1998.

Archival Sources

Archivo General Militar (AGM), Legajo (File) 246, SECCIÓN 2, DIVISIÓN 10.

AGM, Legajo M-3204, SECCIÓN 1, DIVISIÓN 1.

British Documents on Foreign Affairs: Reports and Papers from the Foreign Office Confidential Print. Edited by Anthony Adamthwaite. Part II, Series F, Europe, 1919–39, Vol. 27, Spain, July 1936–January 1940. Frederick, MD: University Publications of America, 1990.

DOL, Negociado de Campaña, July 1921.

Documents on German Foreign Policy, Ser. D (1937–1945), Vol. III. Germany and the Spanish Civil War. Washington DC: USGPO, 1950.

Donovan Papers, Office of Strategic Services. U.S. Military History Institute, Carlisle Barracks, PA.

Resumen Historico De La Legión, Diario de Operaciones de la Legión (Serrallo de la Legión), Plana Mayor del Tercio, Archivo General, Ceuta.

Servicio Historico Militar, Colección Legislative del Ejército—1920—Ministerio de la Guerra 49 (Legislative Collection of the Army) 35 (28-I-1920). Madrid: Talleres del Deposito de la Guerra, 1920.

Servicio Historico Militar, DO 22 (29-I-1920), Tomo (Volume) I, Año de 1920, Primer Trimestre, Madrid: Talleres del Deposito de la Guerra, 1920.

Subinspección de La Legión, ed. *La Legión Española (Cincuenta años de historia) 1920–1936.* Madrid: Leganes, 1975.

Arriba

Defensa

Ejército

Revista Española de Defensa

Revista General de Marina

YA

Index

214   Index

About the Contributors

Michael Alpert is Professor Emeritus of Modern and Contemporary History of Spain at the University of Westminster. He has published several books and articles on Spanish history, including *An International History of the Spanish Civil War* (Palgrave, 2003).

José E. Alvarez is Associate Professor of History at the University of Houston-Downtown. A specialist in Morocco and the Spanish Foreign Legion, he is the author of *The Betrothed of Death: The Spanish Foreign Legion During the Rif Rebellion, 1920–1927* (Greenwood, 2001), as well as articles on armored and amphibious warfare.

Wayne H. Bowen is Associate Professor of History at Ouachita Baptist University. He is the author of *Spaniards and Nazi Germany: Collaboration in the New Order* (Missouri, 2000), *Spain During World War II* (Missouri, 2006), and *Undoing Saddam: From Occupation to Sovereignty in Northern Iraq* (Potomac Books, 2007).

George Esenwein teaches history at the University of Florida. He has published numerous articles and reviews on modern Spanish and European history, as well as three books: *Anarchist Ideology and the Working-Class Movement in Spain* (Berkeley, 1989), *Spain at War* with Adrian Shubert (Longman, 1995), and *The Spanish Civil War: A Modern Tragedy* (Routledge, 2005).

Kenneth W. Estes is the author of several books on European and U.S. military history and has written extensively in defense and academic journals. As a U.S. Marine Corps officer, he served in a variety of command and staff assignments until his retirement in 1993. He has taught at Duke University, the U.S. Naval Academy, and College for International Studies in Madrid.

Shannon E. Fleming is the author of *Primo de Rivera and Abd-el-Krim: The Struggle in Spanish Morocco, 1923–1927* (Garland, 1991). He has also written a number of articles on modern Spanish–Moroccan relations for various scholarly journals.

Geoffrey Jensen is the John Biggs '30 Cincinnati Chair in Military History at Virginia Military Institute. He is the author of *Irrational Triumph: Cultural Despair, Military Nationalism and the Ideological Origins of Franco's*

Spain (Nevada, 2002) and *Franco: Soldier, Commander, Dictator* (Potomac, 2005).

José A. Olmeda is Professor of Political Science and Administration at the Universidad Nacional de Educación a Distancia [Distance Learning National University] in Madrid, Spain. The author, editor, or coauthor of several books on the Spanish military, he has conducted extensive research on the transition to democracy, conscription, the creation of an all-volunteer military, and women in the armed forces.

Stanley G. Payne is Professor Emeritus of History at the University of Wisconsin-Madison, where he held the Hilldale-Jaume Vicens Chair. A member of the American Academy of Arts and Sciences, he is the author of more than fifteen books and is the leading historian of modern Spain in the United States.

Javier Ponce is Professor of Contemporary History at the University of Las Palmas de Gran Canaria, Spain. He is a specialist on naval conflict and the strategic role of the Canary Islands, and is the author of several books and articles on Spain during World War I.

José M. Serrano works in the financial services industry in Madrid. He is a veteran of the Spanish Army and co-owner of a military simulations and wargaming company.